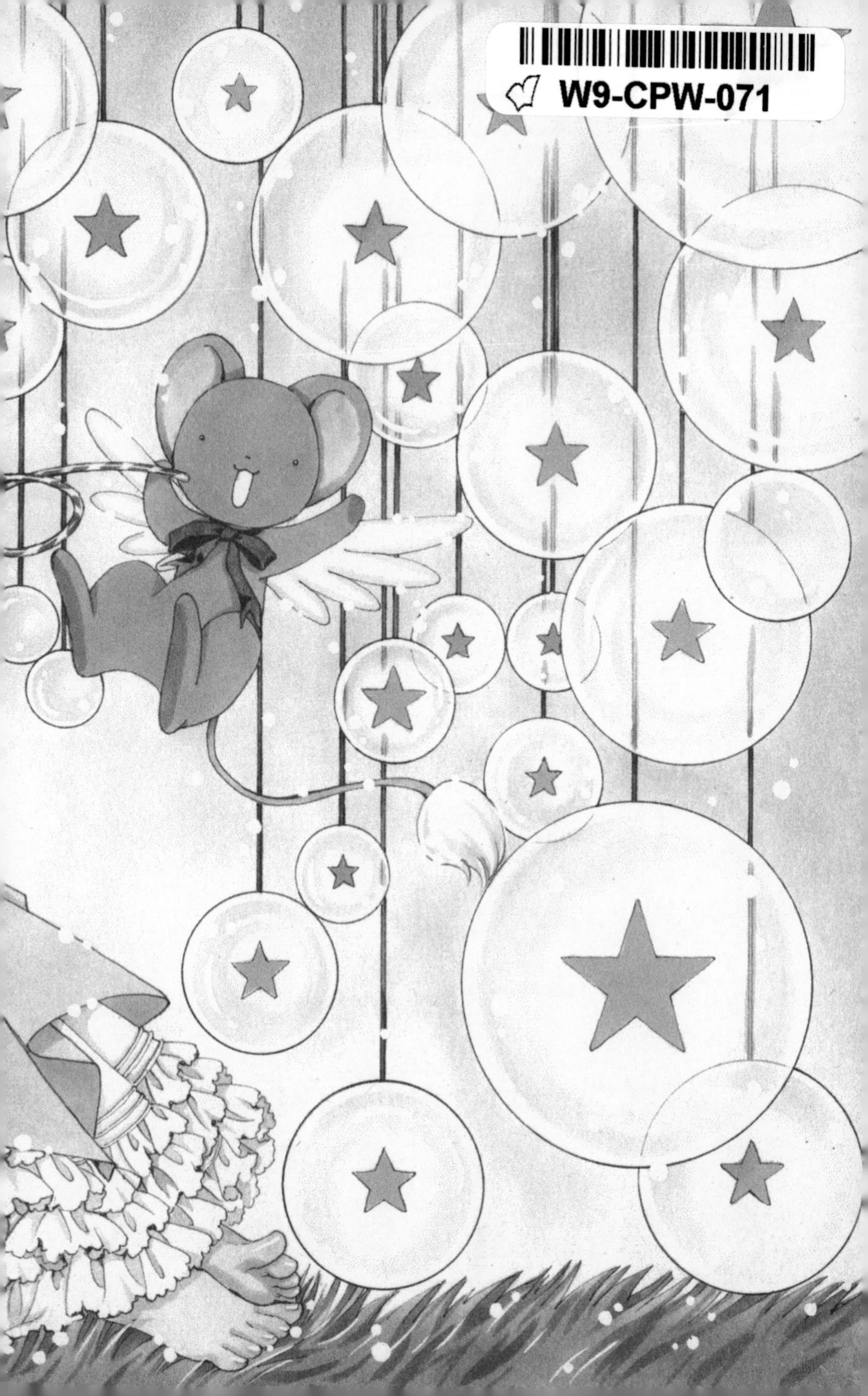

# CLAMP

4

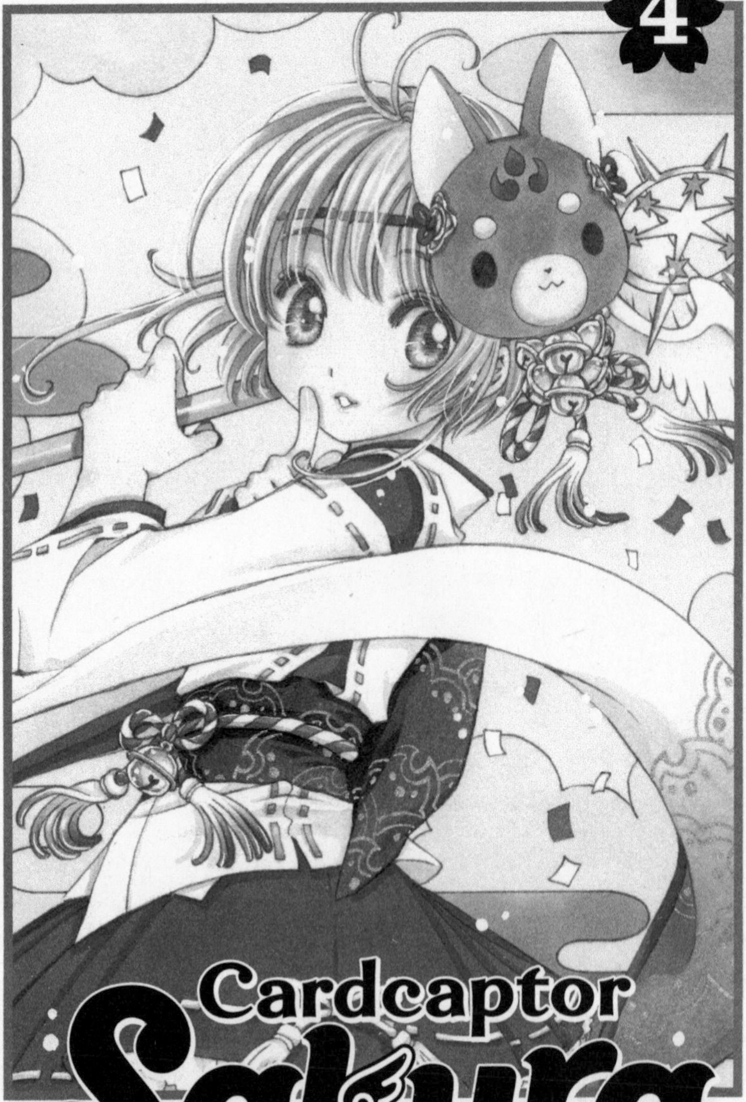

# Cardcaptor Sakura

CLEAR CARD

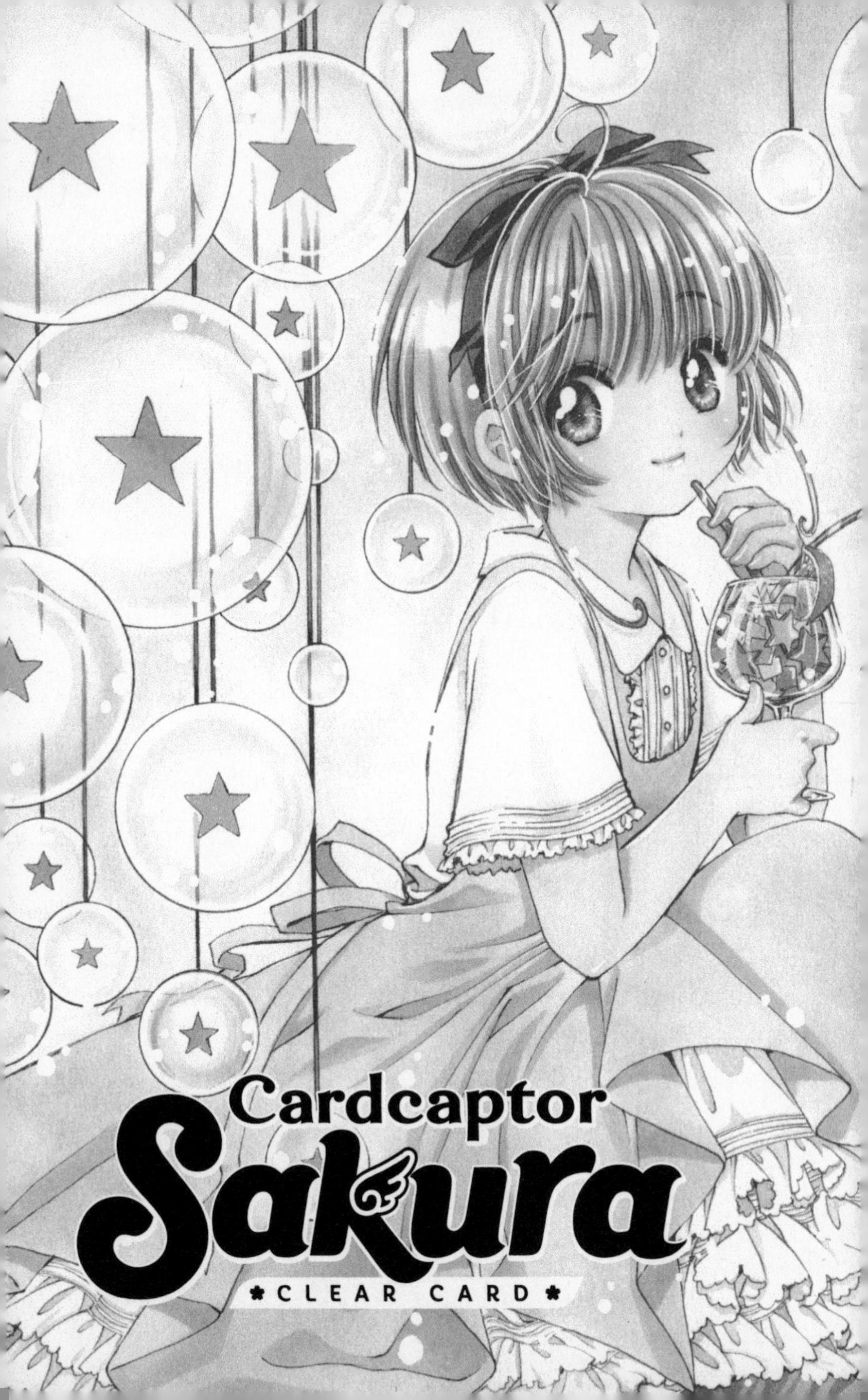
Cardcaptor
Sakura
CLEAR CARD

Cardcaptor
Sakura
CLEAR CARD

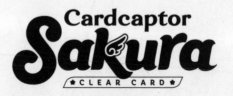

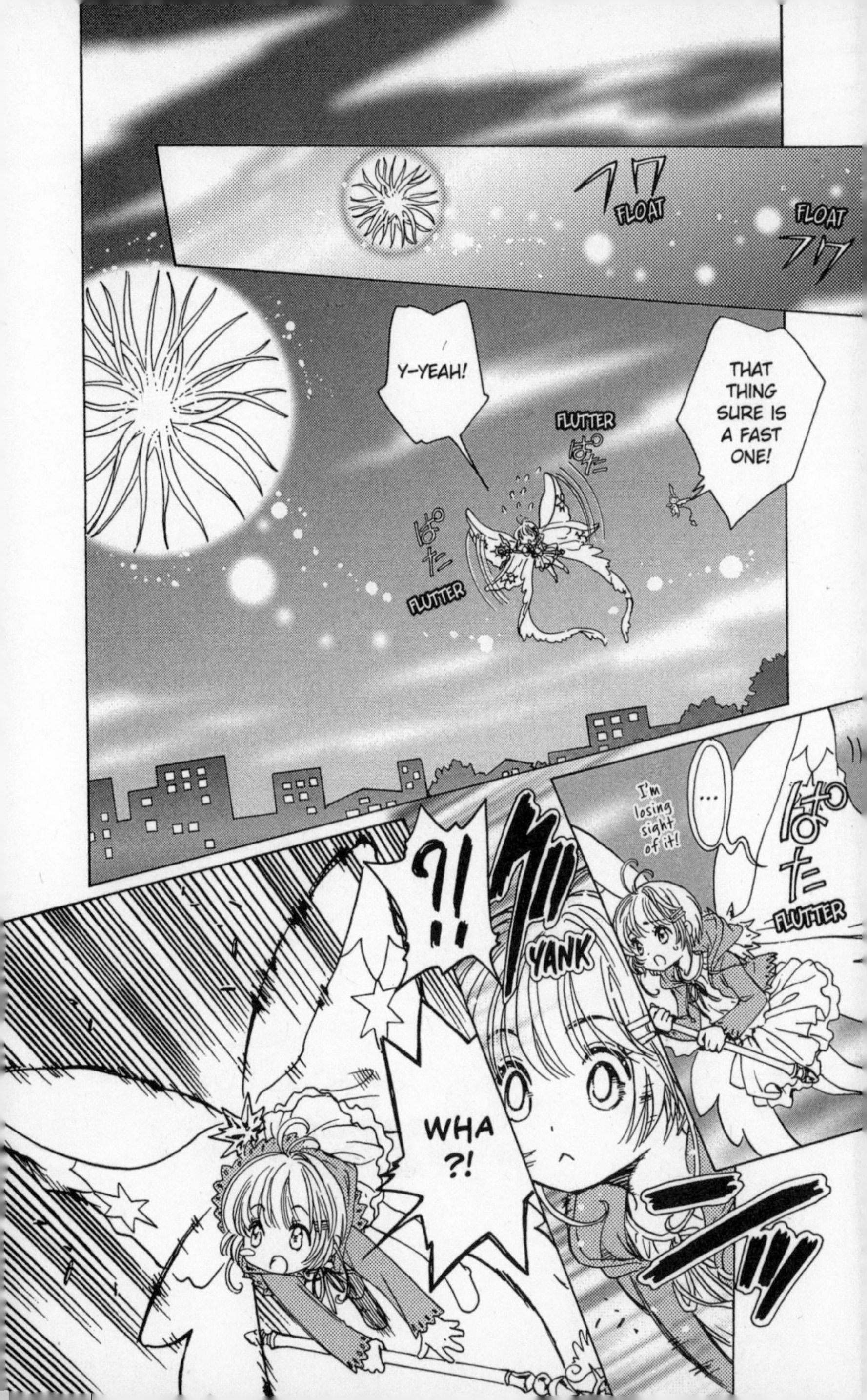

フワ
FLOAT
FLOAT
フワ
THAT THING SURE IS A FAST ONE!
Y-YEAH!
FLUTTER
ぱた
ぱた
FLUTTER
...
I'm losing sight of it!
ぱた
FLUTTER
?!!
YANK
WHA?!

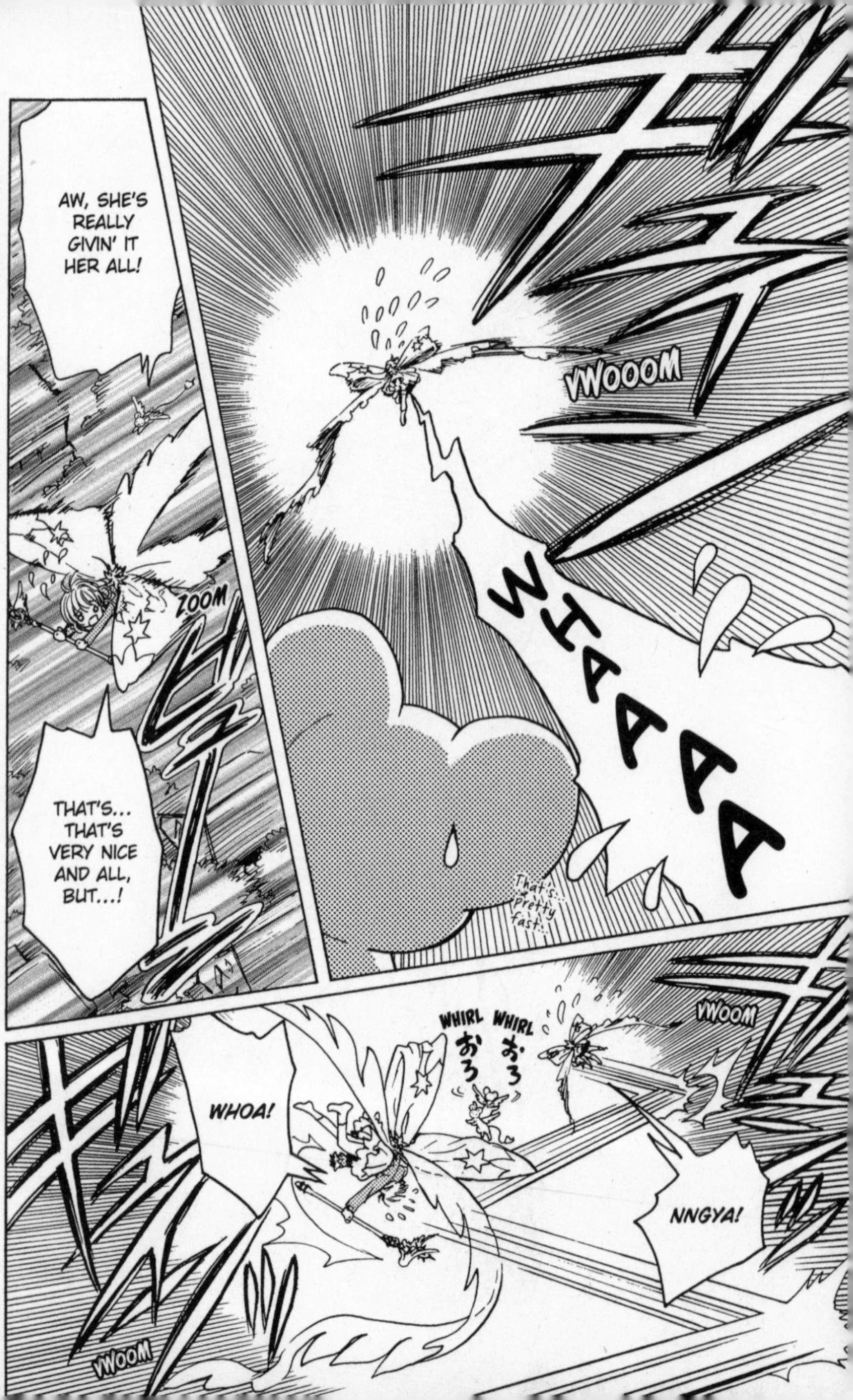
VWOOOM
WHIAAAA
That's... pretty fast...
AW, SHE'S REALLY GIVIN' IT HER ALL!
ZOOM
THAT'S... THAT'S VERY NICE AND ALL, BUT...!
VWOOM
WHIRL おろ
WHIRL おろ
NNGYA!
WHOA!
VWOOM

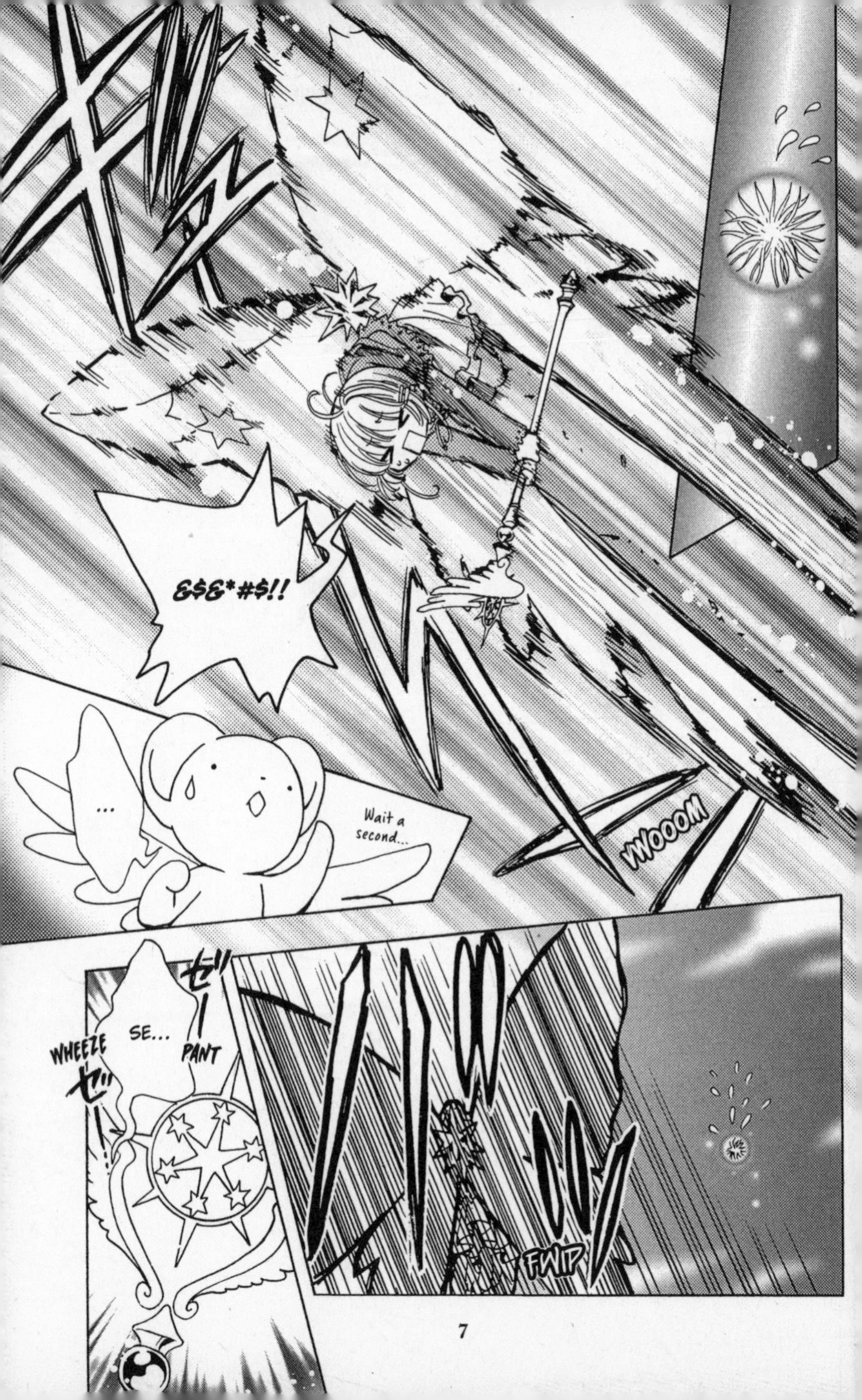
&$&*#$!!
VWOOOM
...
Wait a second...
FWIP
ゼー
PANT
SE...
WHEEZE
ゼー

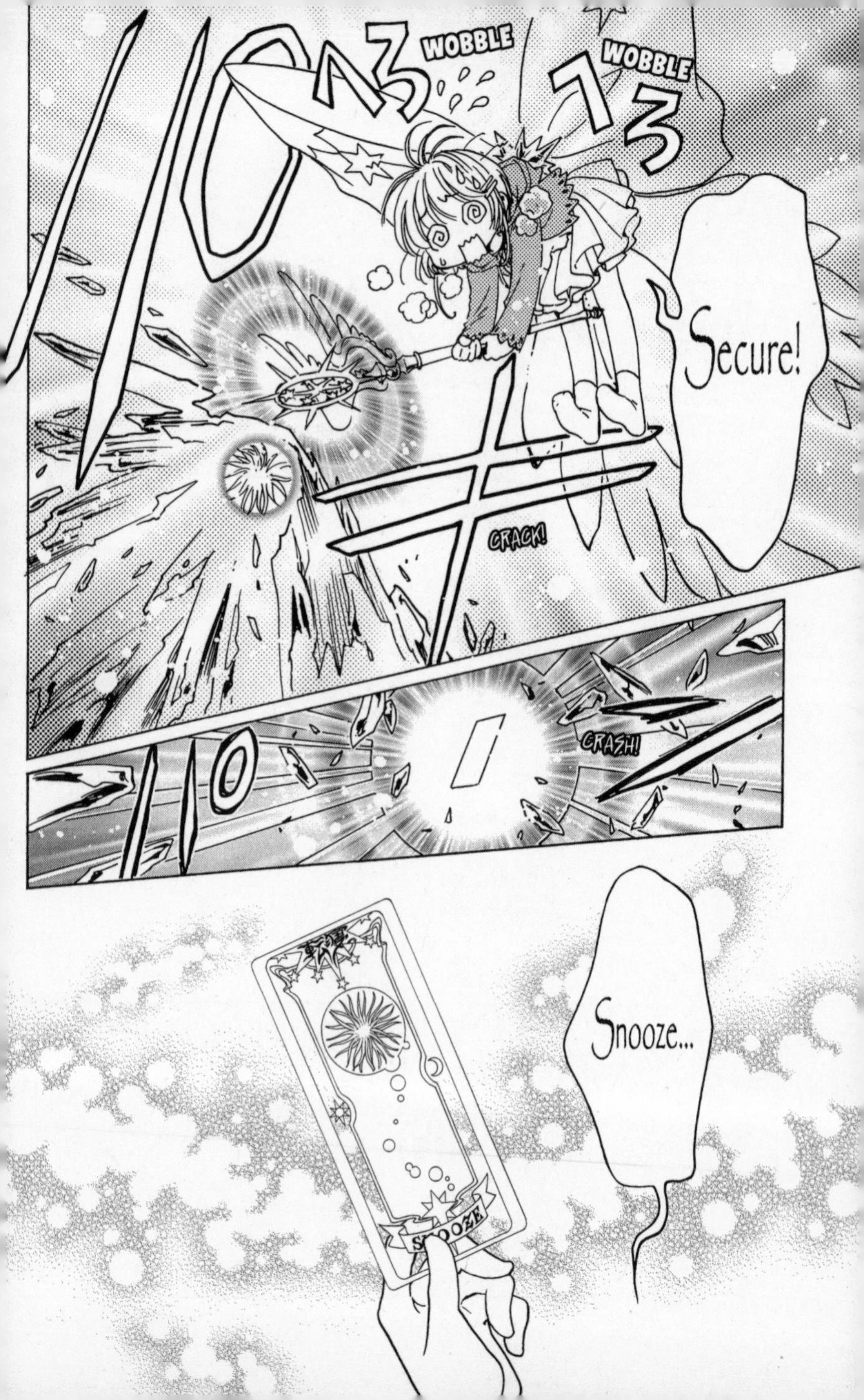
WOBBLE
Secure!
WOBBLE
CRACK!
CRASH!
Snooze...
SNOOZE

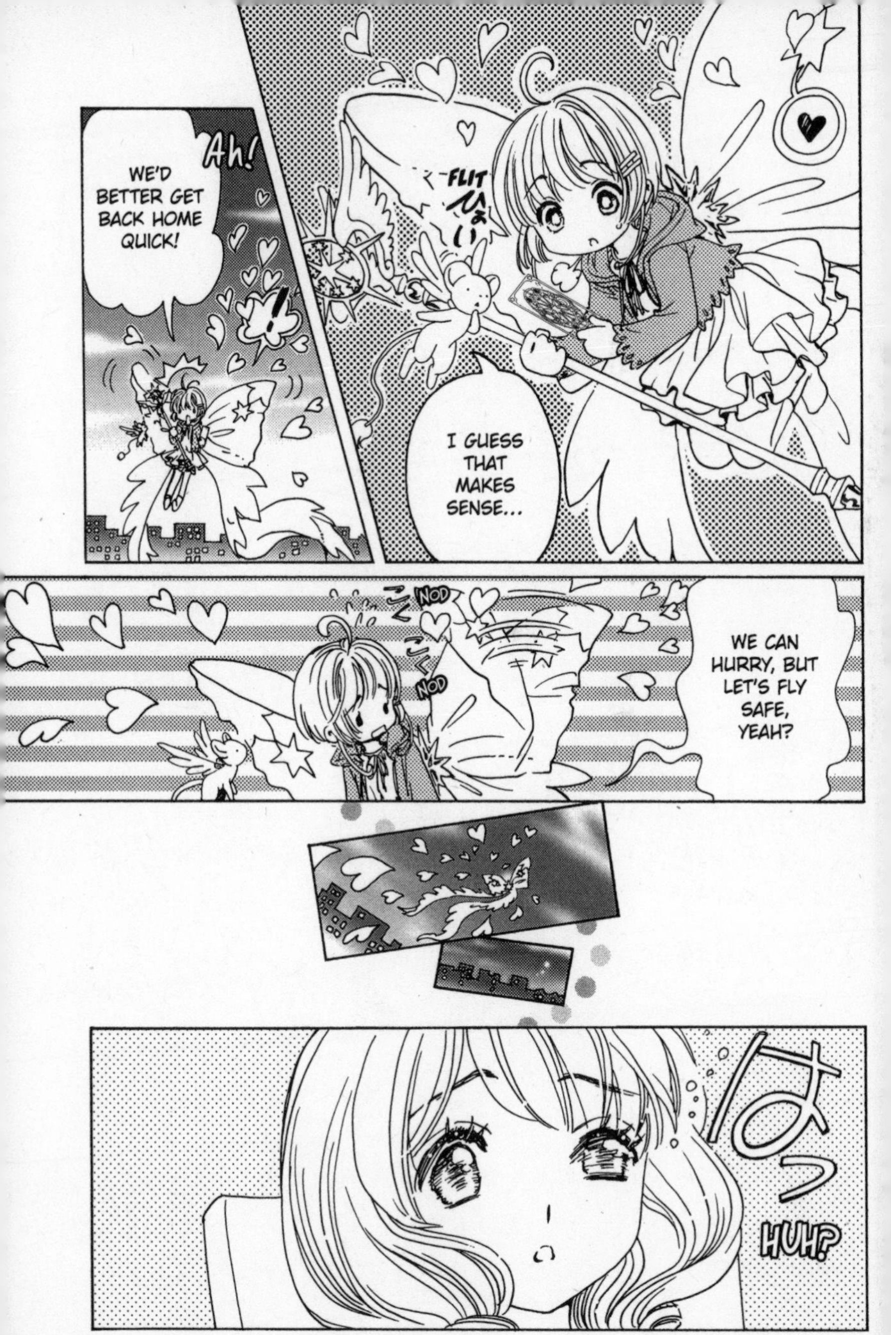
FLIT
ひょい
I GUESS THAT MAKES SENSE...
Ah!
WE'D BETTER GET BACK HOME QUICK!
WE CAN HURRY, BUT LET'S FLY SAFE, YEAH?
NOD
こく
NOD
こく
はっ
HUH?

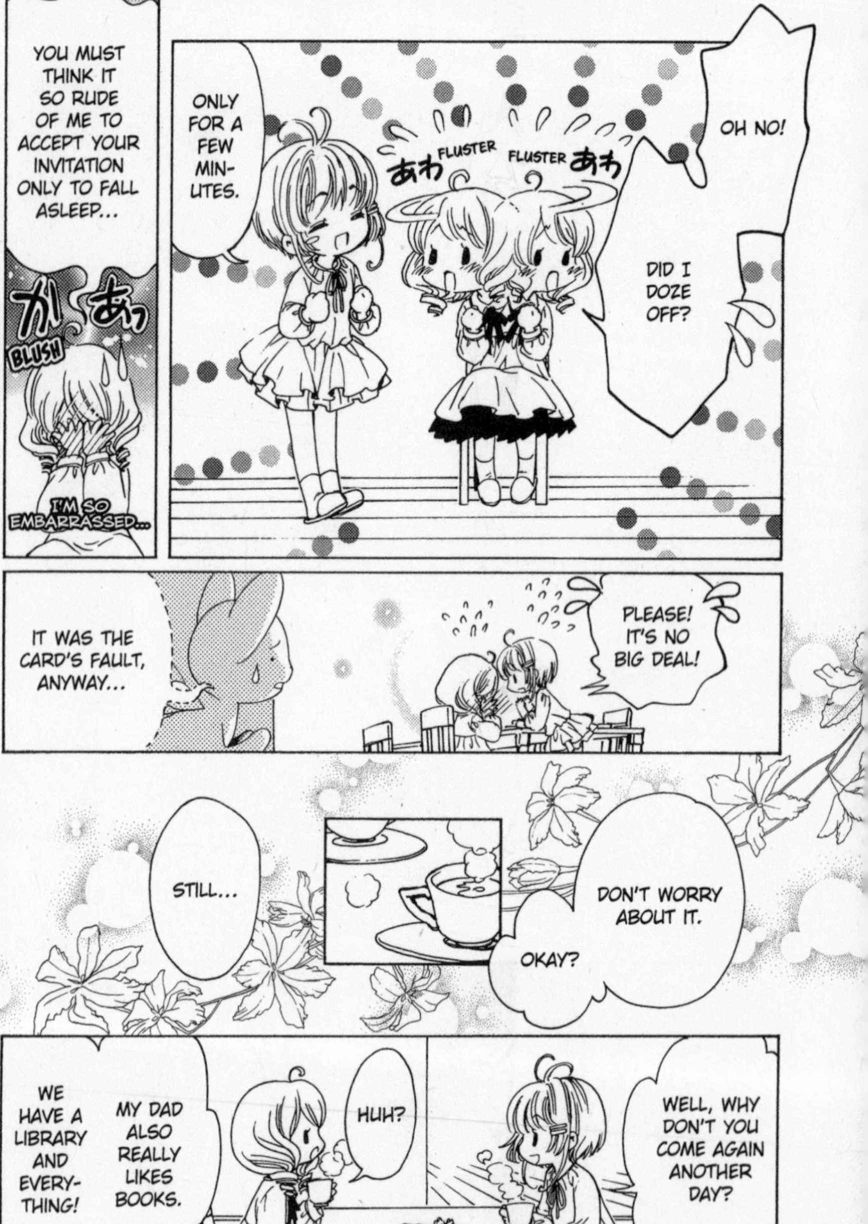
OH NO!
DID I DOZE OFF?
FLUSTER あわ
あわ FLUSTER
ONLY FOR A FEW MIN-UTES.
YOU MUST THINK IT SO RUDE OF ME TO ACCEPT YOUR INVITATION ONLY TO FALL ASLEEP...
かぁっ BLUSH
I'M SO EMBARRASSED...
PLEASE! IT'S NO BIG DEAL!
IT WAS THE CARD'S FAULT, ANYWAY...
DON'T WORRY ABOUT IT.
OKAY?
STILL...
WELL, WHY DON'T YOU COME AGAIN ANOTHER DAY?
HUH?
MY DAD ALSO REALLY LIKES BOOKS.
WE HAVE A LIBRARY AND EVERY-THING!

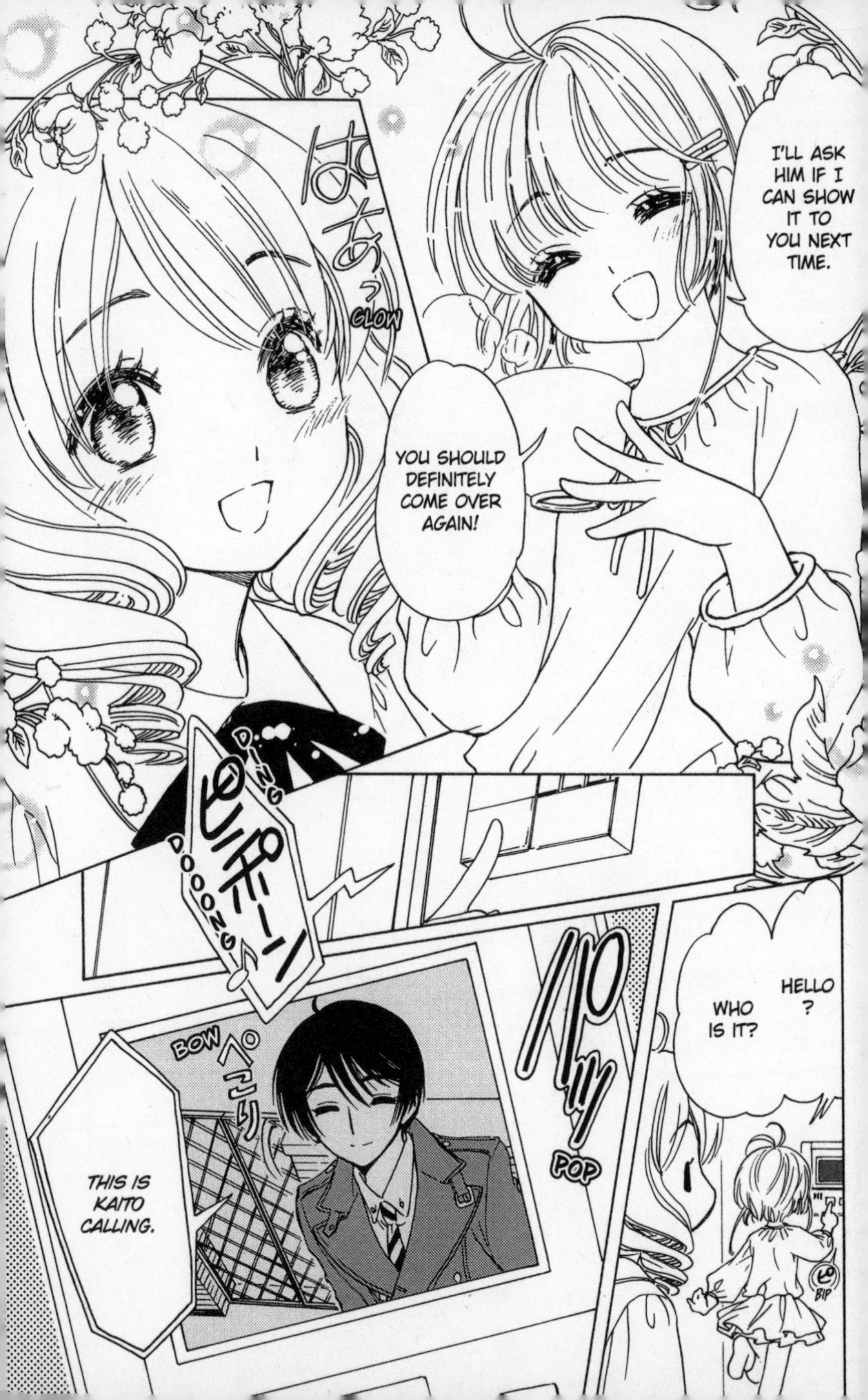
I'LL ASK HIM IF I CAN SHOW IT TO YOU NEXT TIME.
はあっ
GLOW
YOU SHOULD DEFINITELY COME OVER AGAIN!
ピンポーン
DING DOOOONG
HELLO?
WHO IS IT?
ピ
BIP
パッ
POP
ぺこり
BOW
THIS IS KAITO CALLING.

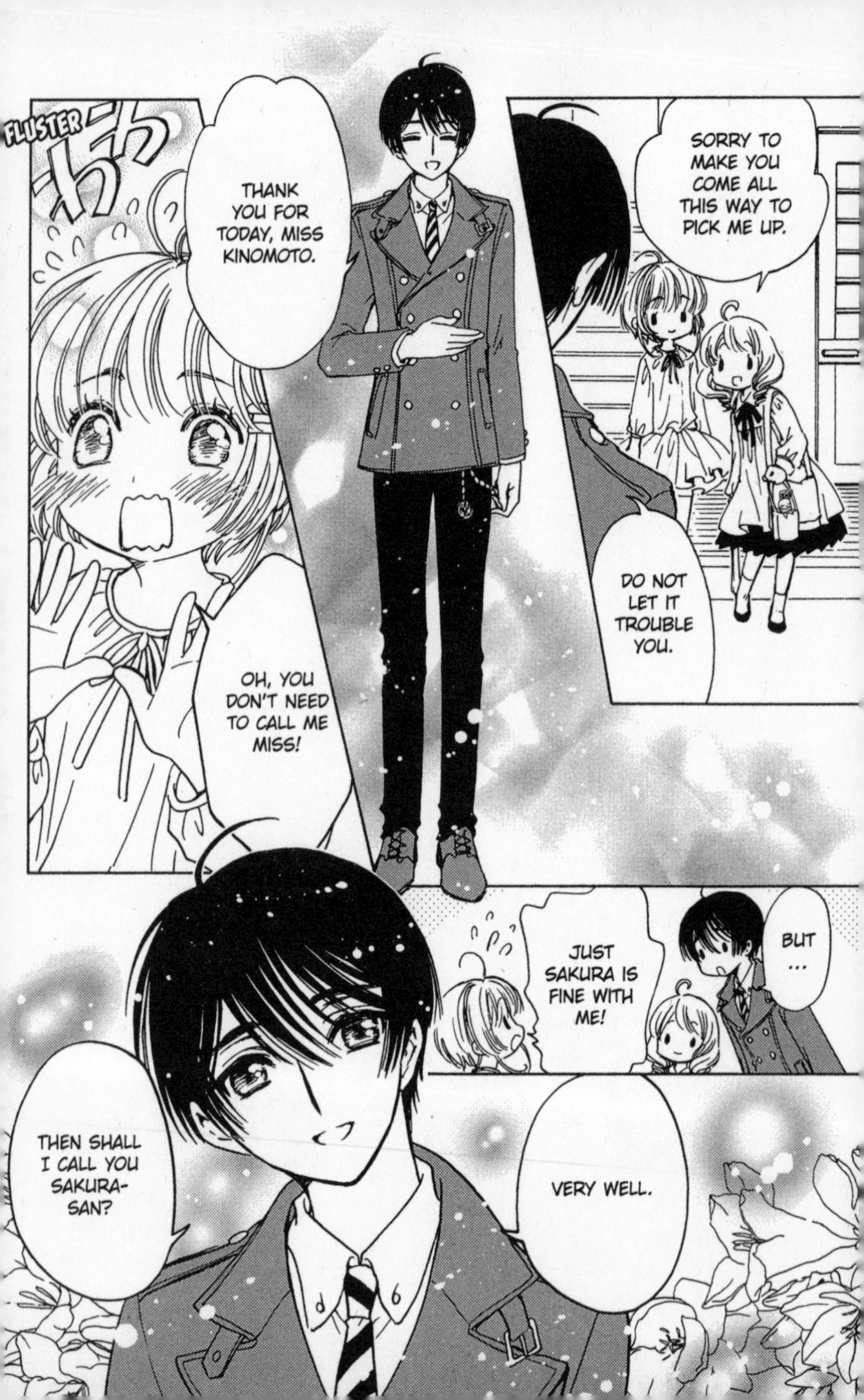

SORRY TO MAKE YOU COME ALL THIS WAY TO PICK ME UP.
DO NOT LET IT TROUBLE YOU.
THANK YOU FOR TODAY, MISS KINOMOTO.
FLUSTER
OH, YOU DON'T NEED TO CALL ME MISS!
BUT ...
JUST SAKURA IS FINE WITH ME!
VERY WELL.
THEN SHALL I CALL YOU SAKURA-SAN?

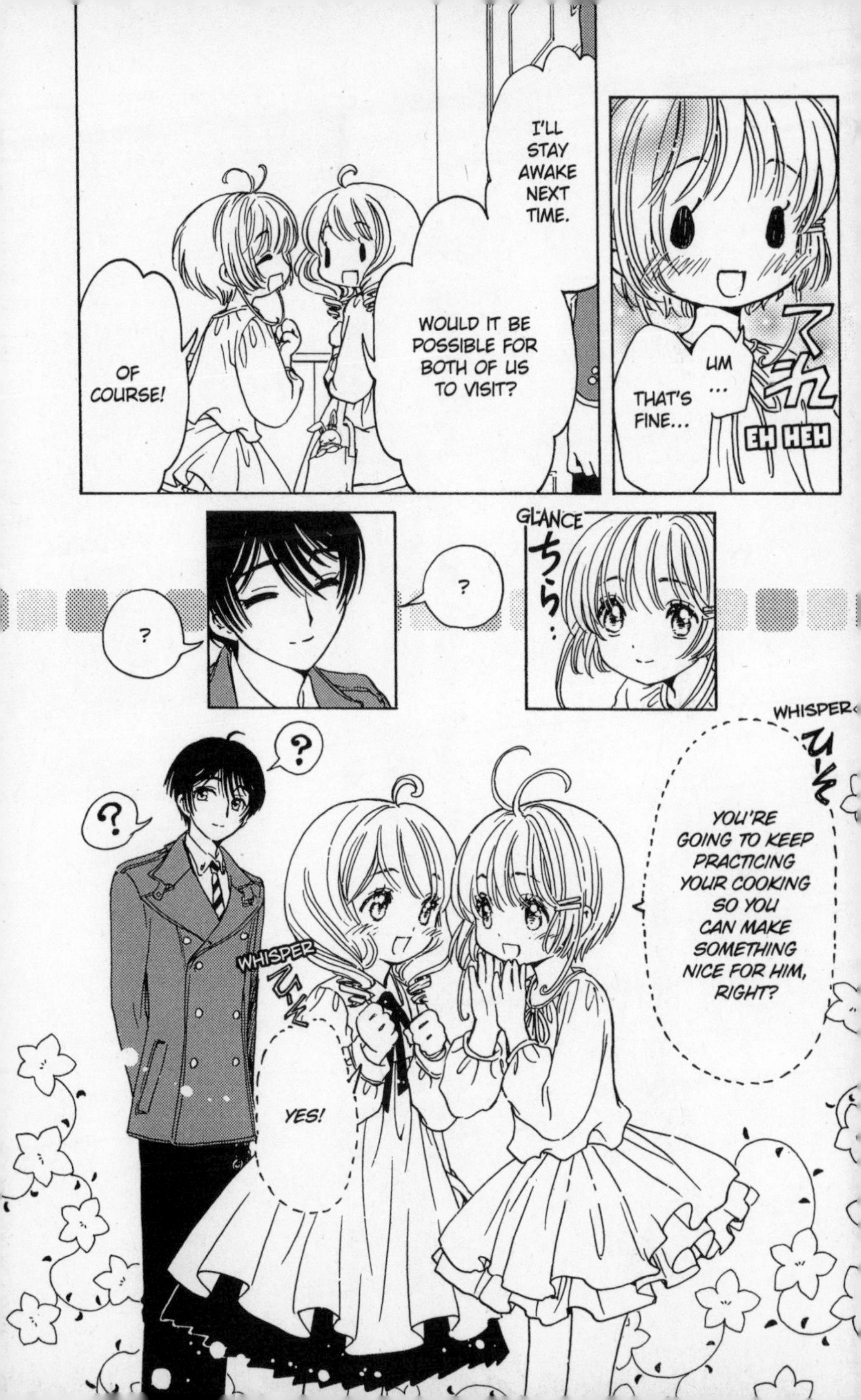
てれ
EH HEH
UM ...
THAT'S FINE...
I'LL STAY AWAKE NEXT TIME.
WOULD IT BE POSSIBLE FOR BOTH OF US TO VISIT?
OF COURSE!
GLANCE
ちら...
?
?
WHISPER
ひそ
YOU'RE GOING TO KEEP PRACTICING YOUR COOKING SO YOU CAN MAKE SOMETHING NICE FOR HIM, RIGHT?
?
?
WHISPER
ひそ
YES!

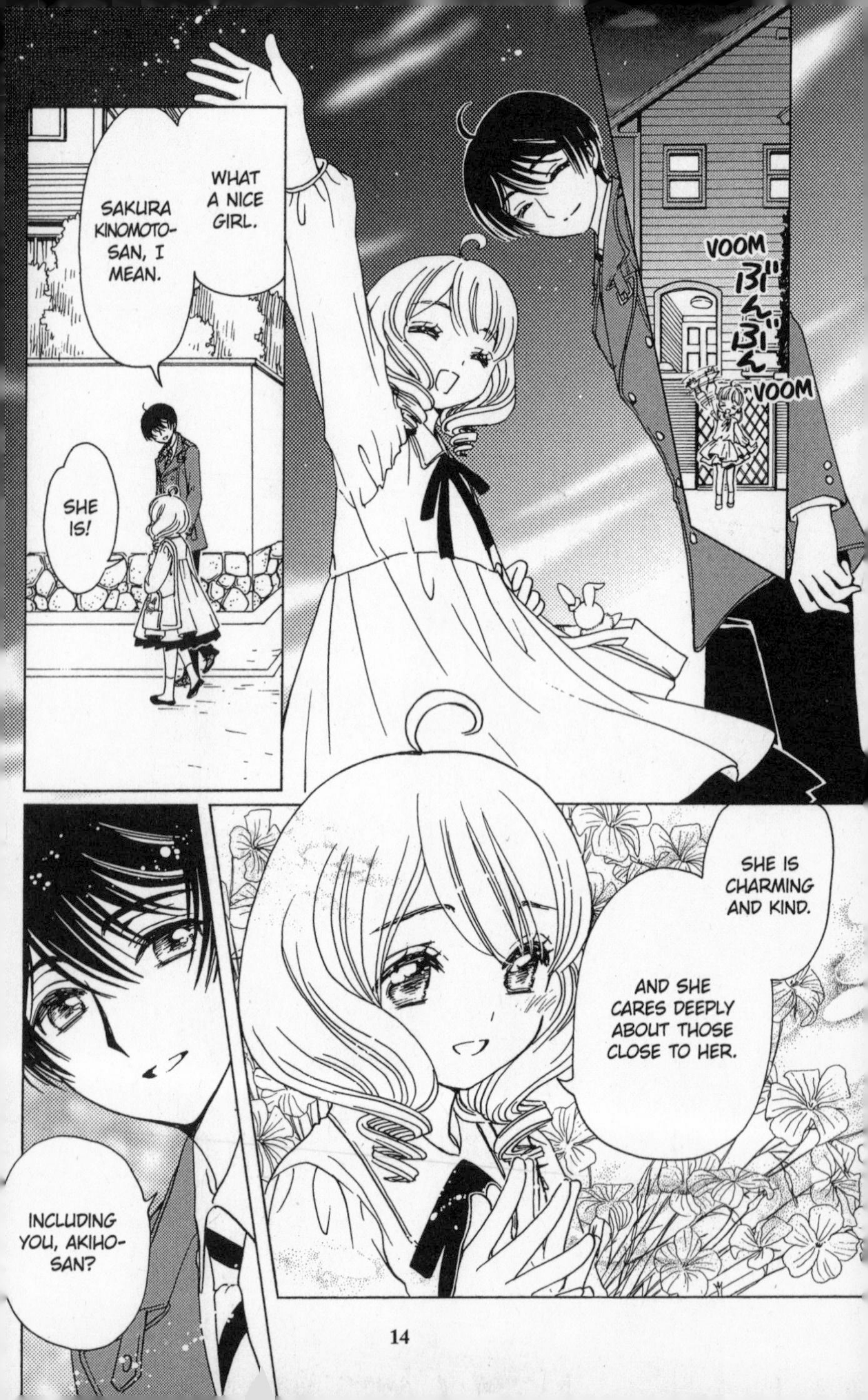

VOOM
ぶんぶん
VOOM
WHAT A NICE GIRL.
SAKURA KINOMOTO-SAN, I MEAN.
SHE IS!
SHE IS CHARMING AND KIND.
AND SHE CARES DEEPLY ABOUT THOSE CLOSE TO HER.
INCLUDING YOU, AKIHO-SAN?

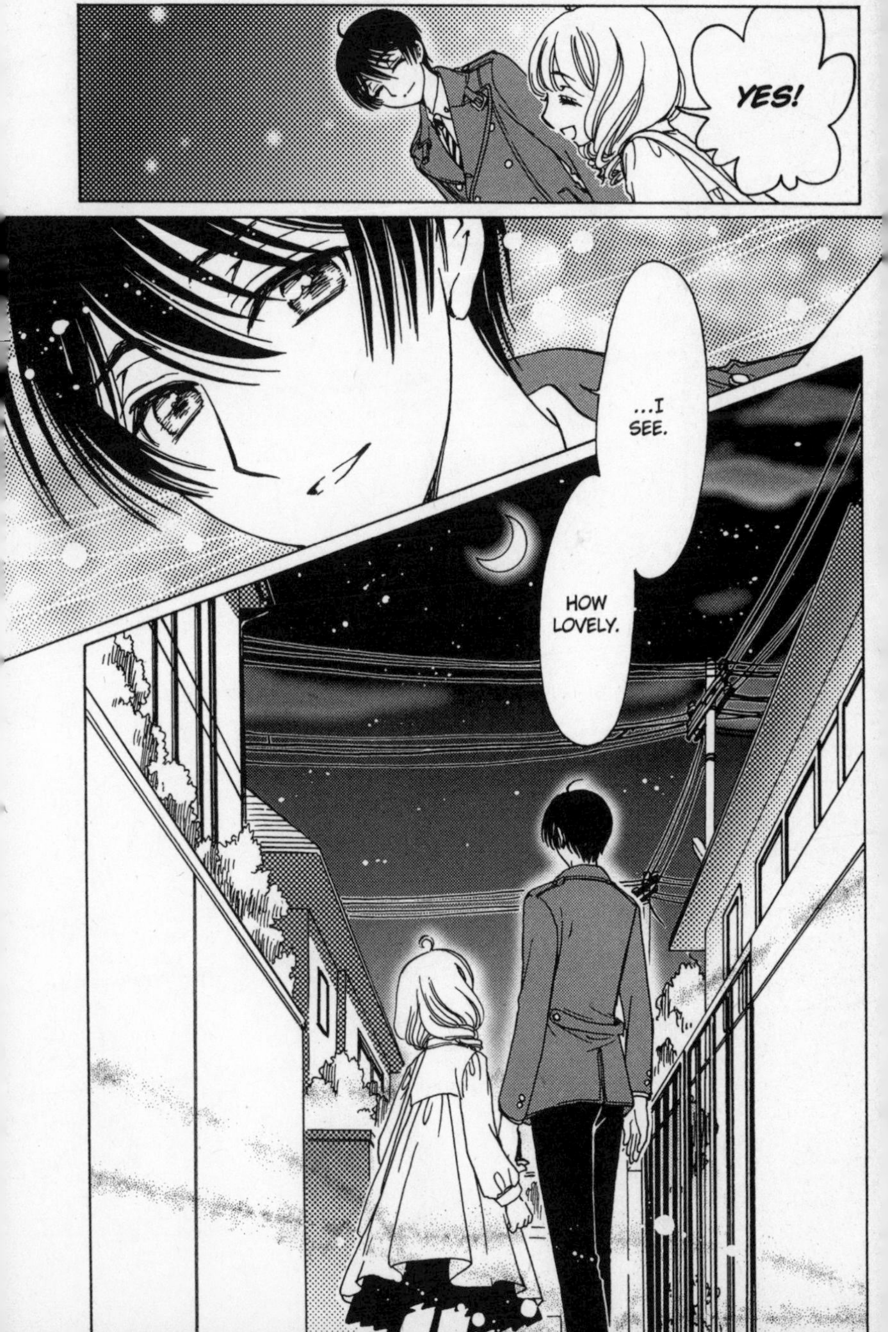
YES!
...I SEE.
HOW LOVELY.

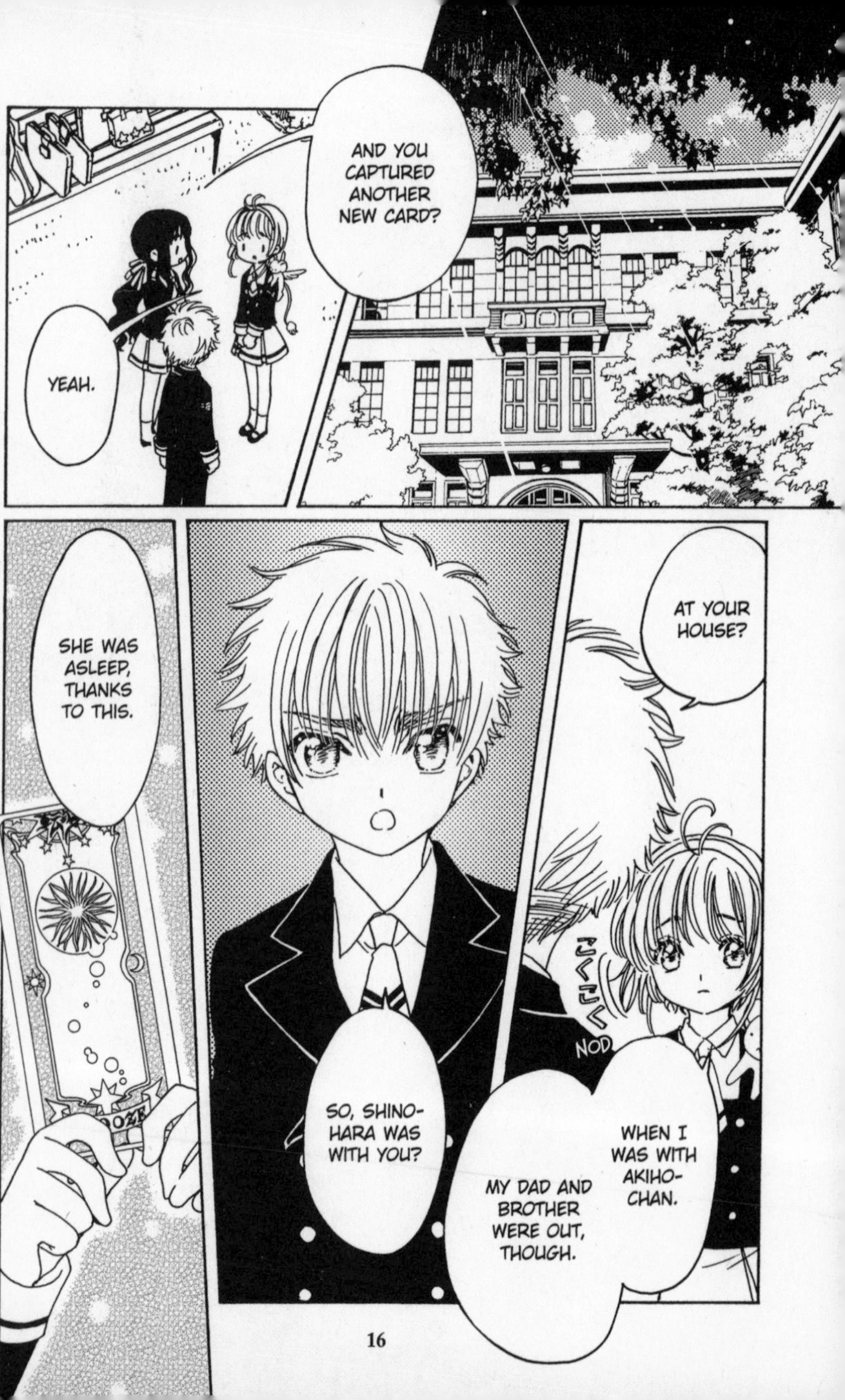
AND YOU CAPTURED ANOTHER NEW CARD?
YEAH.
AT YOUR HOUSE?
NOD
WHEN I WAS WITH AKIHO-CHAN.
MY DAD AND BROTHER WERE OUT, THOUGH.
SO, SHINO-HARA WAS WITH YOU?
SHE WAS ASLEEP, THANKS TO THIS.

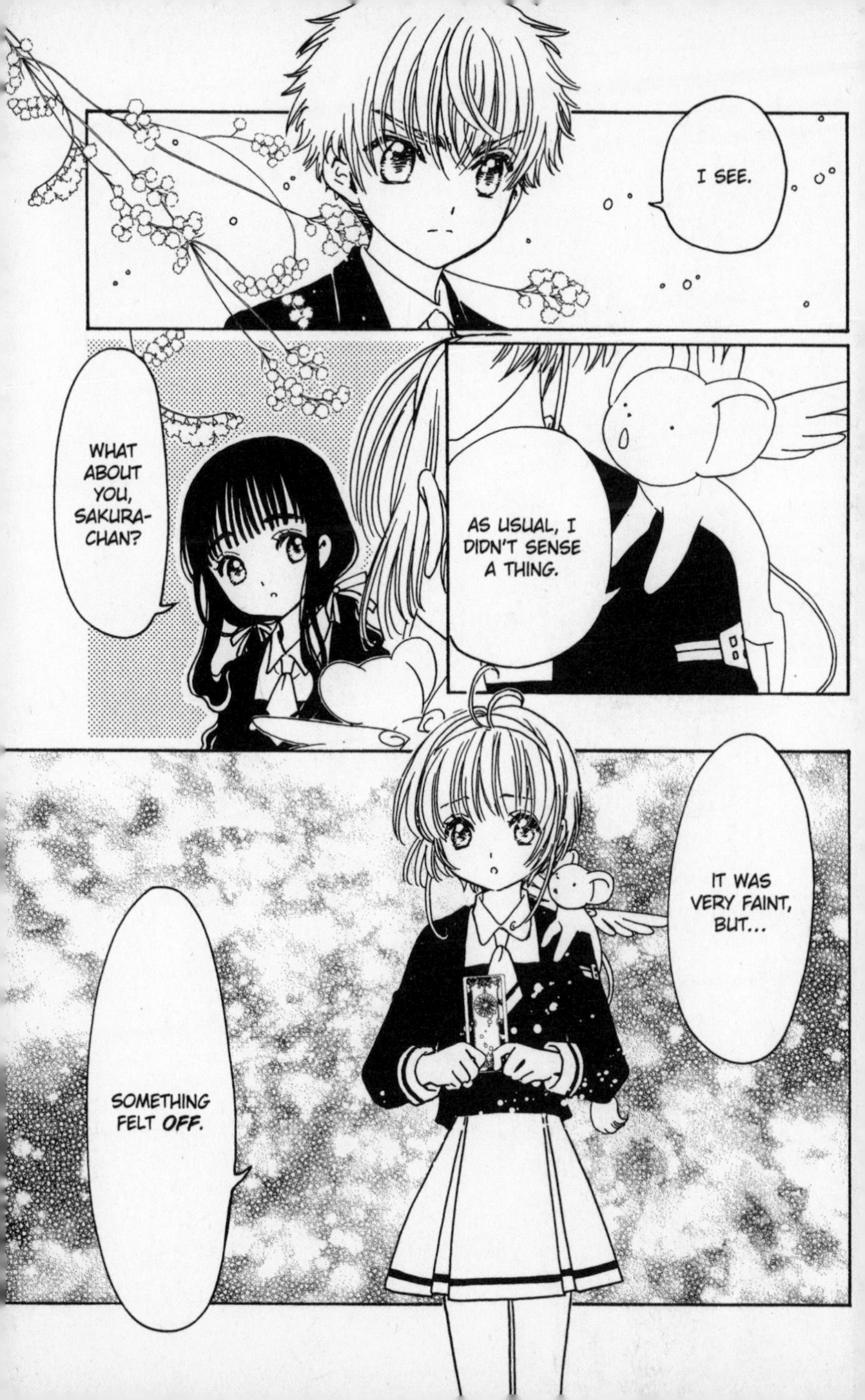
I SEE.
AS USUAL, I DIDN'T SENSE A THING.
WHAT ABOUT YOU, SAKURA-CHAN?
IT WAS VERY FAINT, BUT...
SOMETHING FELT *OFF*.

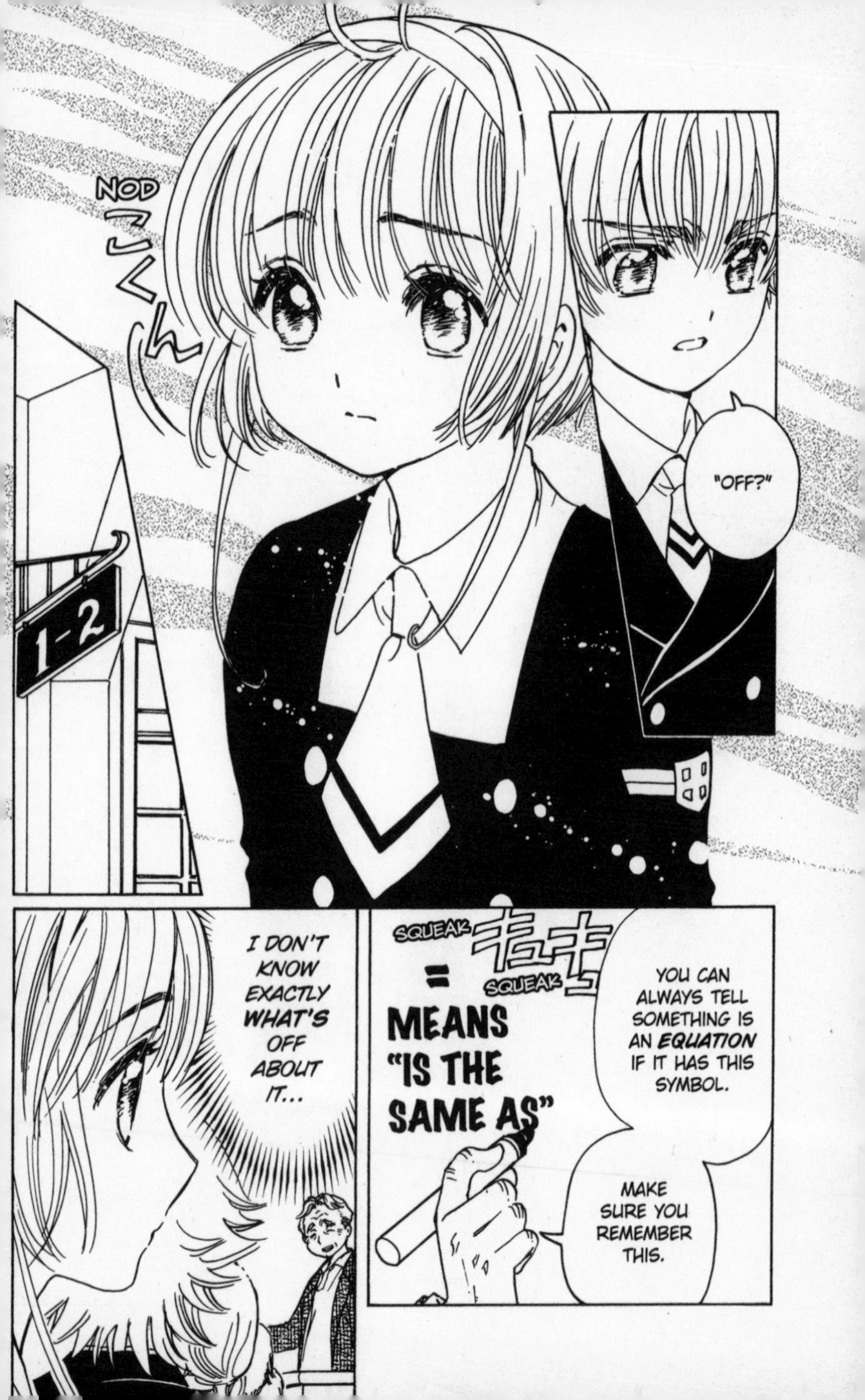
"OFF?"
NOD
1-2
YOU CAN ALWAYS TELL SOMETHING IS AN *EQUATION* IF IT HAS THIS SYMBOL.
SQUEAK SQUEAK
= MEANS "IS THE SAME AS"
MAKE SURE YOU REMEMBER THIS.
I DON'T KNOW EXACTLY **WHAT'S** OFF ABOUT IT...

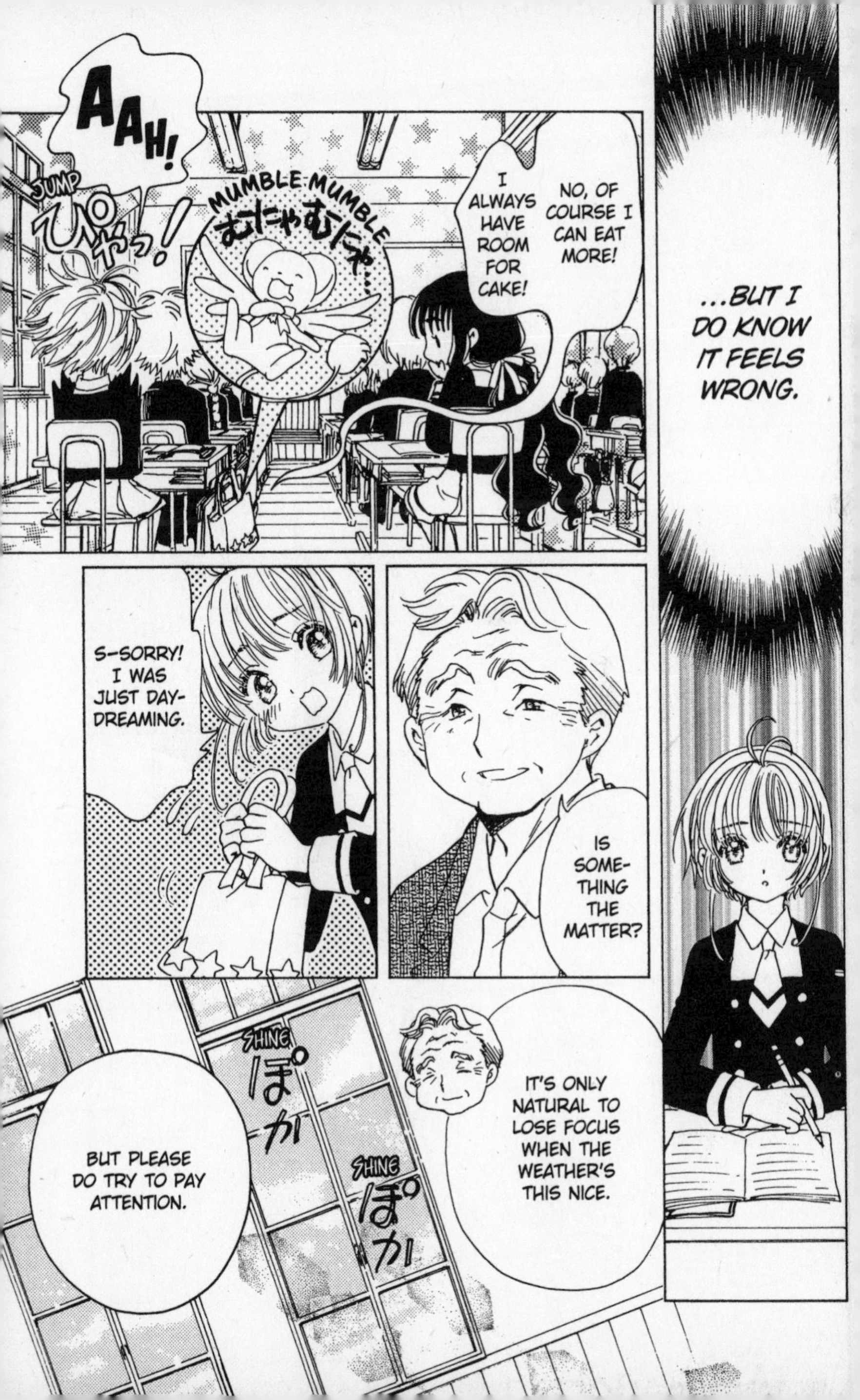
...BUT I DO KNOW IT FEELS WRONG.
NO, OF COURSE I CAN EAT MORE!
I ALWAYS HAVE ROOM FOR CAKE!
MUMBLE MUMBLE
むにゃむにゃ…
JUMP
ぴゃっ!
AAH!
IS SOMETHING THE MATTER?
S-SORRY! I WAS JUST DAY-DREAMING.
IT'S ONLY NATURAL TO LOSE FOCUS WHEN THE WEATHER'S THIS NICE.
SHINE
ぽか
SHINE
ぽか
BUT PLEASE DO TRY TO PAY ATTENTION.

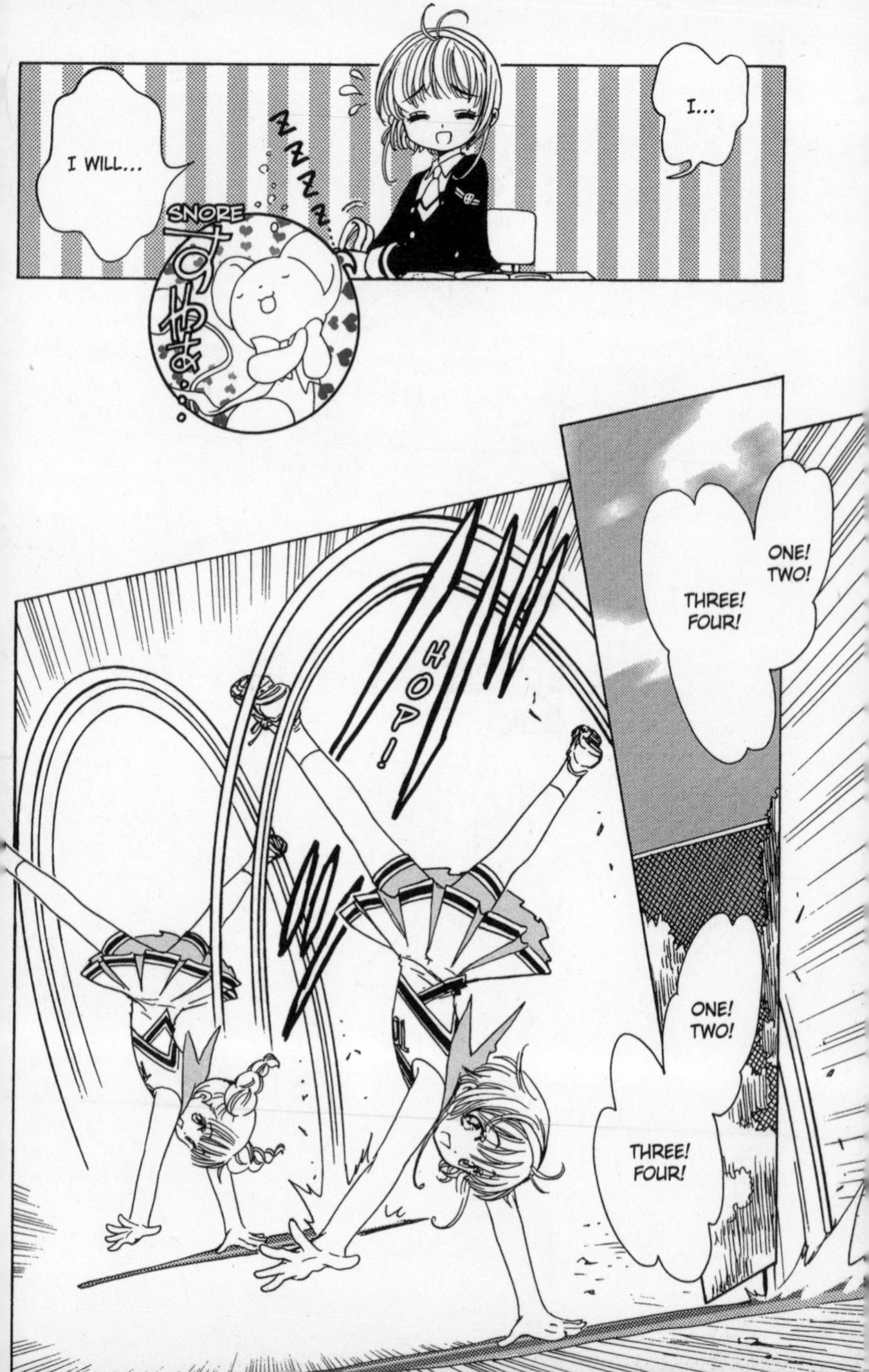
I...
I WILL...
SNORE
ONE! TWO! THREE! FOUR!
HOP!
ONE! TWO! THREE! FOUR!

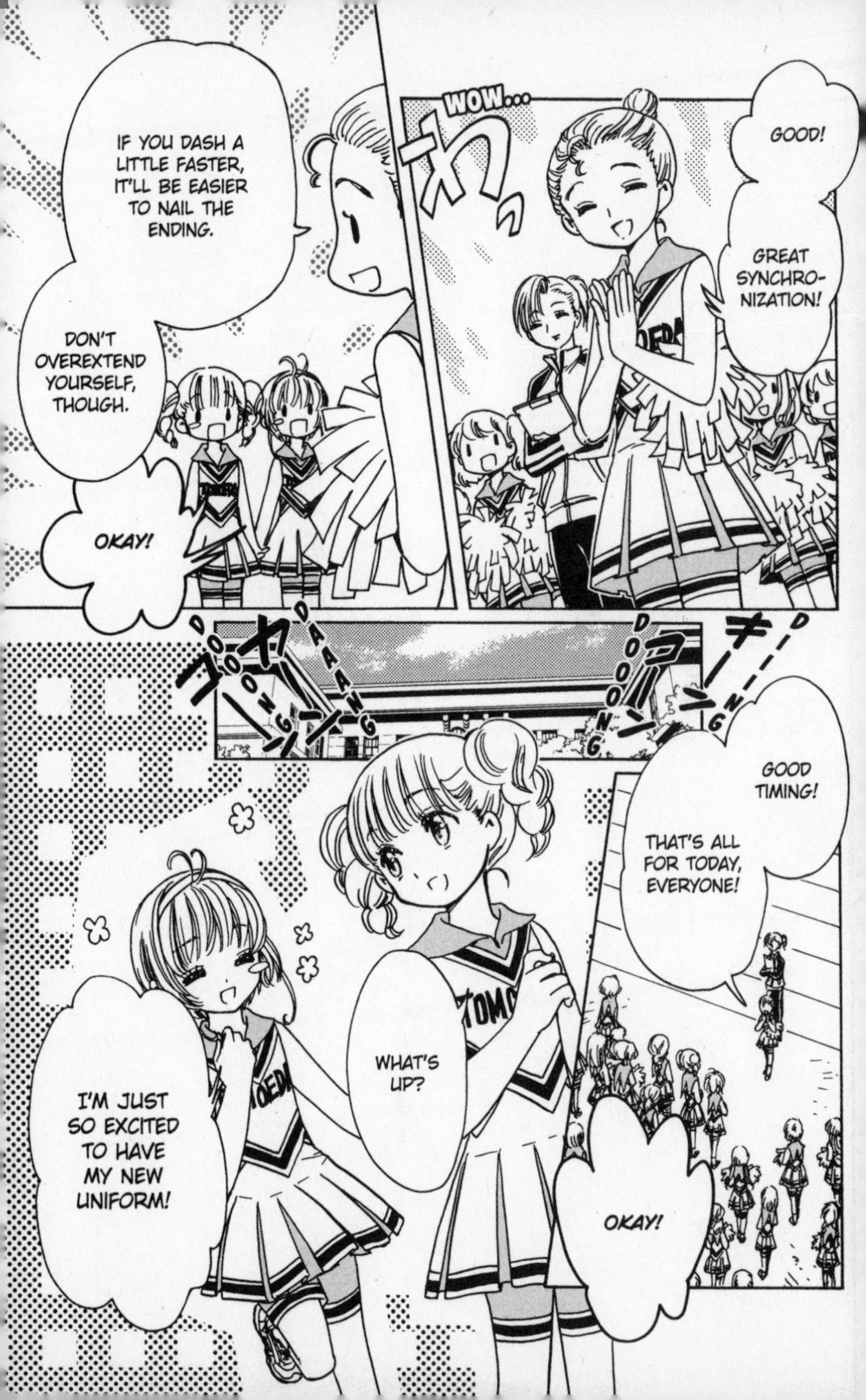
WOW...
GOOD!
GREAT SYNCHRONIZATION!
IF YOU DASH A LITTLE FASTER, IT'LL BE EASIER TO NAIL THE ENDING.
DON'T OVEREXTEND YOURSELF, THOUGH.
OKAY!
DING
DOOOONG
DAAAANG
DOOOONG
GOOD TIMING!
THAT'S ALL FOR TODAY, EVERYONE!
OKAY!
WHAT'S UP?
I'M JUST SO EXCITED TO HAVE MY NEW UNIFORM!

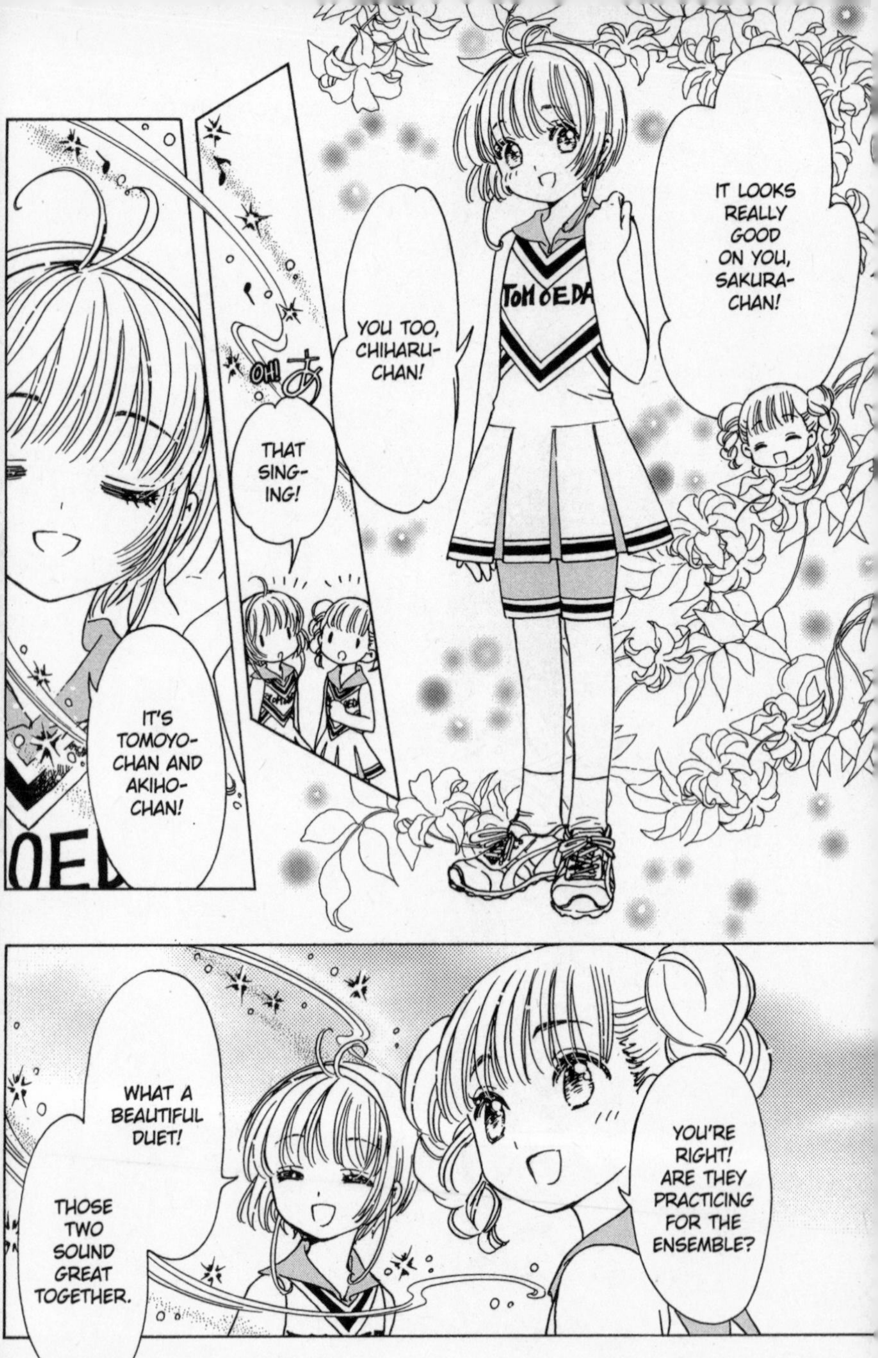
IT LOOKS REALLY GOOD ON YOU, SAKURA-CHAN!
YOU TOO, CHIHARU-CHAN!
TOMOEDA
OH!
THAT SINGING!
IT'S TOMOYO-CHAN AND AKIHO-CHAN!
YOU'RE RIGHT! ARE THEY PRACTICING FOR THE ENSEMBLE?
WHAT A BEAUTIFUL DUET!
THOSE TWO SOUND GREAT TOGETHER.

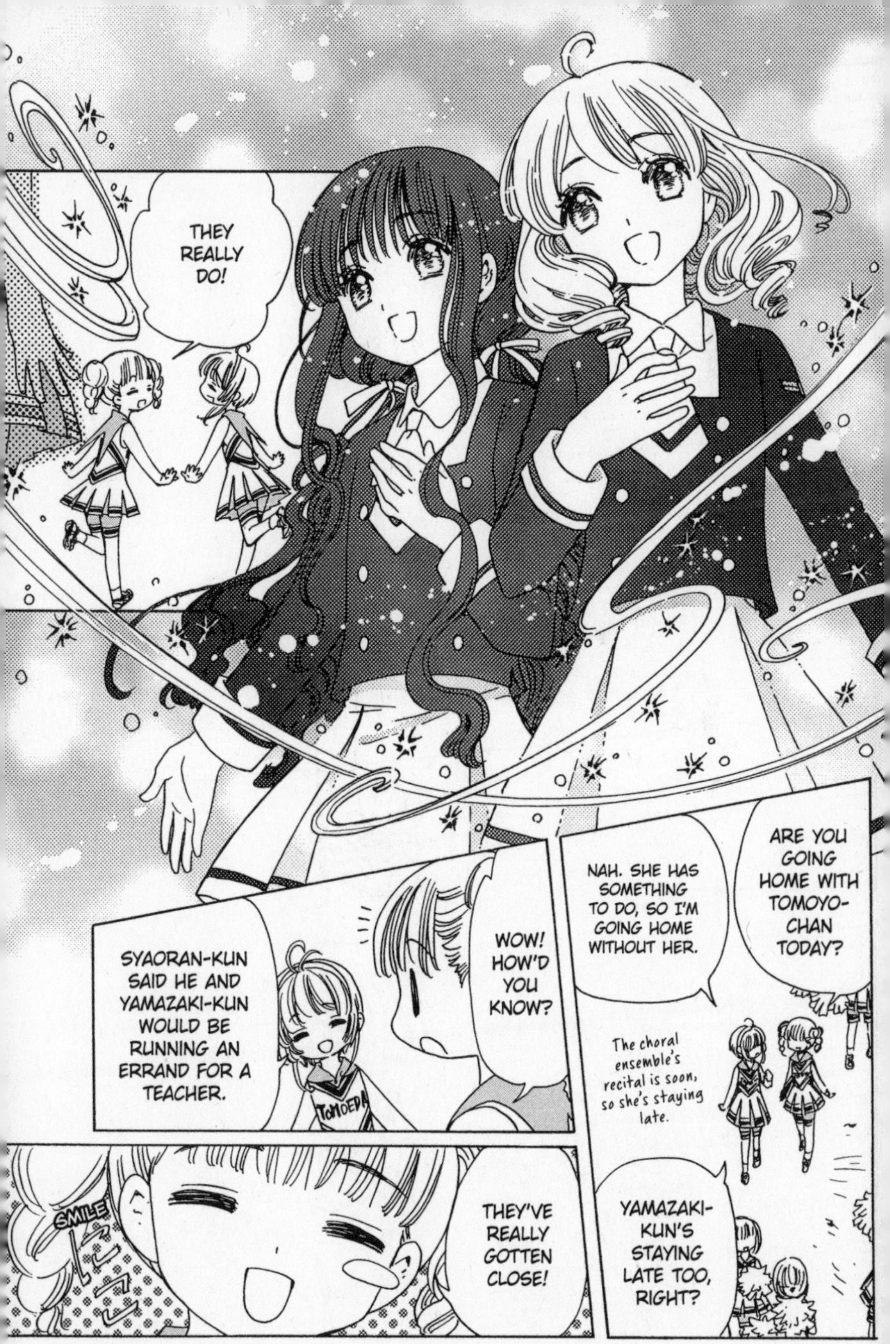
THEY REALLY DO!
ARE YOU GOING HOME WITH TOMOYO-CHAN TODAY?
NAH. SHE HAS SOMETHING TO DO, SO I'M GOING HOME WITHOUT HER.
The choral ensemble's recital is soon, so she's staying late.
YAMAZAKI-KUN'S STAYING LATE TOO, RIGHT?
WOW! HOW'D YOU KNOW?
SYAORAN-KUN SAID HE AND YAMAZAKI-KUN WOULD BE RUNNING AN ERRAND FOR A TEACHER.
THEY'VE REALLY GOTTEN CLOSE!
SMILE

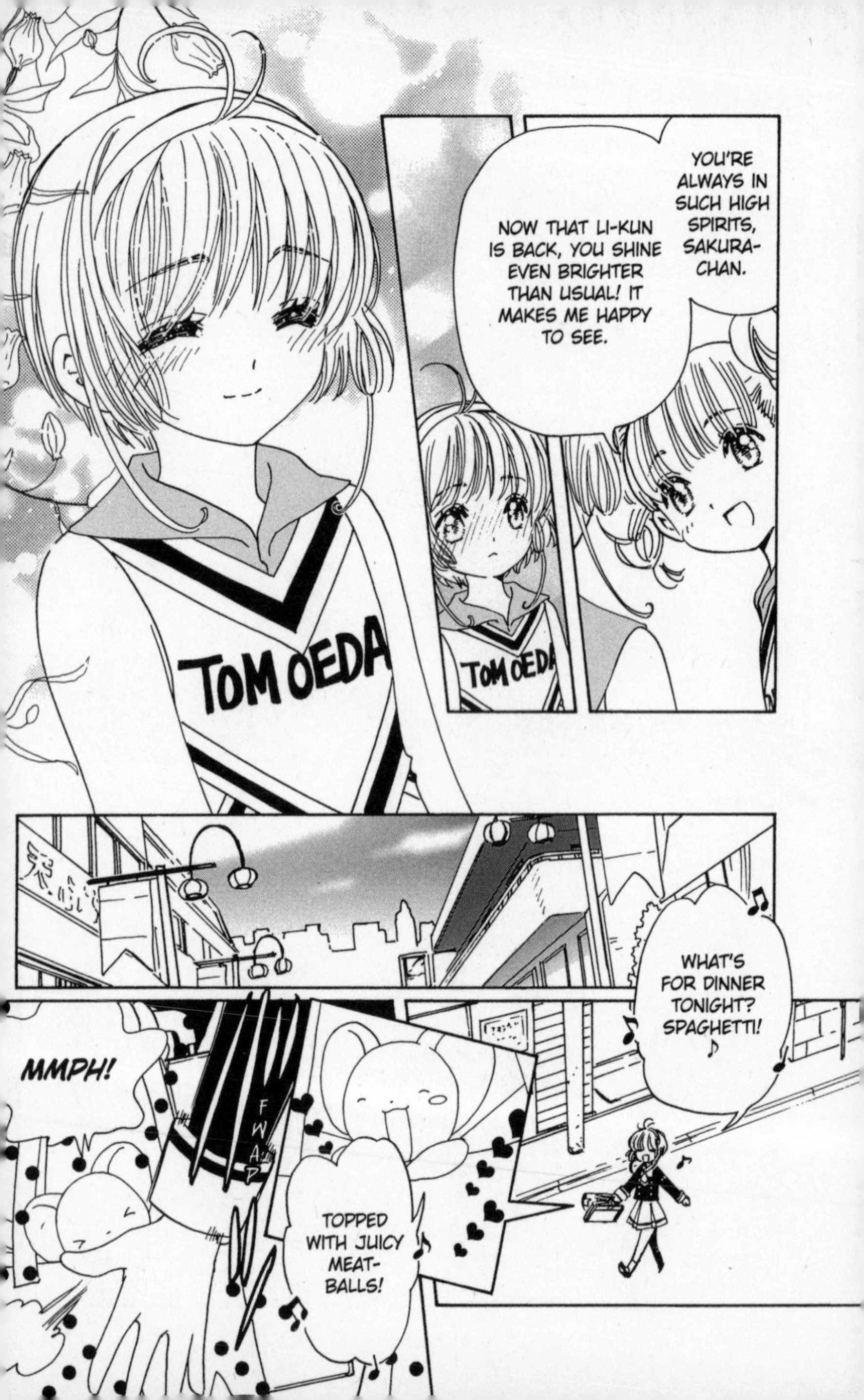
YOU'RE ALWAYS IN SUCH HIGH SPIRITS, SAKURA-CHAN.
NOW THAT LI-KUN IS BACK, YOU SHINE EVEN BRIGHTER THAN USUAL! IT MAKES ME HAPPY TO SEE.
TOMOEDA
TOMOEDA
WHAT'S FOR DINNER TONIGHT? SPAGHETTI! ♪
FWAP
TOPPED WITH JUICY MEAT-BALLS!
MMPH!

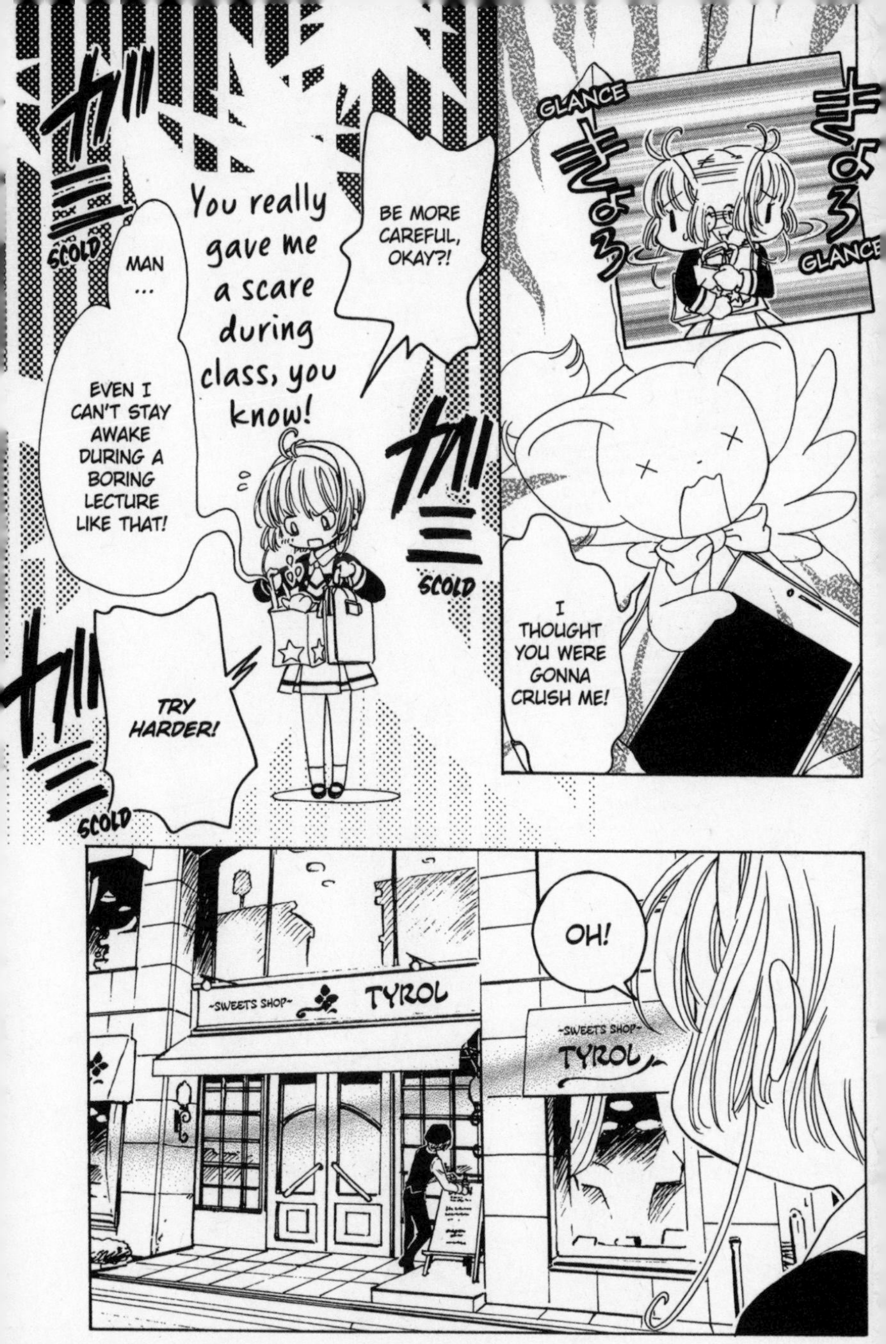
GLANCE
きょろ
きょろ
GLANCE
I THOUGHT YOU WERE GONNA CRUSH ME!
ガミ
SCOLD
BE MORE CAREFUL, OKAY?!
You really gave me a scare during class, you know!
ガミ
SCOLD
MAN ...
EVEN I CAN'T STAY AWAKE DURING A BORING LECTURE LIKE THAT!
TRY HARDER!
ガミ
SCOLD
OH!
~SWEETS SHOP~ TYROL
~SWEETS SHOP~ TYROL

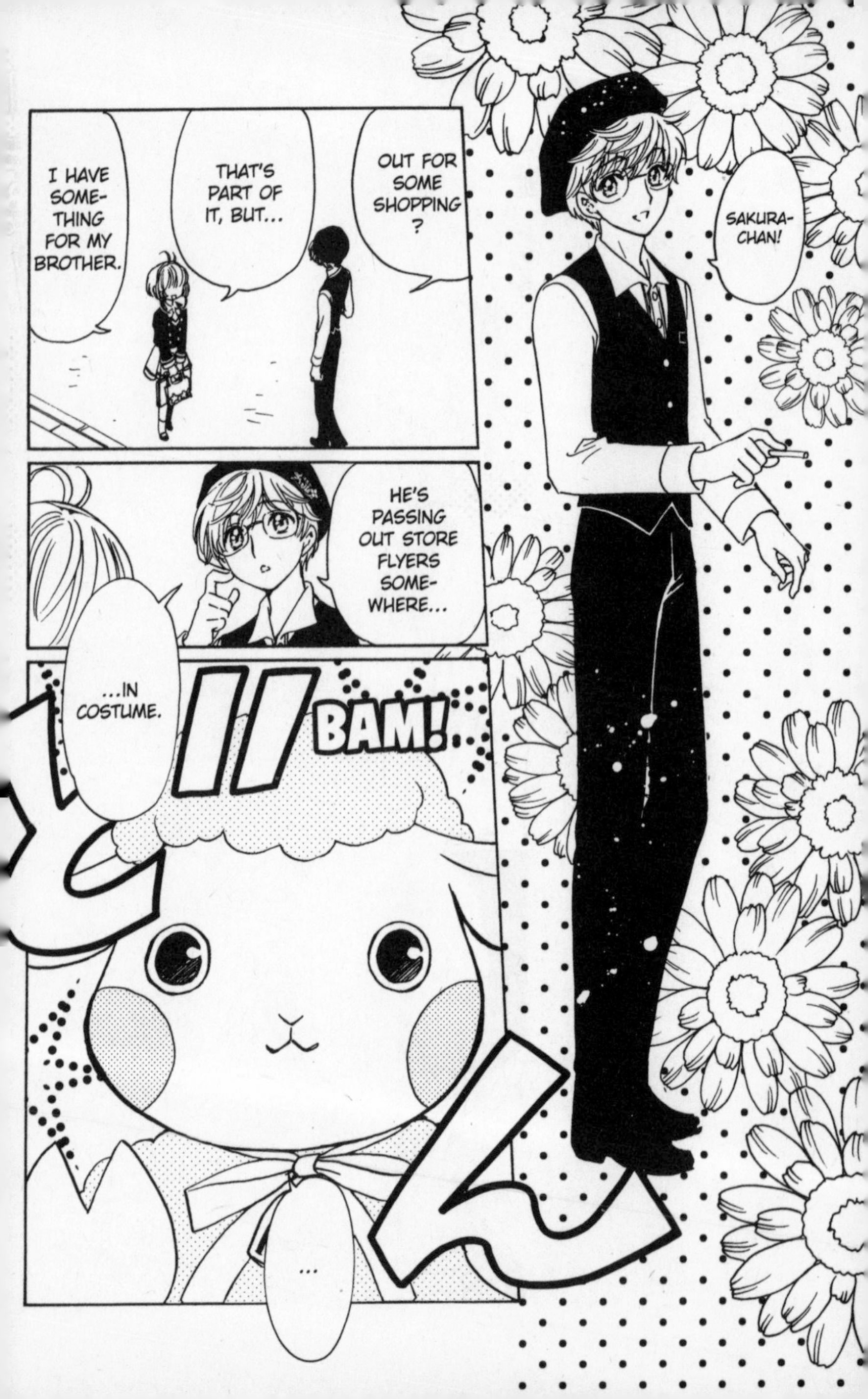
SAKURA-CHAN!
OUT FOR SOME SHOPPING?
THAT'S PART OF IT, BUT...
I HAVE SOMETHING FOR MY BROTHER.
HE'S PASSING OUT STORE FLYERS SOMEWHERE...
...IN COSTUME.
BAM!
...

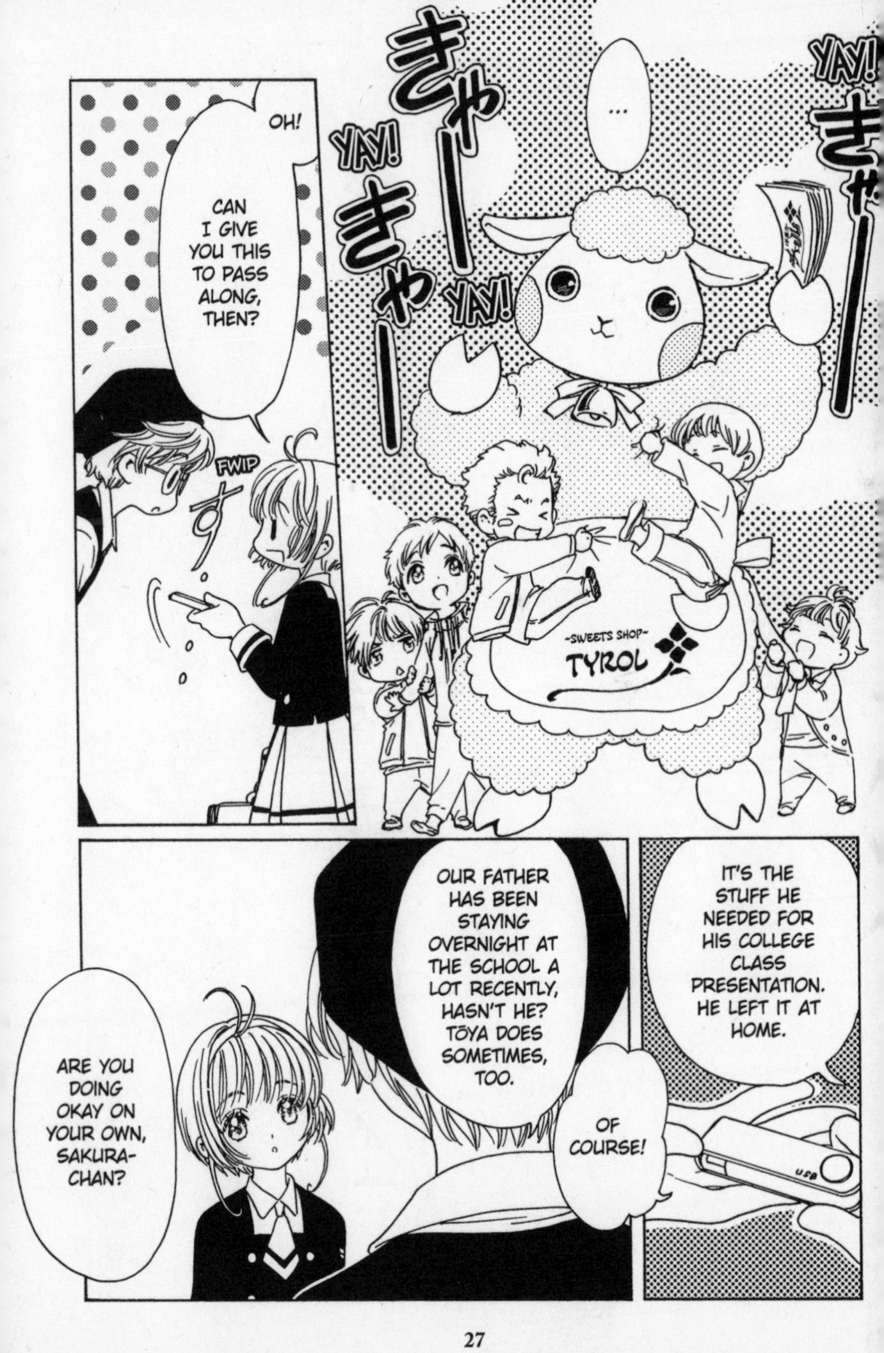

YAY!
...
きゃーきゃー
YAY!
YAY!
~SWEETS SHOP~
TYROL
OH!
CAN I GIVE YOU THIS TO PASS ALONG, THEN?
FWIP
す
IT'S THE STUFF HE NEEDED FOR HIS COLLEGE CLASS PRESENTATION. HE LEFT IT AT HOME.
OUR FATHER HAS BEEN STAYING OVERNIGHT AT THE SCHOOL A LOT RECENTLY, HASN'T HE? TŌYA DOES SOMETIMES, TOO.
ARE YOU DOING OKAY ON YOUR OWN, SAKURA-CHAN?
OF COURSE!

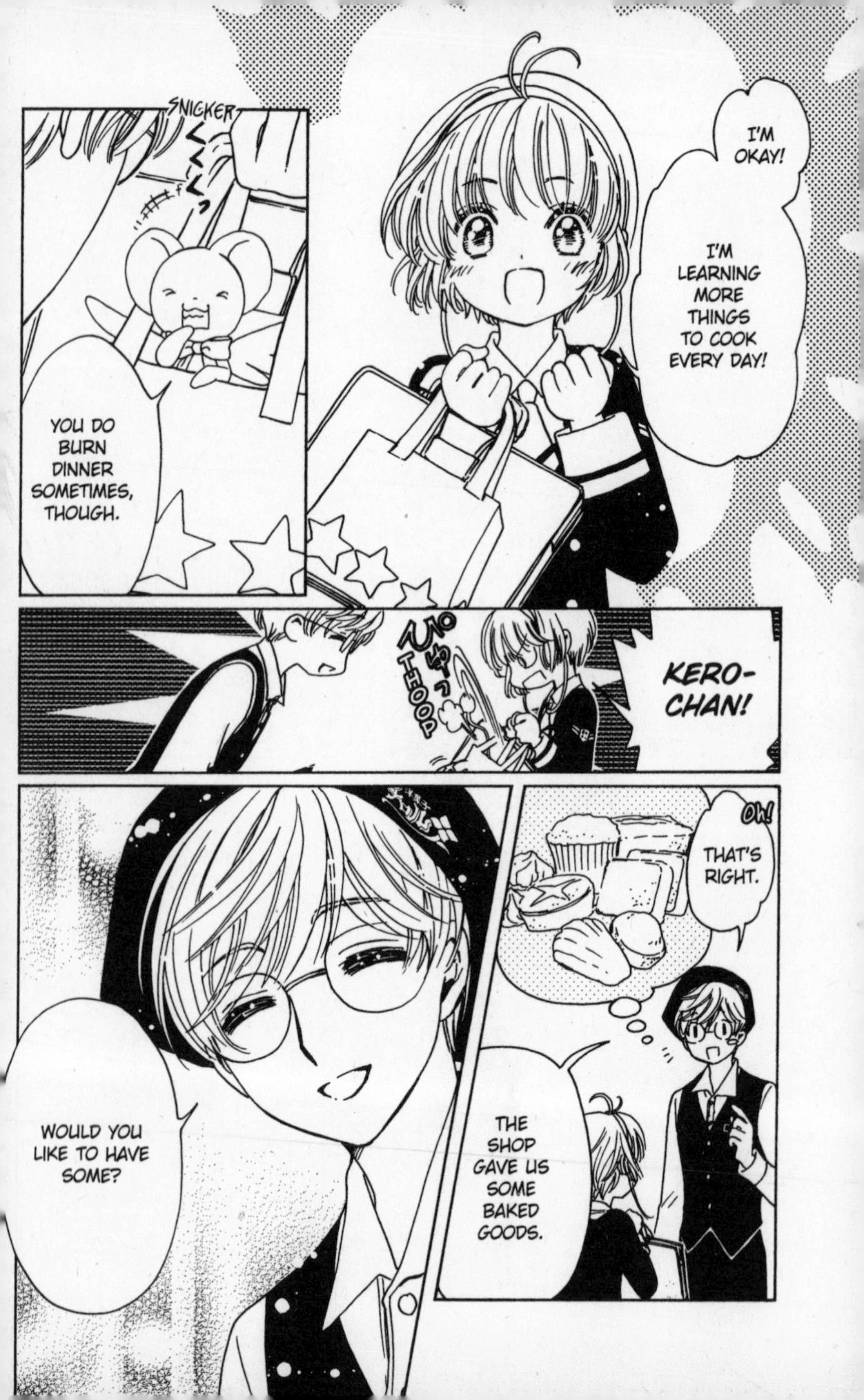
I'M OKAY!
I'M LEARNING MORE THINGS TO COOK EVERY DAY!
SNICKER
YOU DO BURN DINNER SOMETIMES, THOUGH.
KERO-CHAN!
THOOP
OH!
THAT'S RIGHT.
THE SHOP GAVE US SOME BAKED GOODS.
WOULD YOU LIKE TO HAVE SOME?

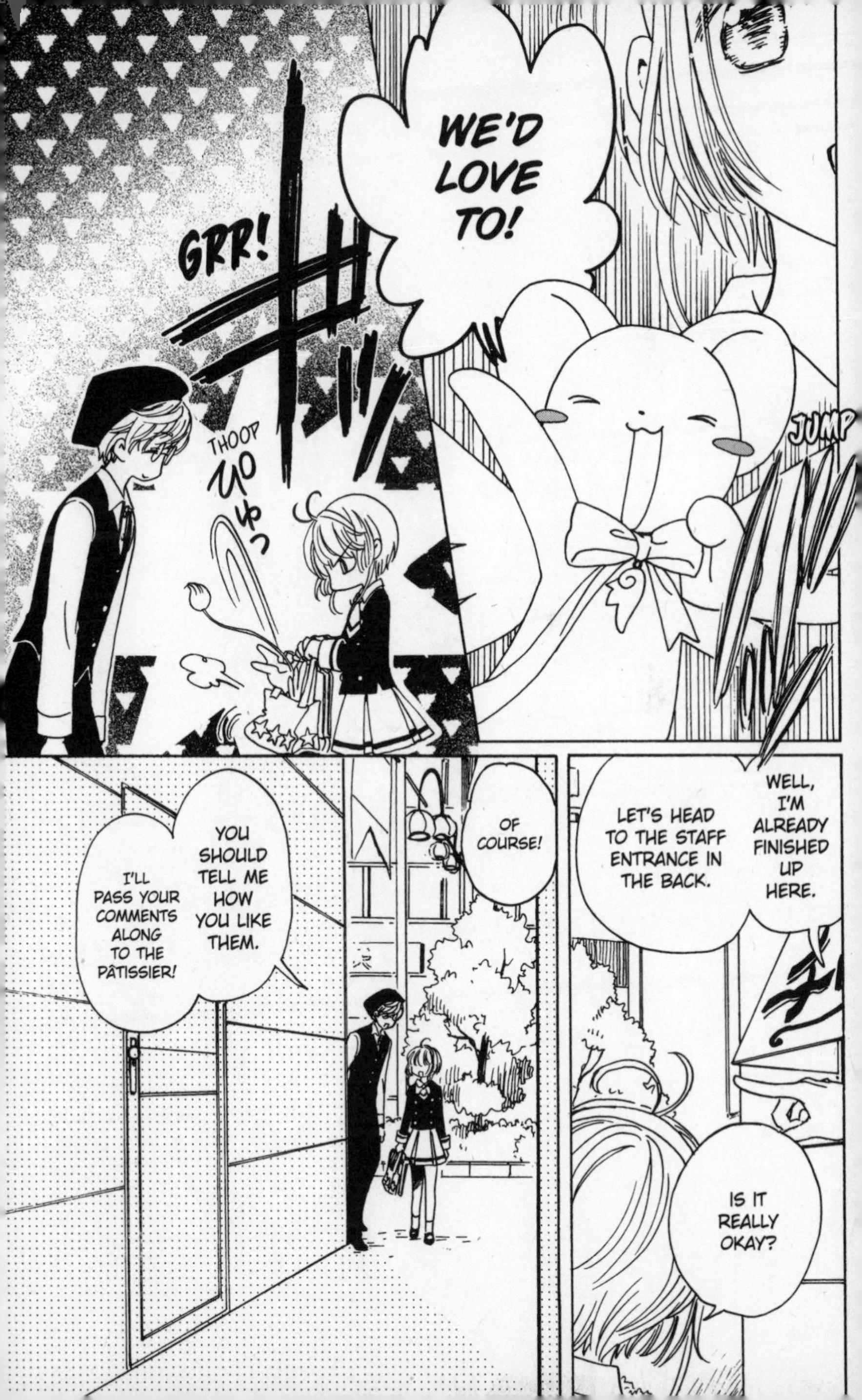
WE'D LOVE TO!
JUMP
GRR!
THOOP
ひゅっ
WELL, I'M ALREADY FINISHED UP HERE.
LET'S HEAD TO THE STAFF ENTRANCE IN THE BACK.
IS IT REALLY OKAY?
OF COURSE!
YOU SHOULD TELL ME HOW YOU LIKE THEM.
I'LL PASS YOUR COMMENTS ALONG TO THE PÂTISSIER!

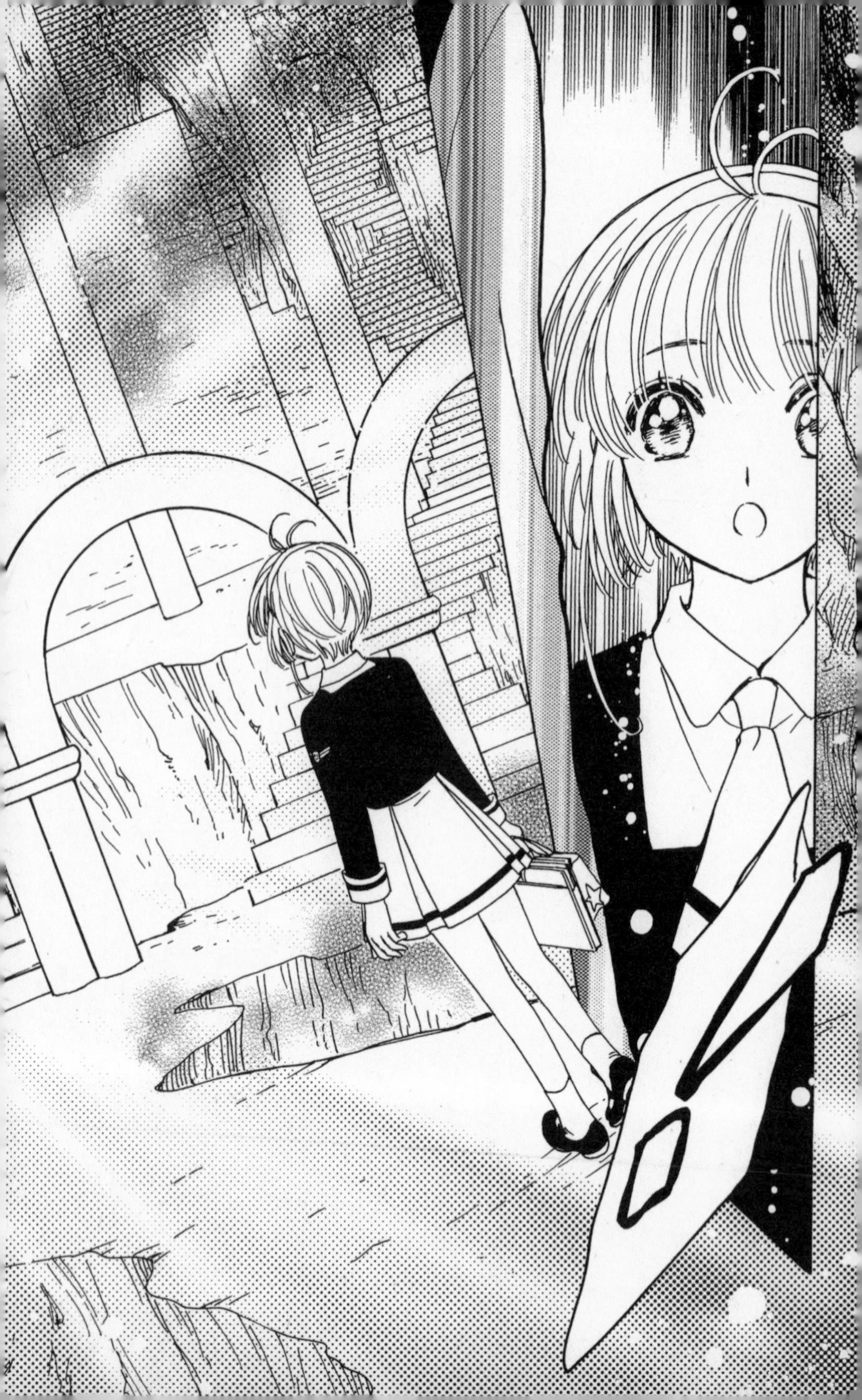

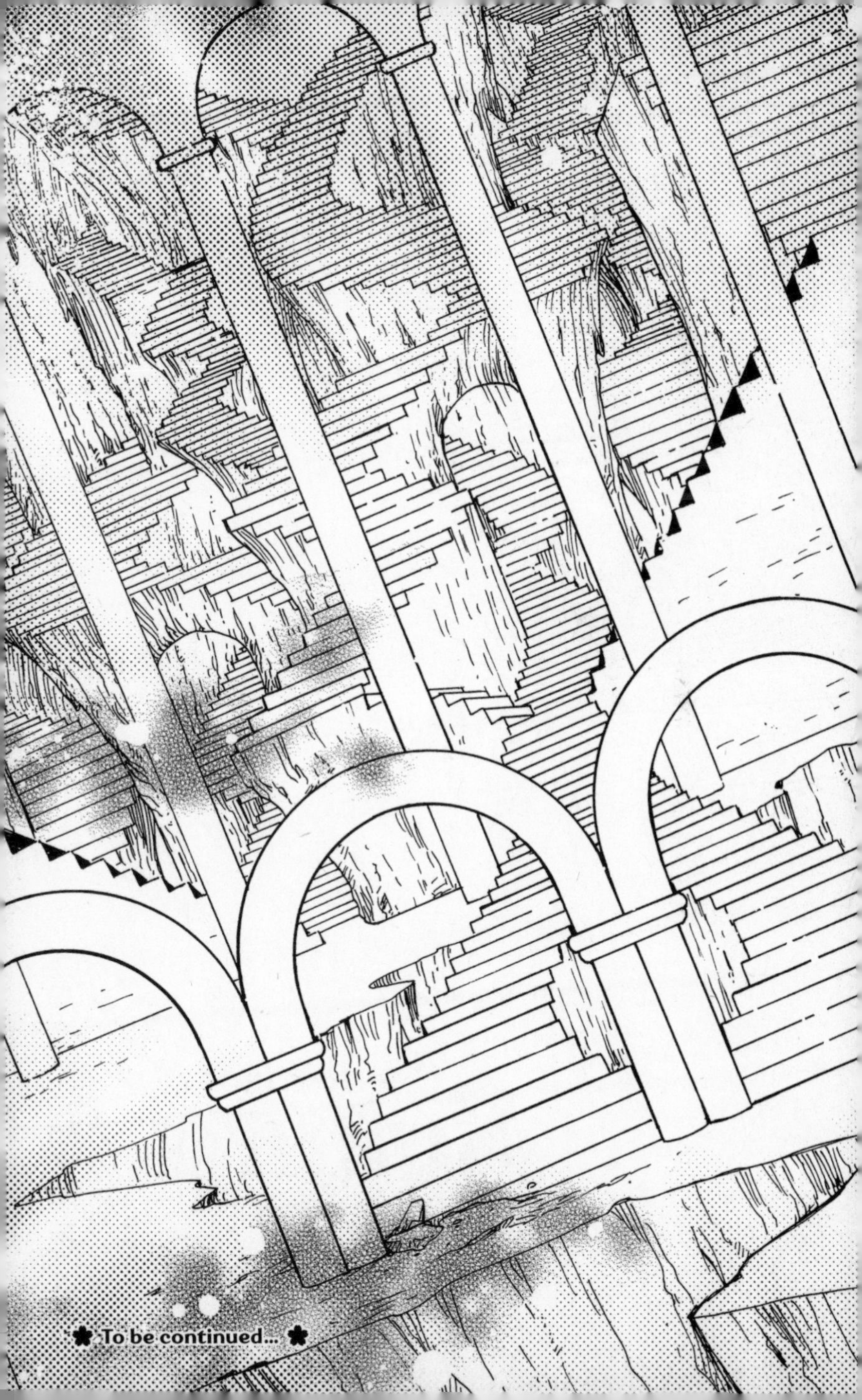
To be continued...

Cardcaptor Sakura
CLEAR CARD

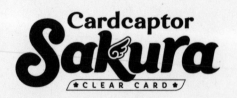

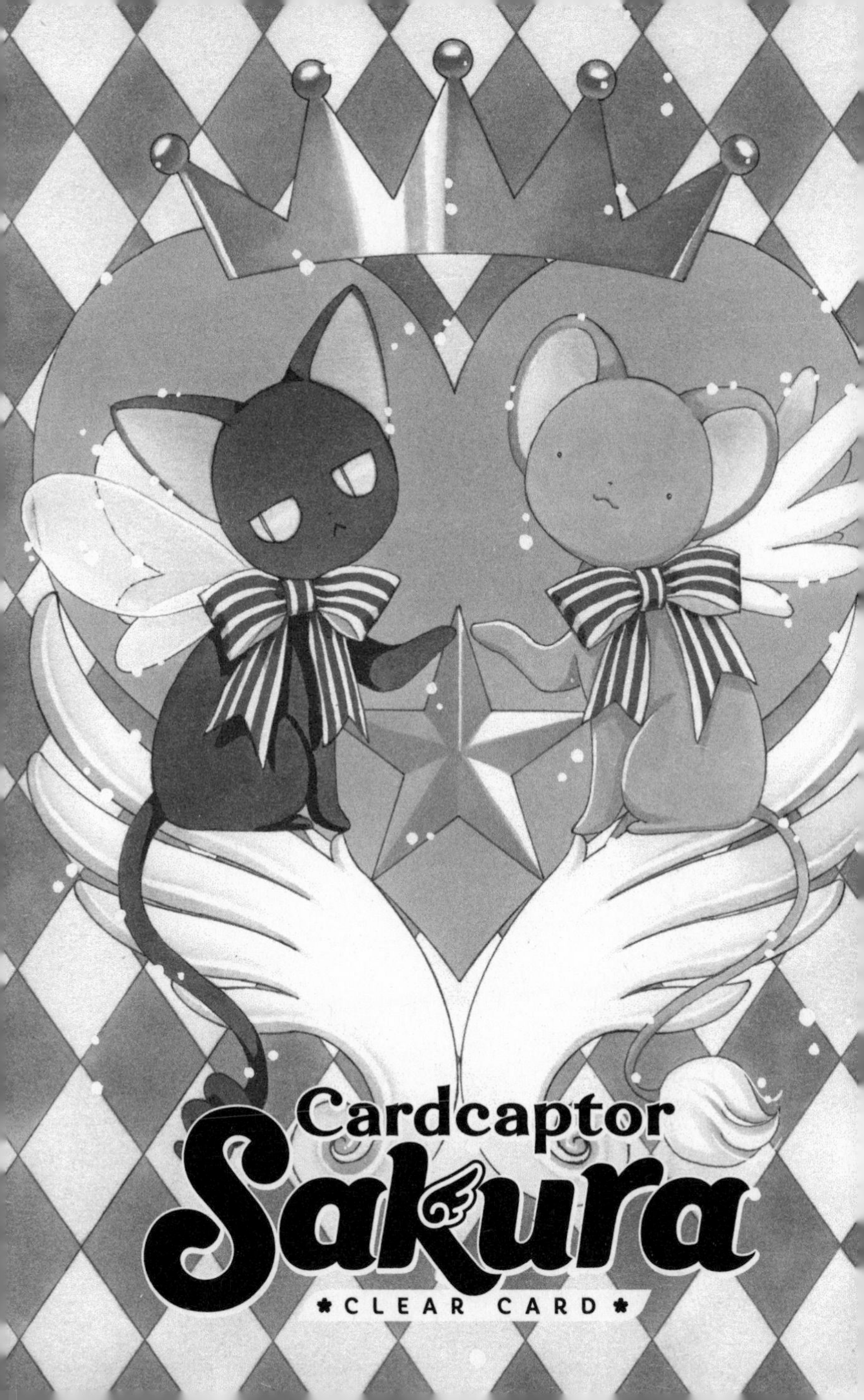
Cardcaptor
Sakura
CLEAR CARD

Cardcaptor Sakura

CLEAR CARD

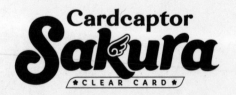

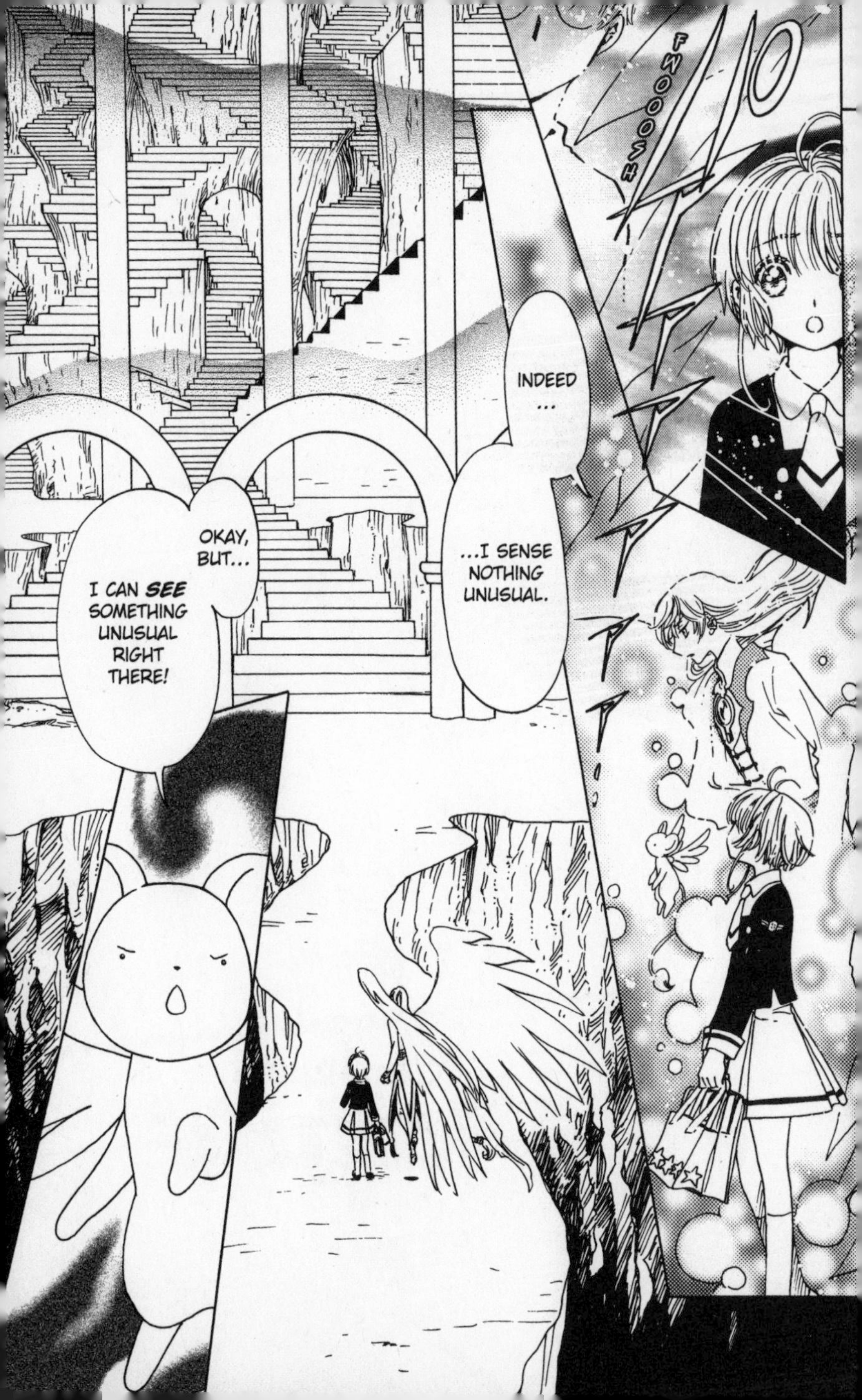
FWOOOSH
INDEED...
...I SENSE NOTHING UNUSUAL.
OKAY, BUT...
I CAN **SEE** SOMETHING UNUSUAL RIGHT THERE!

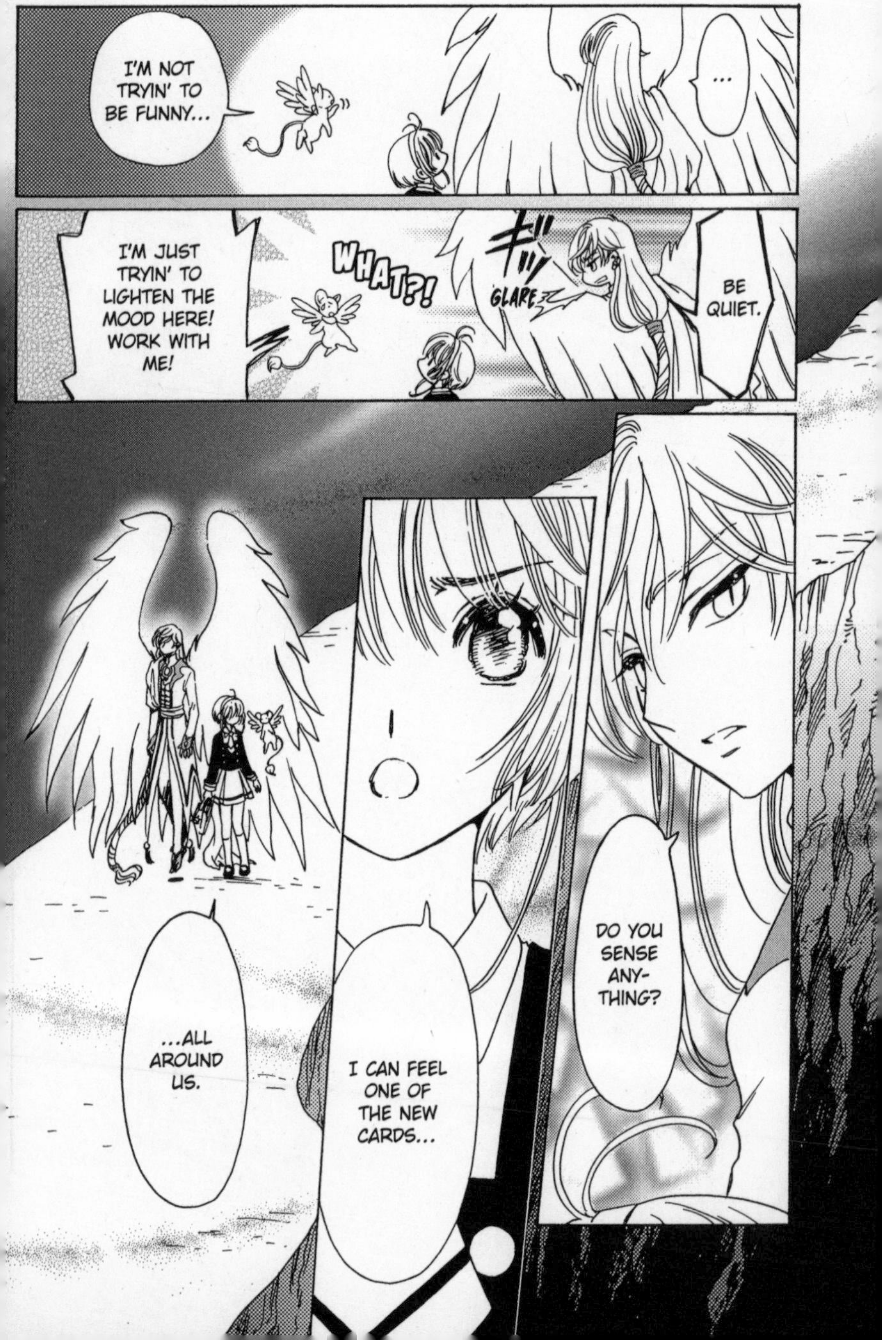
...
I'M NOT TRYIN' TO BE FUNNY...
BE QUIET.
GLARE
WHAT?!
I'M JUST TRYIN' TO LIGHTEN THE MOOD HERE! WORK WITH ME!
DO YOU SENSE ANY-THING?
!
I CAN FEEL ONE OF THE NEW CARDS...
...ALL AROUND US.

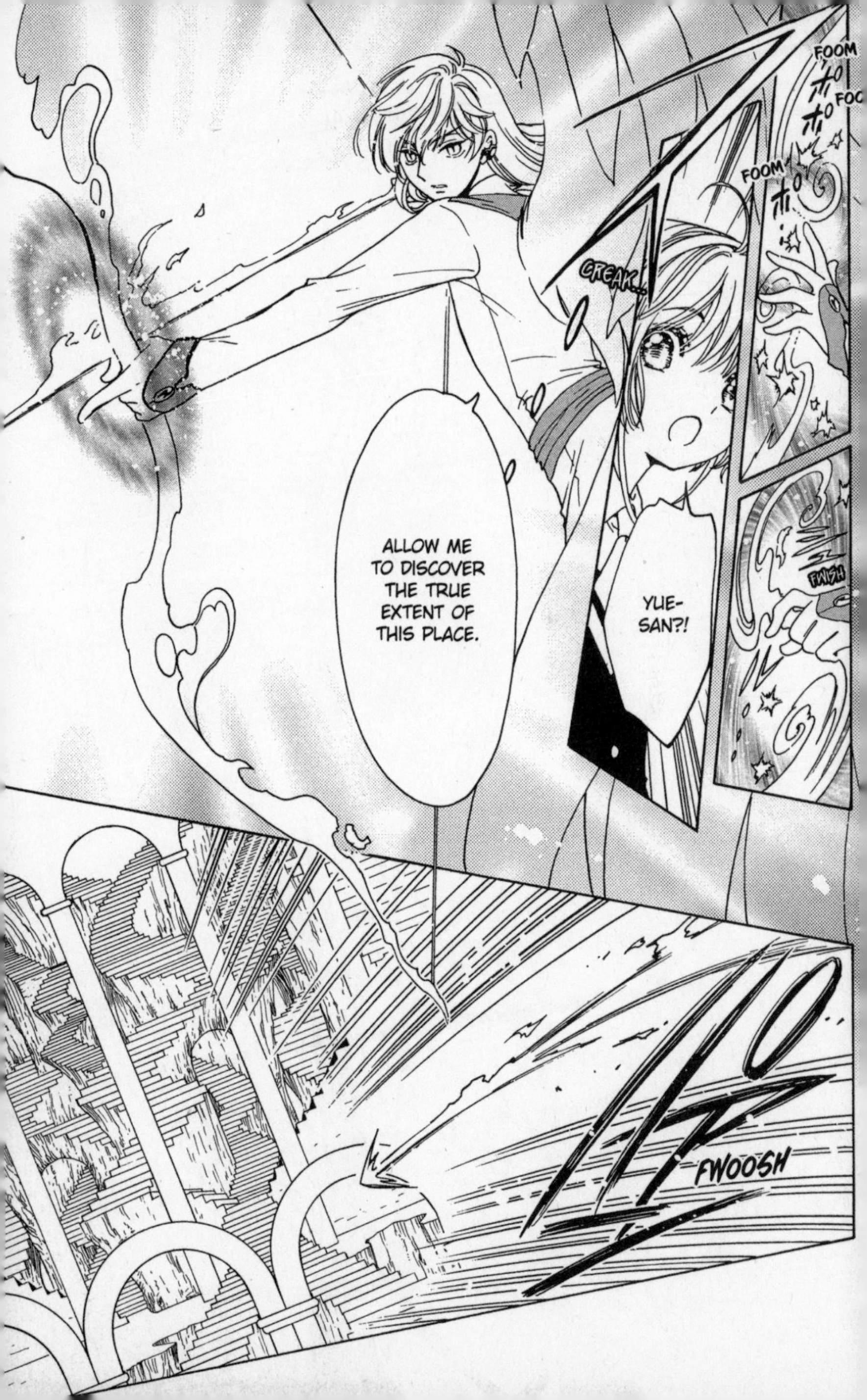
FOOM
FOO
FOOM
FWISH
CREAK...
YUE-SAN?!
ALLOW ME TO DISCOVER THE TRUE EXTENT OF THIS PLACE.
FWOOSH

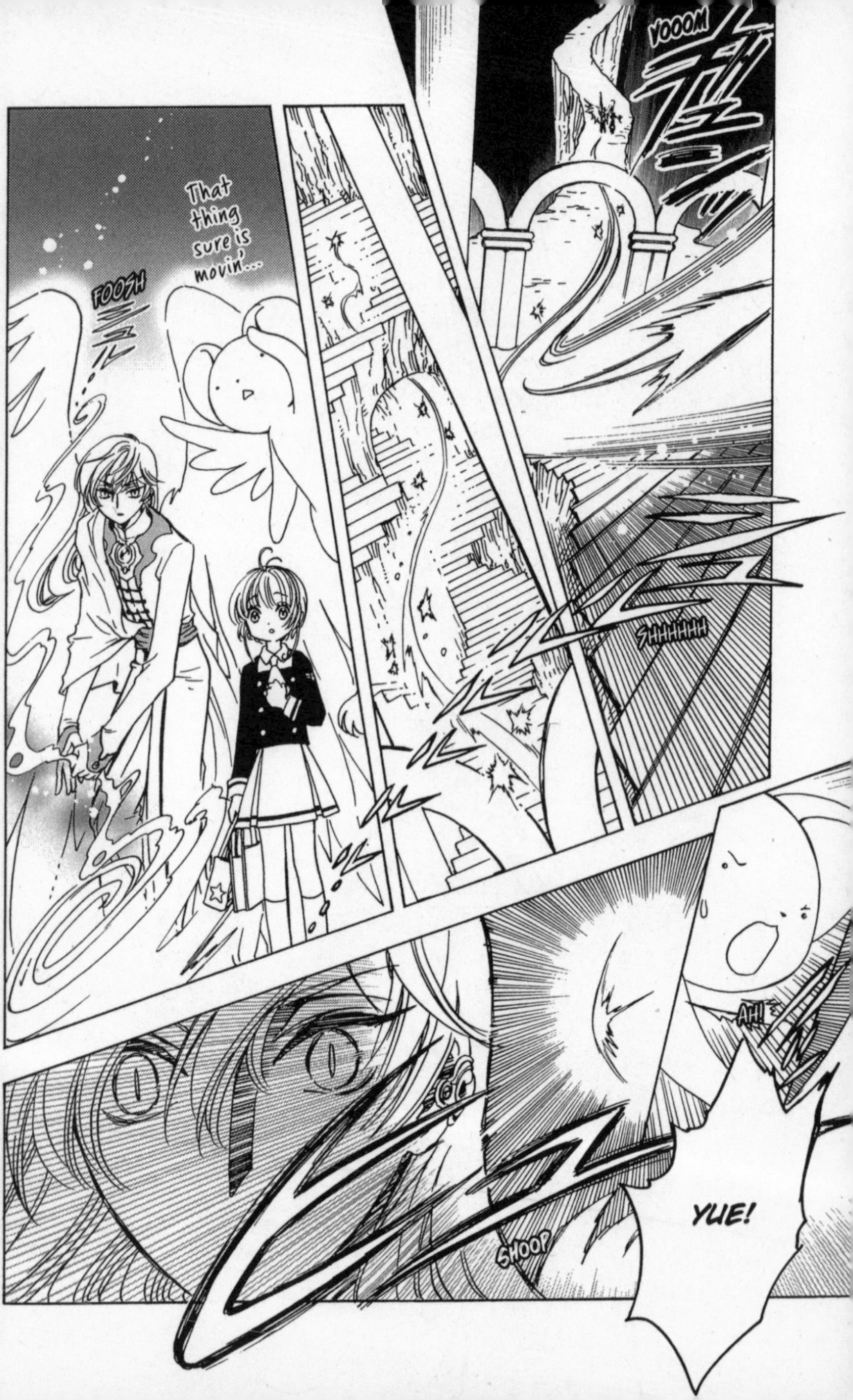
VOOOM
SHHHHHH
That thing sure is movin'...
FOOSH
AH!
YUE!
SHOOP

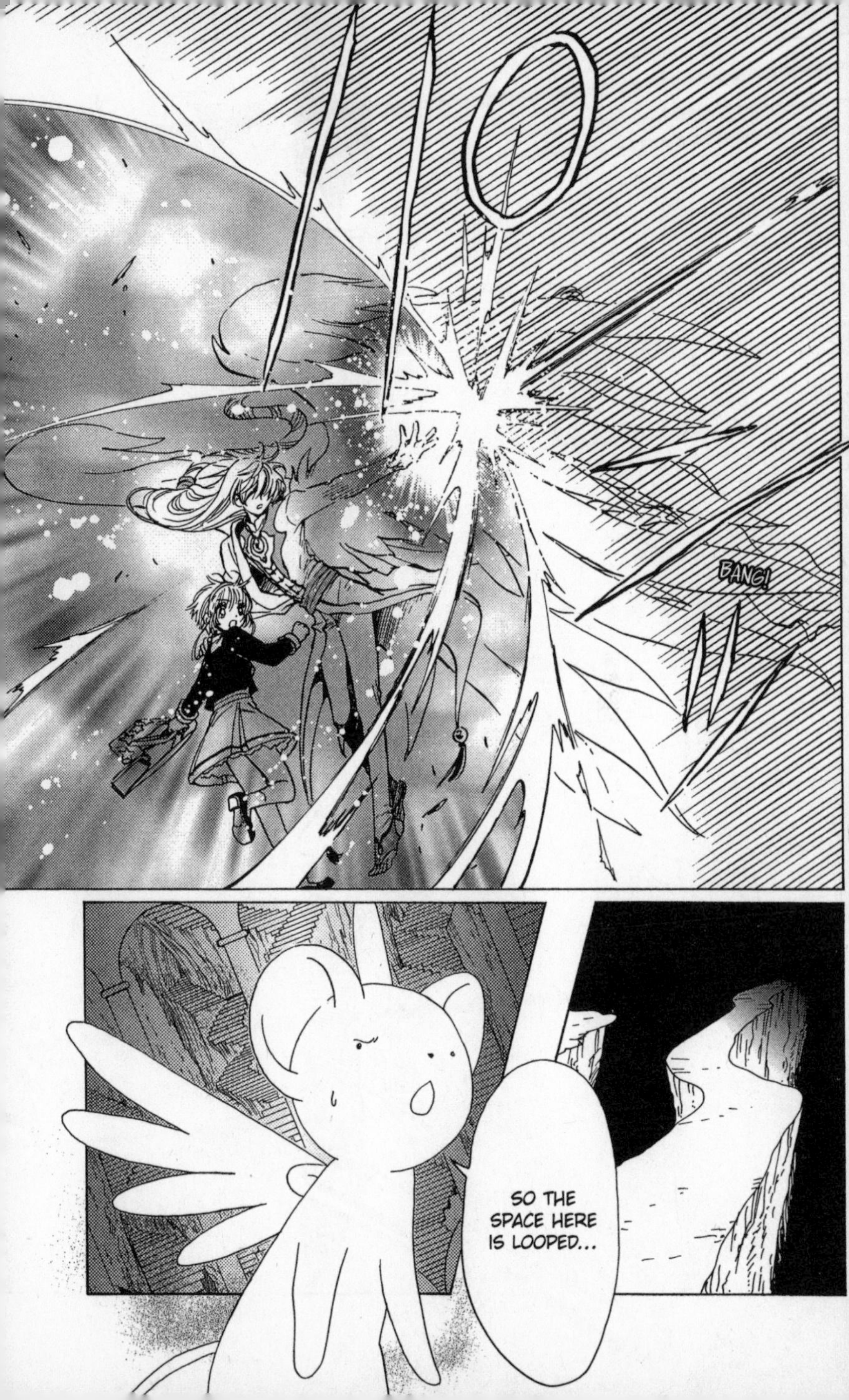
BANG!
SO THE SPACE HERE IS LOOPED...

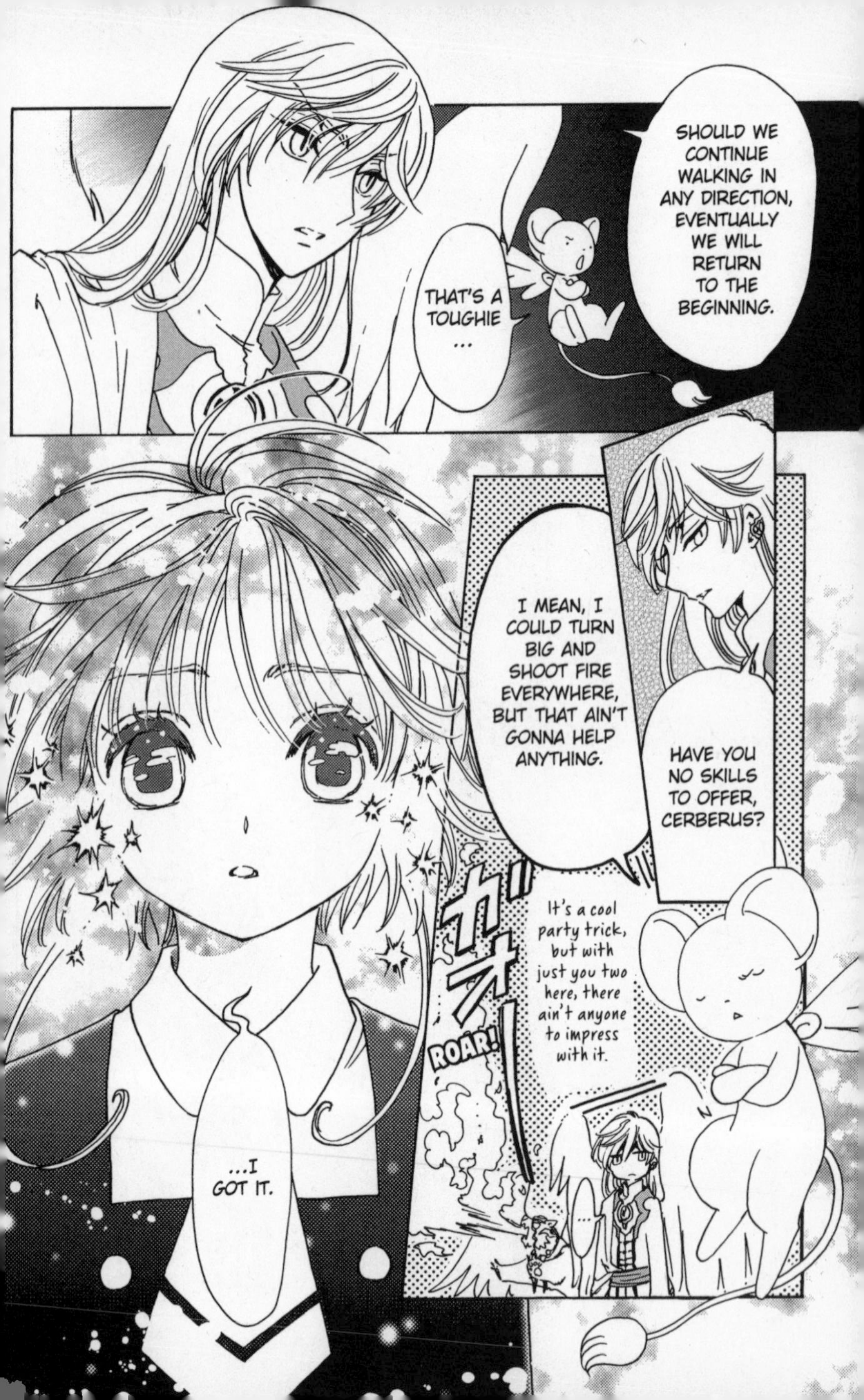
SHOULD WE CONTINUE WALKING IN ANY DIRECTION, EVENTUALLY WE WILL RETURN TO THE BEGINNING.
THAT'S A TOUGHIE ...
HAVE YOU NO SKILLS TO OFFER, CERBERUS?
I MEAN, I COULD TURN BIG AND SHOOT FIRE EVERYWHERE, BUT THAT AIN'T GONNA HELP ANYTHING.
It's a cool party trick, but with just you two here, there ain't anyone to impress with it.
ガオー
ROAR!
...
...I GOT IT.

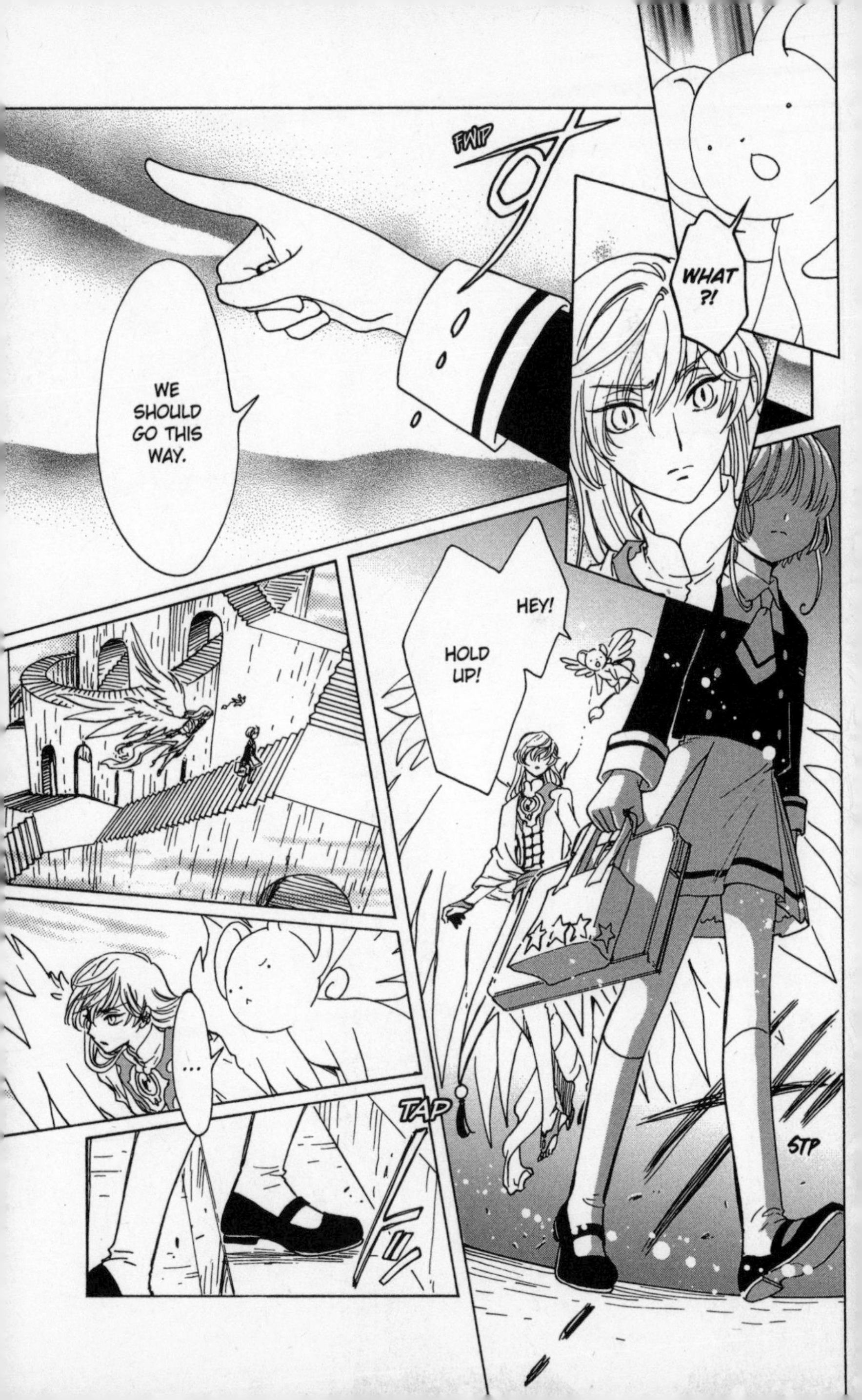
WHAT ?!
FWIP
WE SHOULD GO THIS WAY.
HEY! HOLD UP!
STP
...
TAP

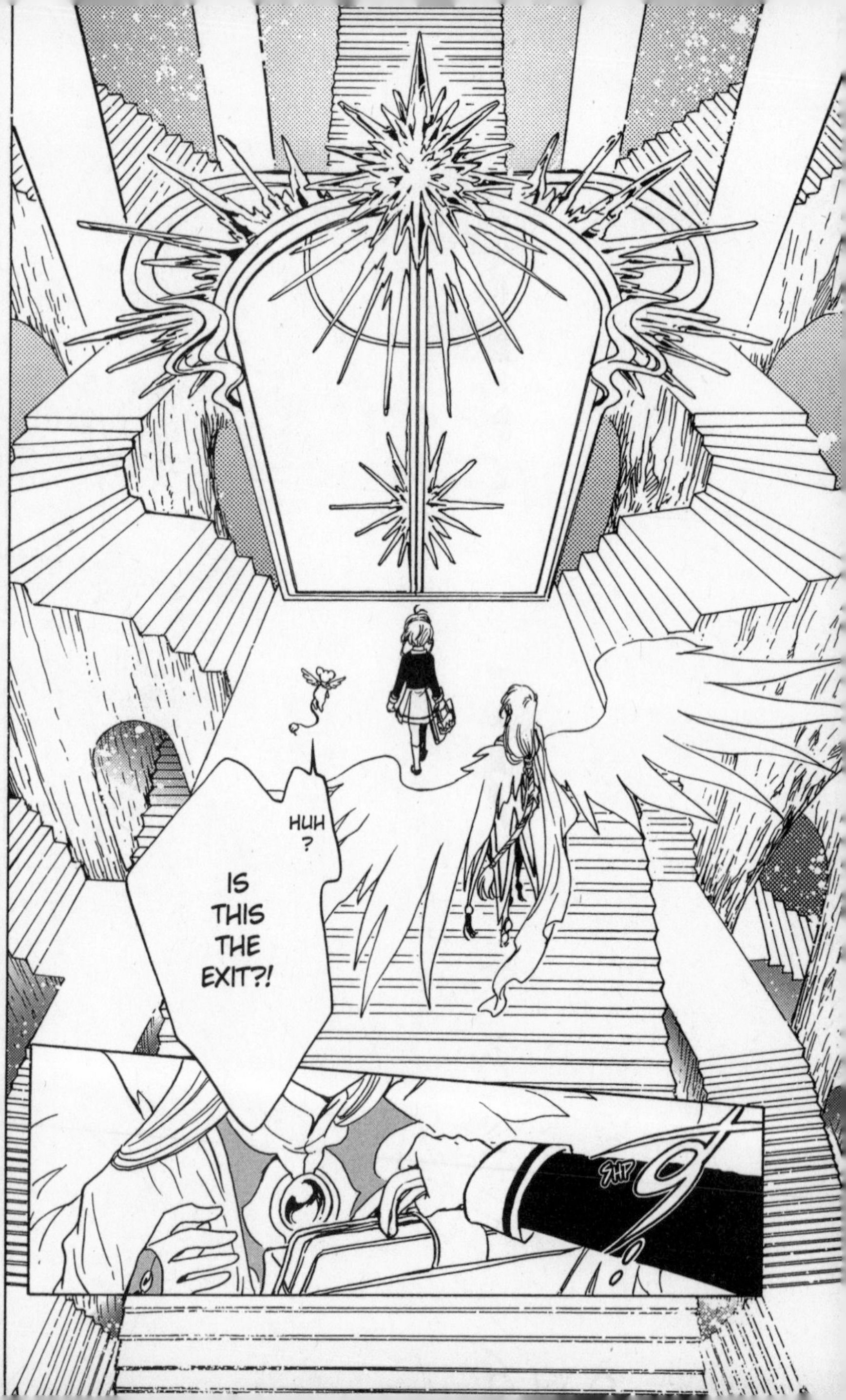
HUH?
IS THIS THE EXIT?!
SHP

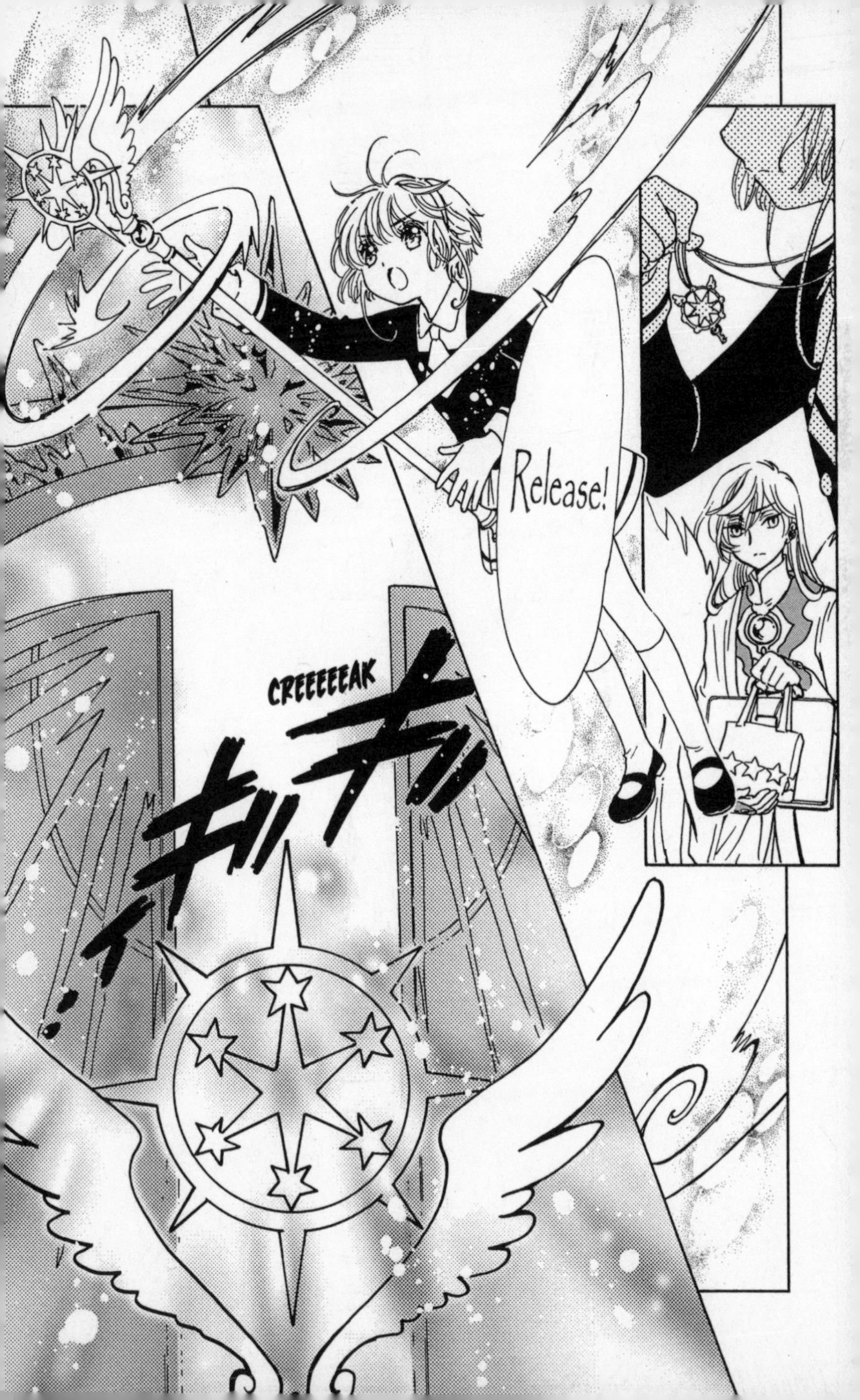
Release!
CREEEEEAK

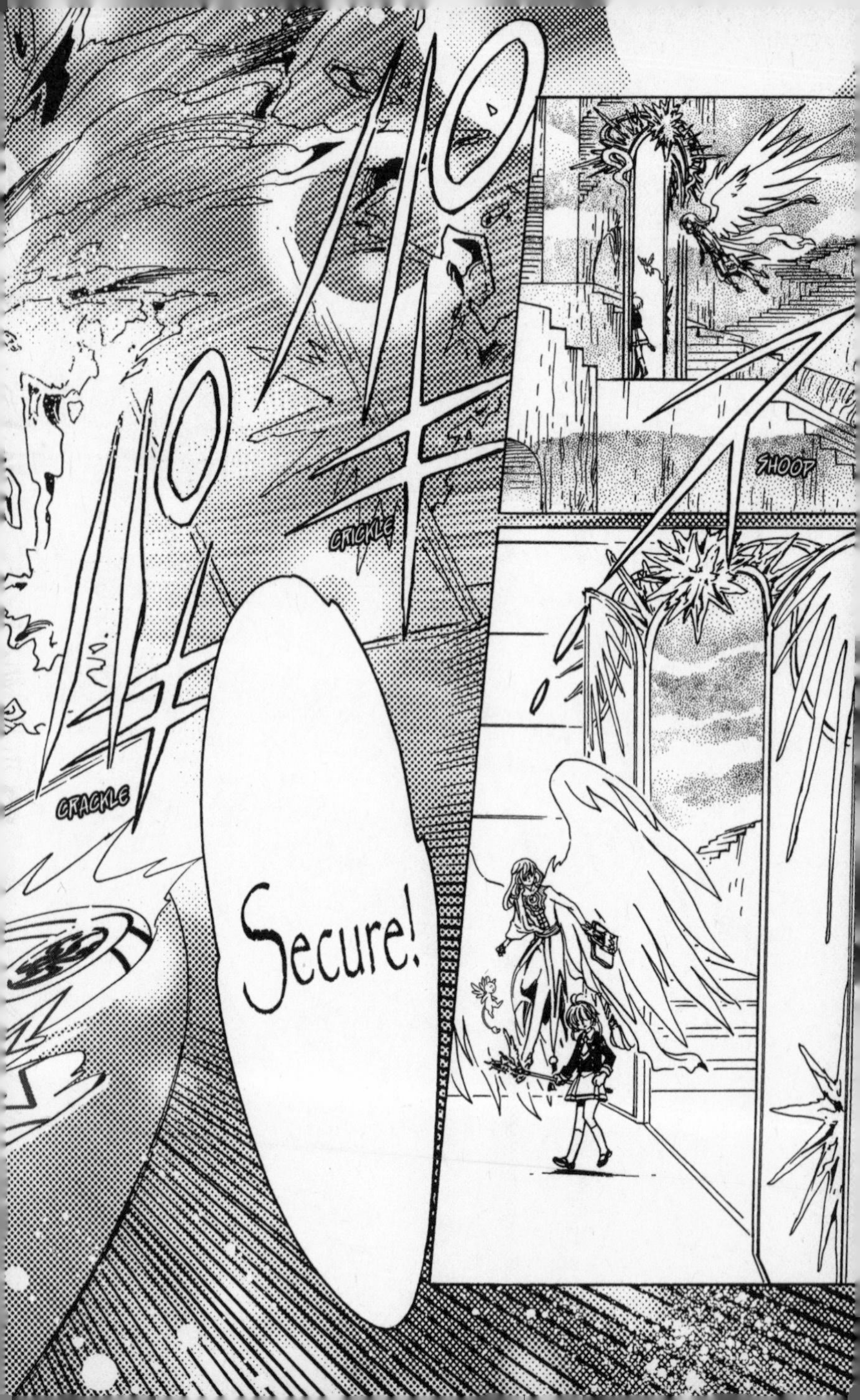
SHOOP
CRICKLE
Secure!
CRACKLE

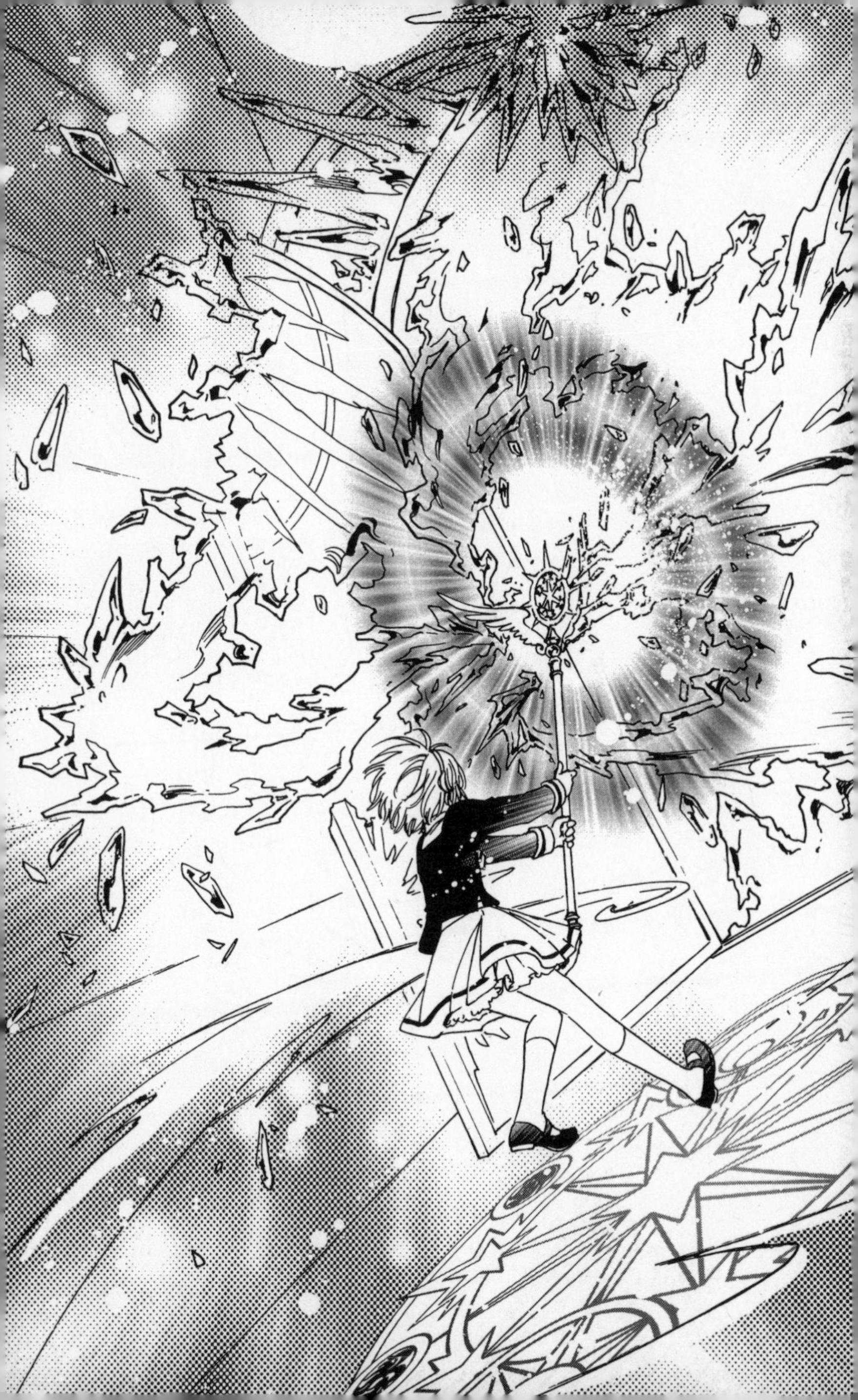

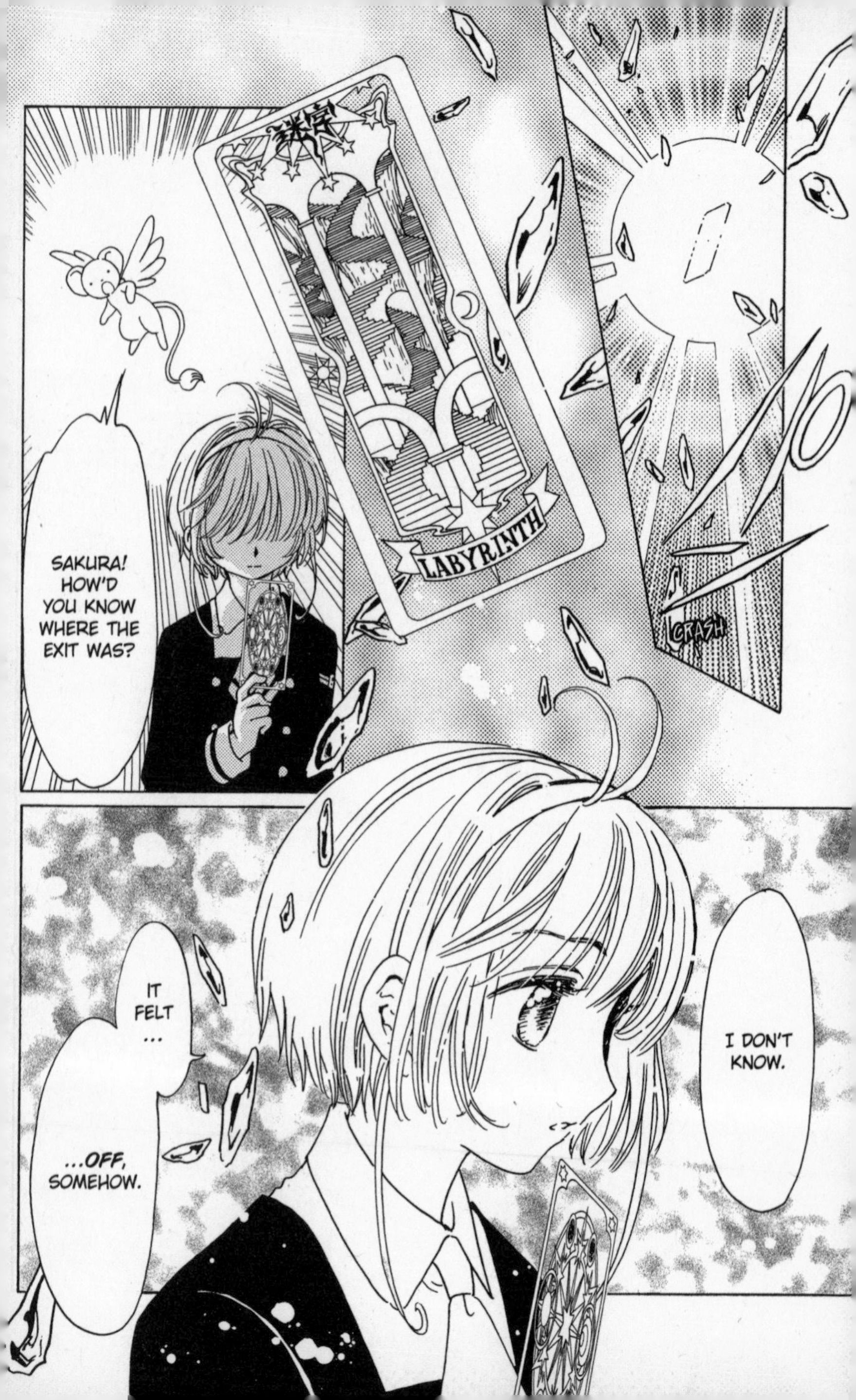
CRASH
LABYRINTH
SAKURA! HOW'D YOU KNOW WHERE THE EXIT WAS?
I DON'T KNOW.
IT FELT ...
...OFF, SOMEHOW.

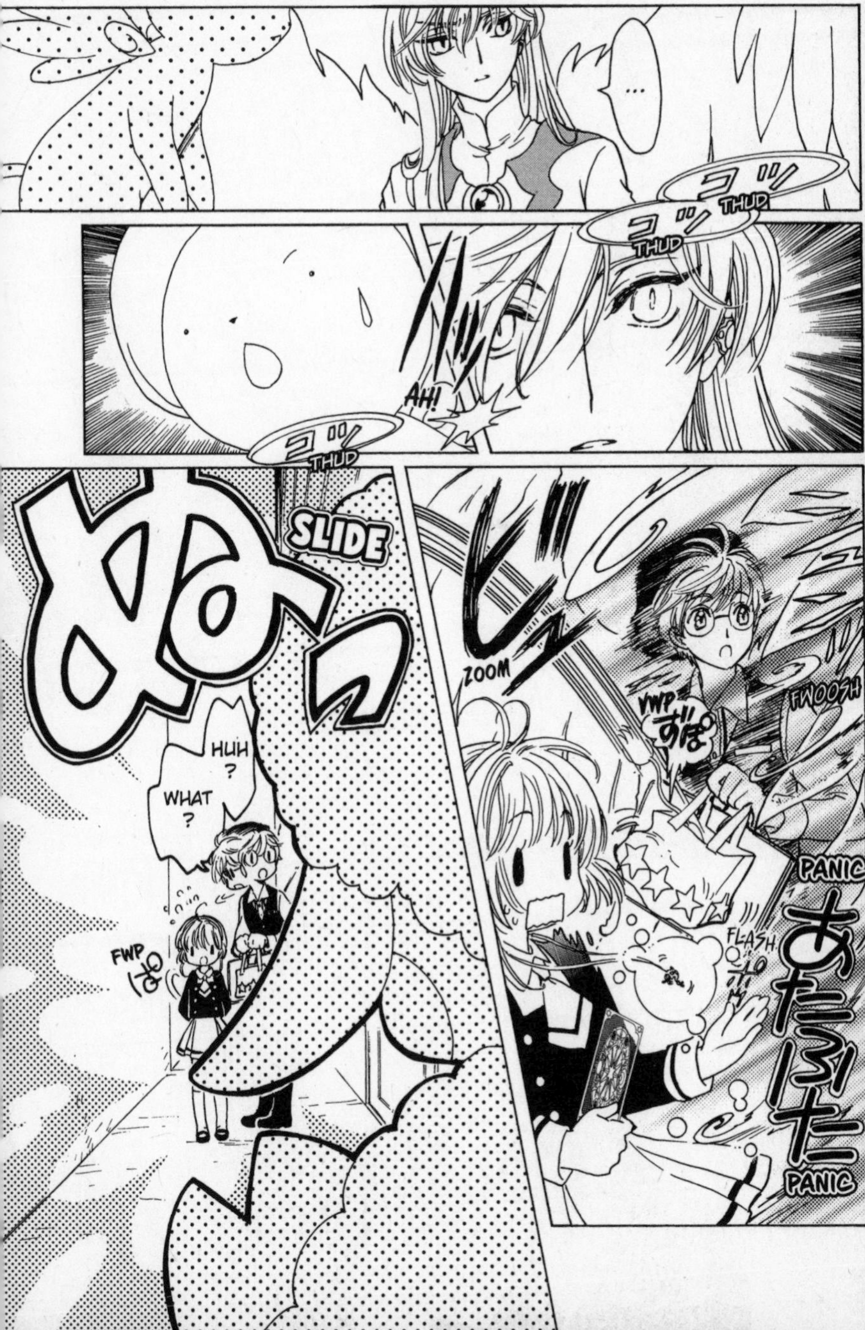
...
THUD
THUD
AH!
THUD
ZOOM
VWP
FWOOSH
PANIC
PANIC
FLASH
SLIDE
HUH?
WHAT?
FWP

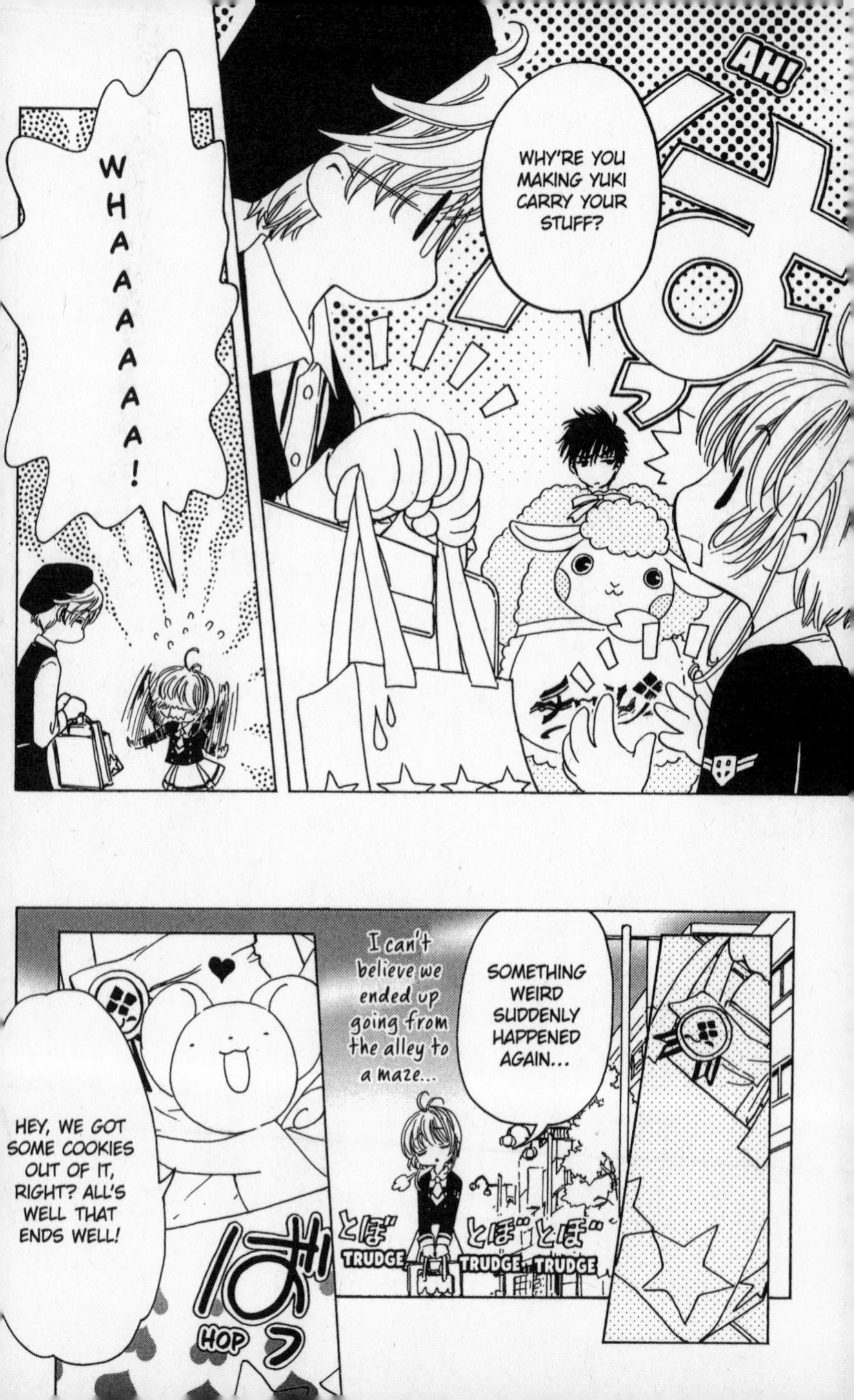
AH!
WHY'RE YOU MAKING YUKI CARRY YOUR STUFF?
WHAAAAAAA!
SOMETHING WEIRD SUDDENLY HAPPENED AGAIN...
I can't believe we ended up going from the alley to a maze...
TRUDGE TRUDGE TRUDGE
HEY, WE GOT SOME COOKIES OUT OF IT, RIGHT? ALL'S WELL THAT ENDS WELL!
HOP

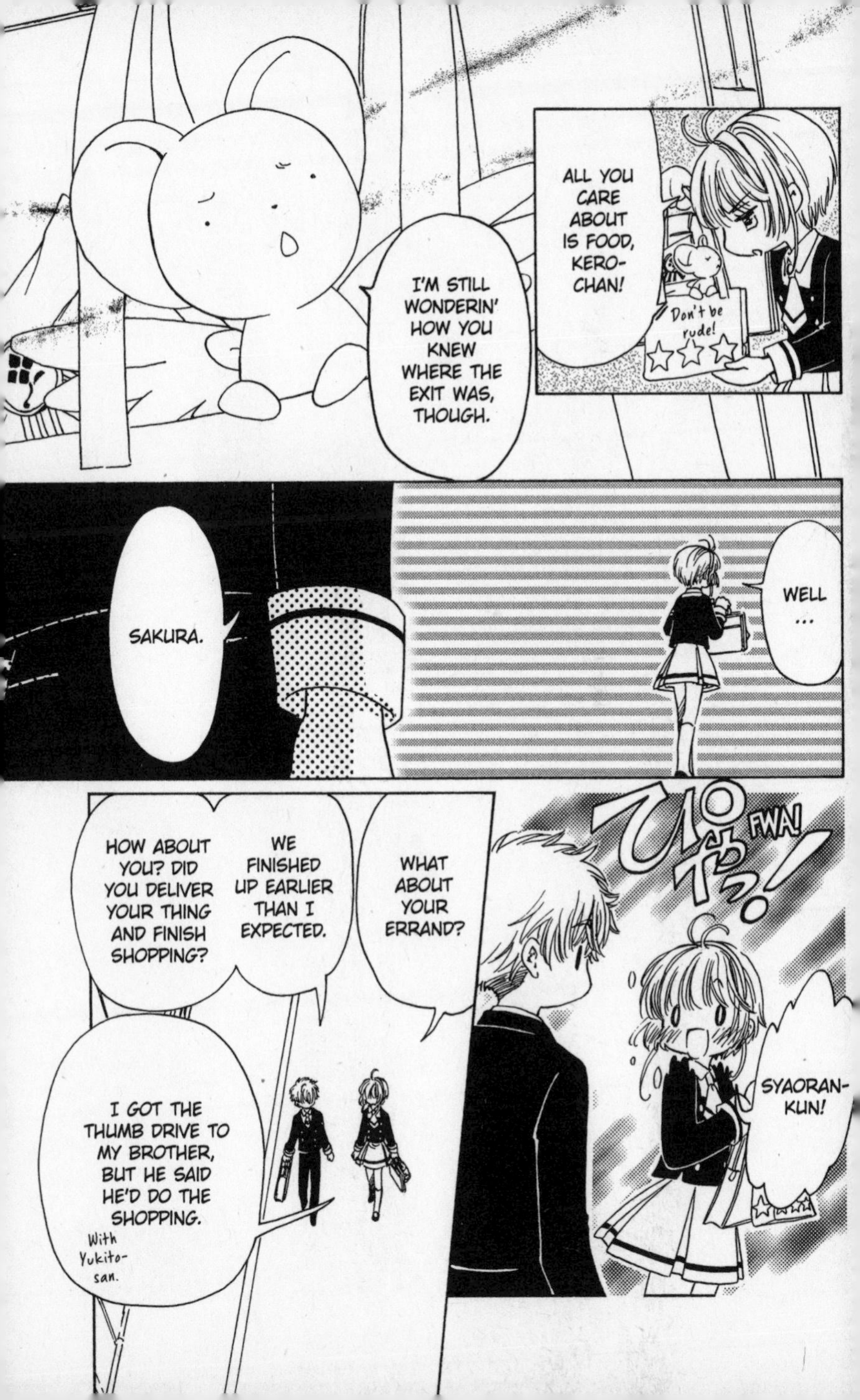

ALL YOU CARE ABOUT IS FOOD, KERO-CHAN!
Don't be rude!
I'M STILL WONDERIN' HOW YOU KNEW WHERE THE EXIT WAS, THOUGH.
WELL ...
SAKURA.
ぴゃっ!
FWA!
SYAORAN-KUN!
WHAT ABOUT YOUR ERRAND?
WE FINISHED UP EARLIER THAN I EXPECTED.
HOW ABOUT YOU? DID YOU DELIVER YOUR THING AND FINISH SHOPPING?
I GOT THE THUMB DRIVE TO MY BROTHER, BUT HE SAID HE'D DO THE SHOPPING.
With Yukito-san.

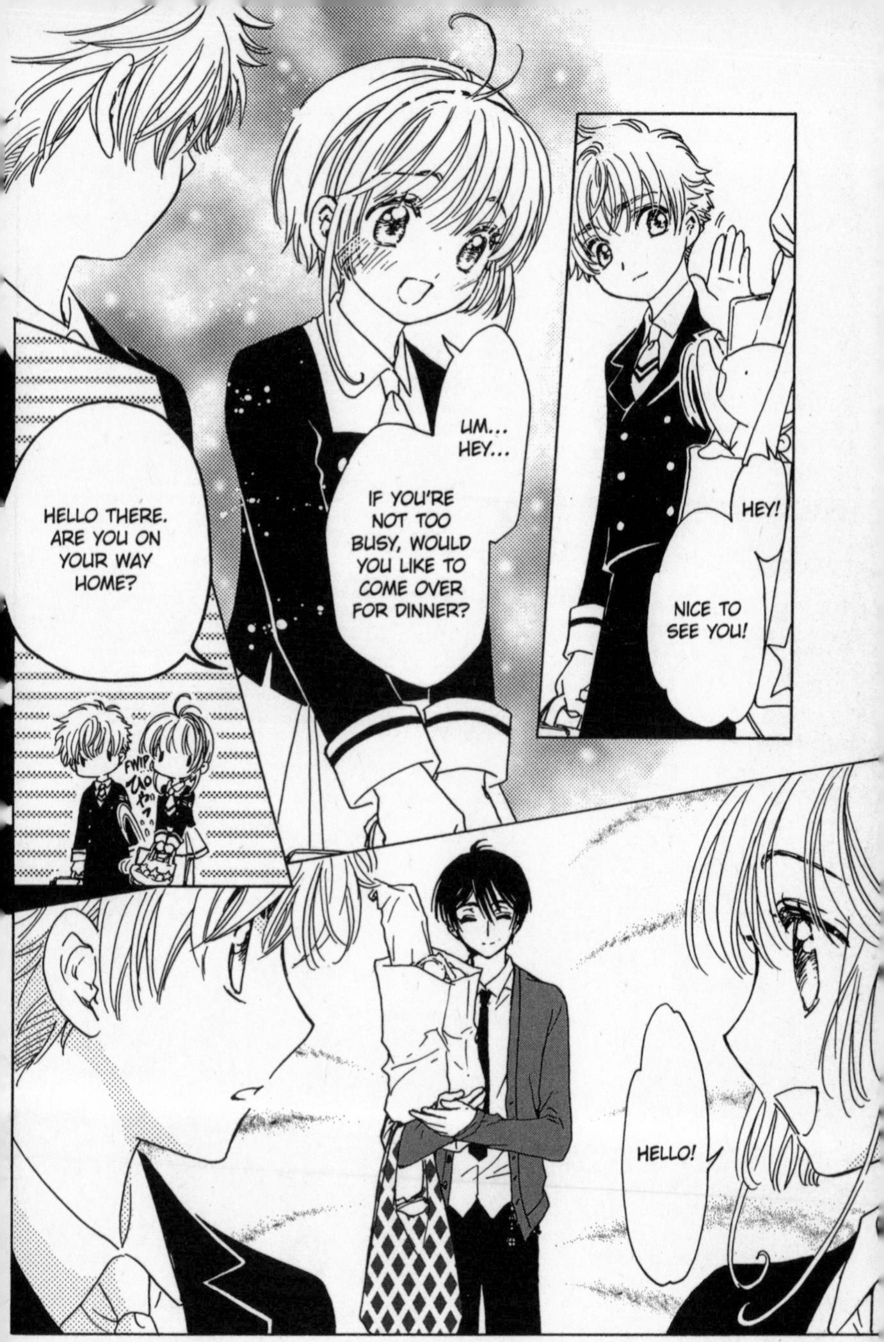
HEY!
NICE TO SEE YOU!
UM... HEY...
IF YOU'RE NOT TOO BUSY, WOULD YOU LIKE TO COME OVER FOR DINNER?
HELLO THERE. ARE YOU ON YOUR WAY HOME?
FWIP!
HELLO!

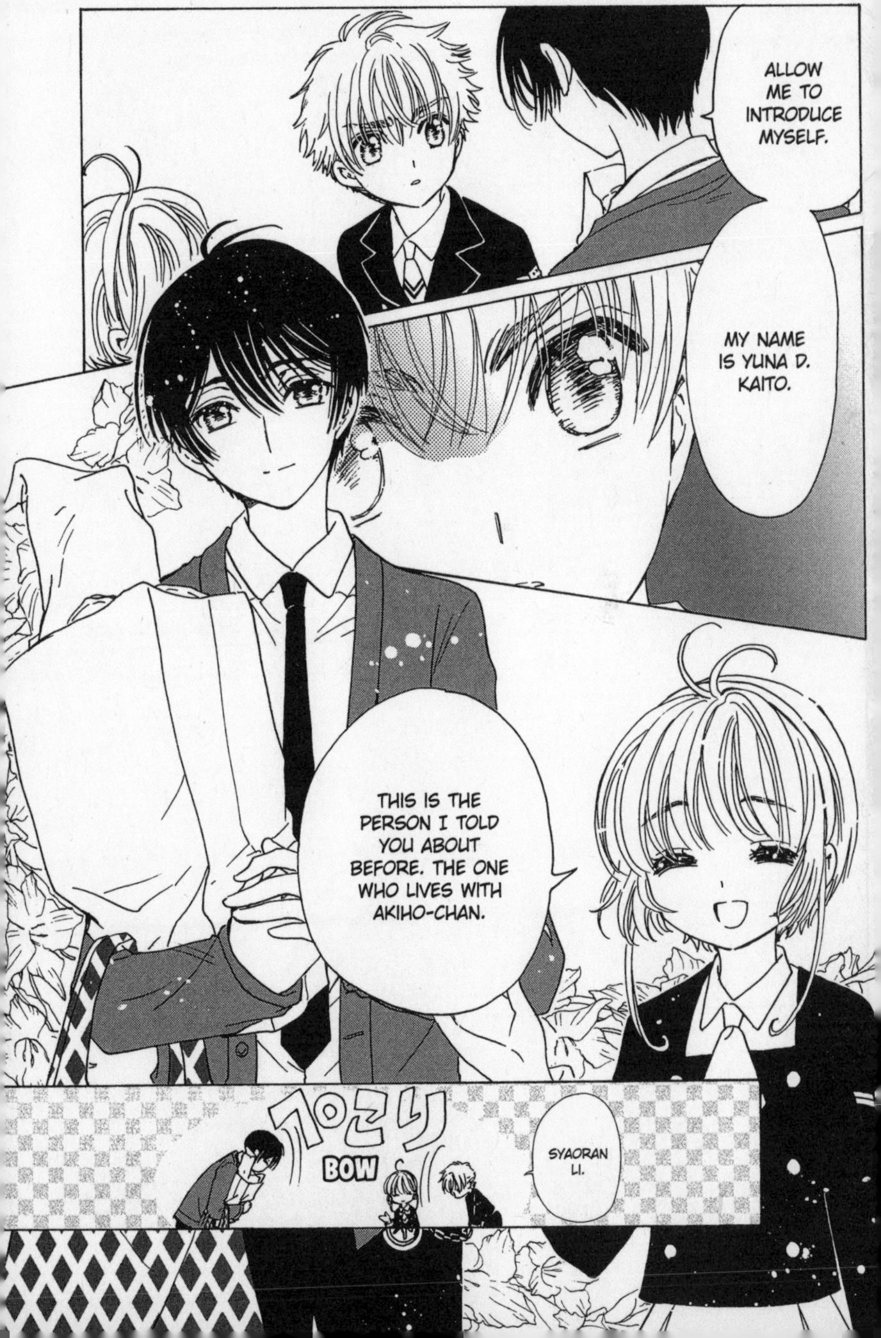
ALLOW ME TO INTRODUCE MYSELF.
MY NAME IS YUNA D. KAITO.
THIS IS THE PERSON I TOLD YOU ABOUT BEFORE. THE ONE WHO LIVES WITH AKIHO-CHAN.
SYAORAN LI.
BOW

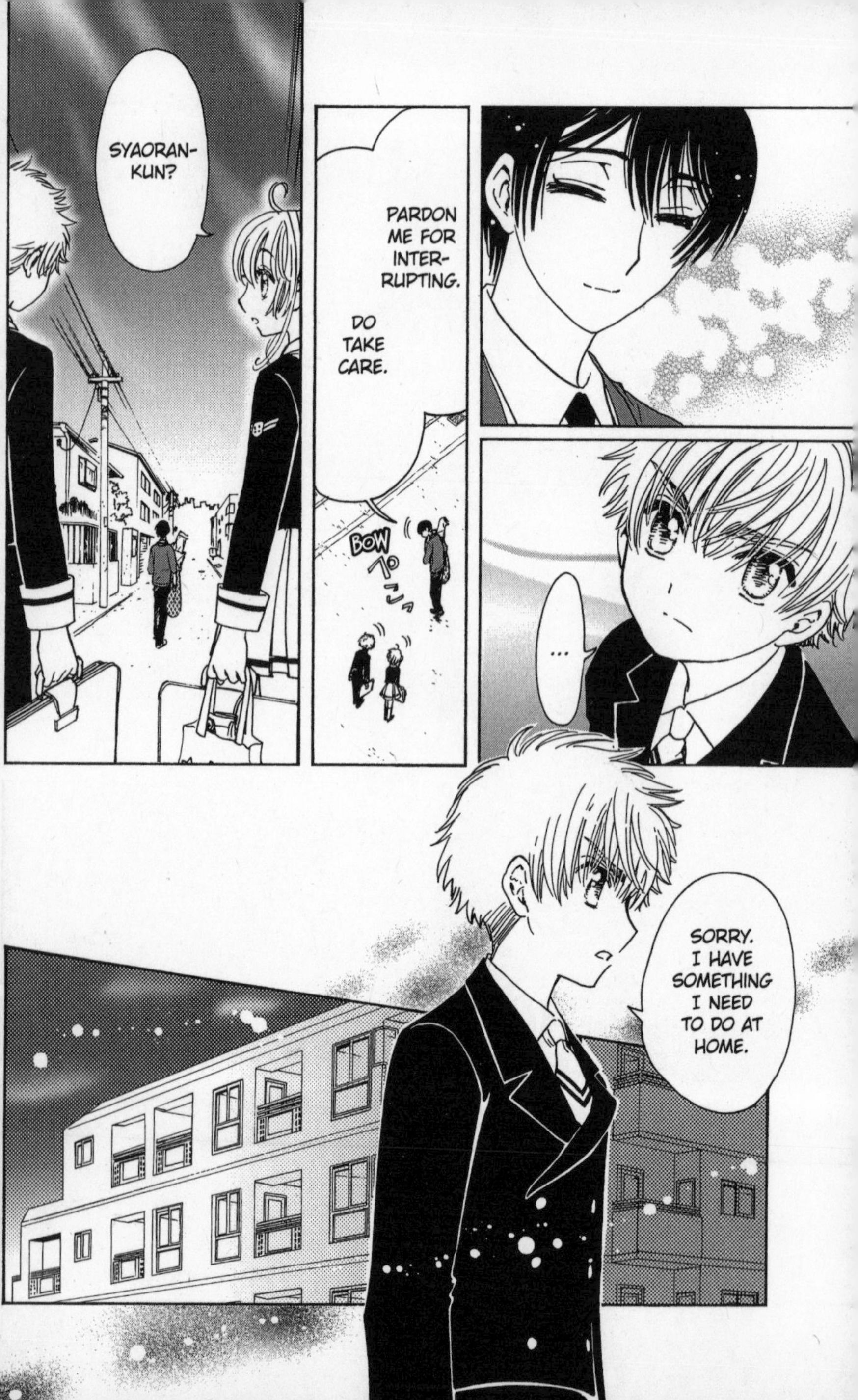
...
PARDON ME FOR INTERRUPTING.
DO TAKE CARE.
BOW
SYAORAN-KUN?
SORRY. I HAVE SOMETHING I NEED TO DO AT HOME.

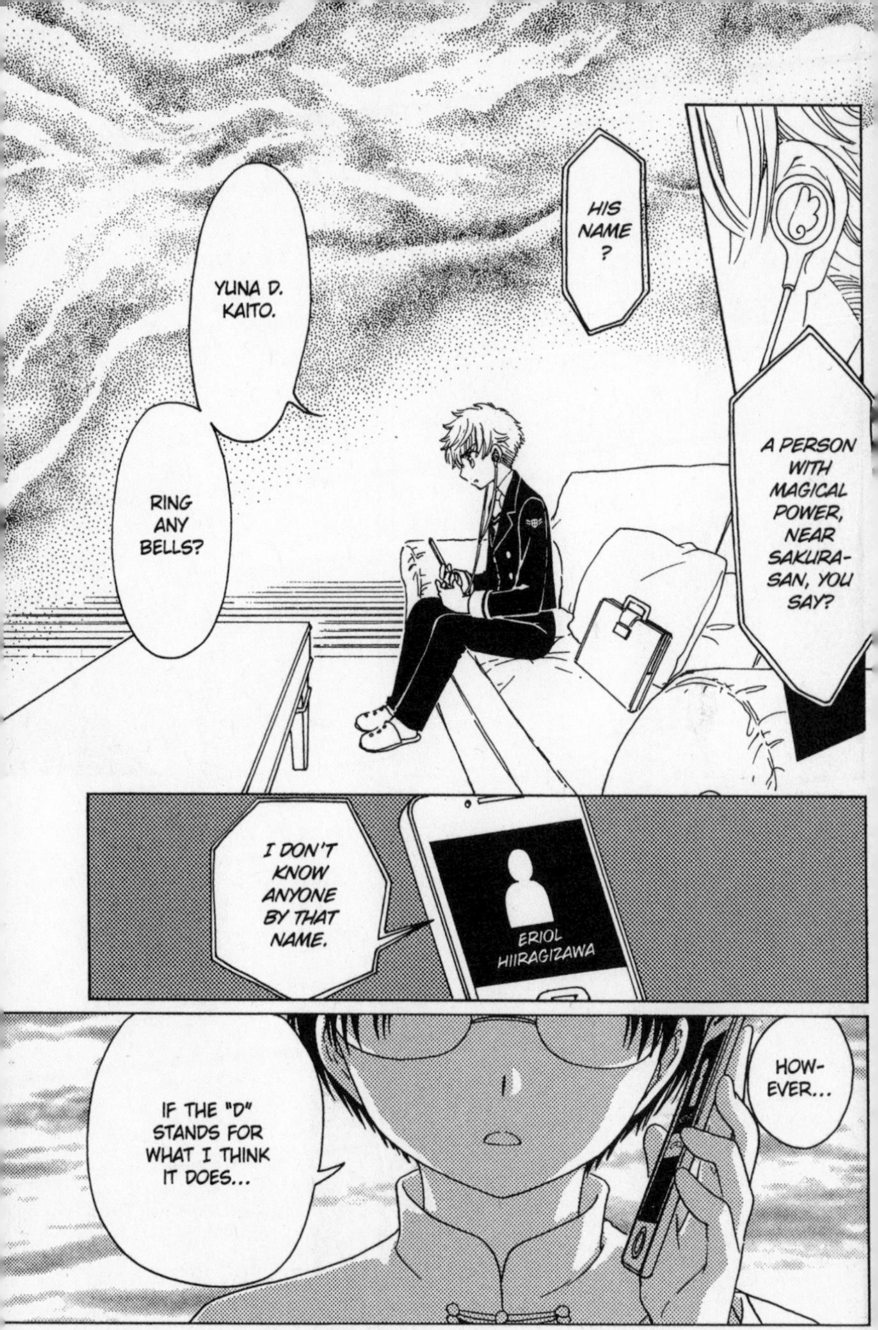
A PERSON WITH MAGICAL POWER, NEAR SAKURA-SAN, YOU SAY?
HIS NAME?
YUNA D. KAITO.
RING ANY BELLS?
I DON'T KNOW ANYONE BY THAT NAME.
ERIOL HIIRAGIZAWA
HOW-EVER...
IF THE "D" STANDS FOR WHAT I THINK IT DOES...

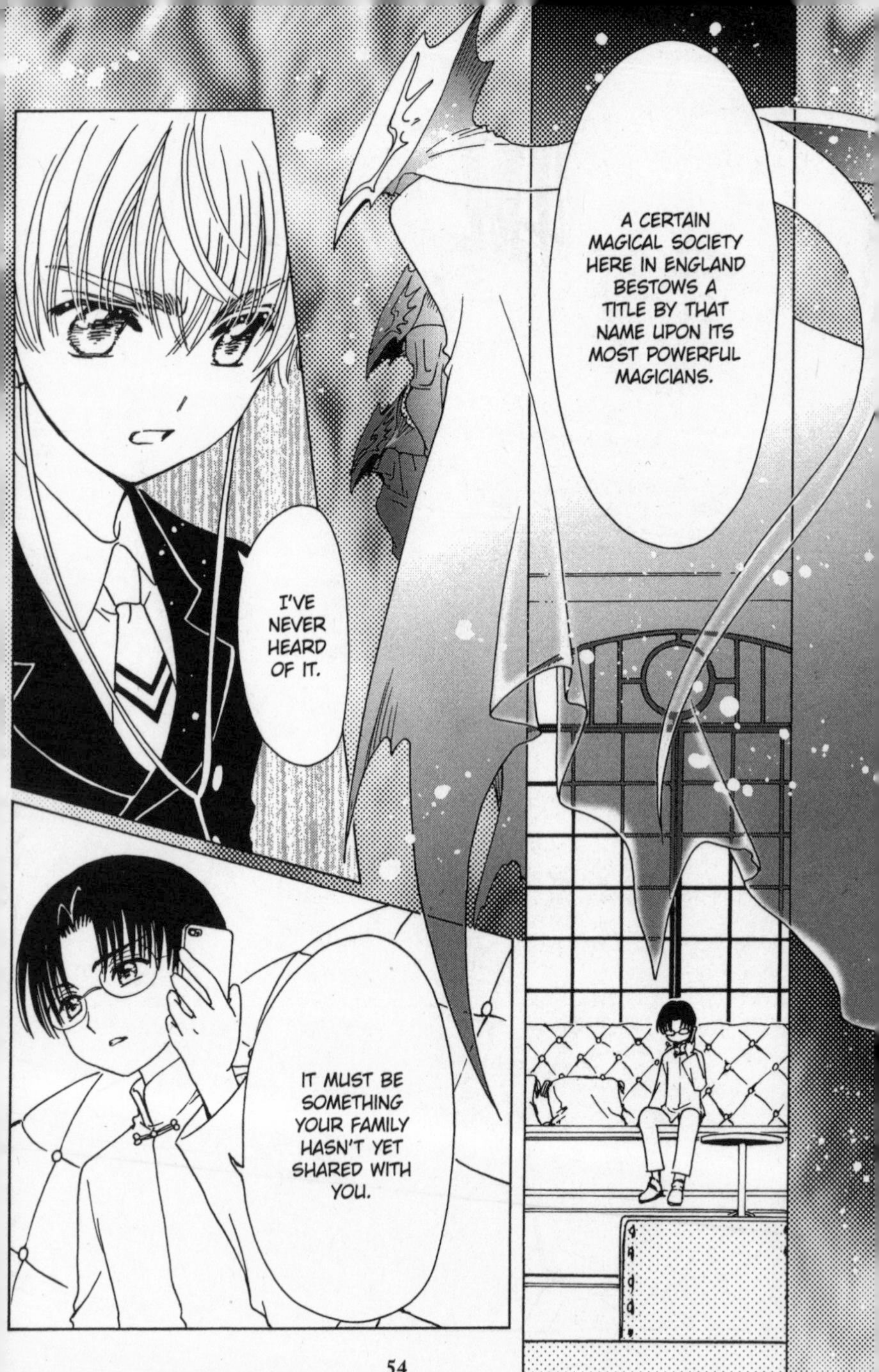
A CERTAIN MAGICAL SOCIETY HERE IN ENGLAND BESTOWS A TITLE BY THAT NAME UPON ITS MOST POWERFUL MAGICIANS.
I'VE NEVER HEARD OF IT.
IT MUST BE SOMETHING YOUR FAMILY HASN'T YET SHARED WITH YOU.

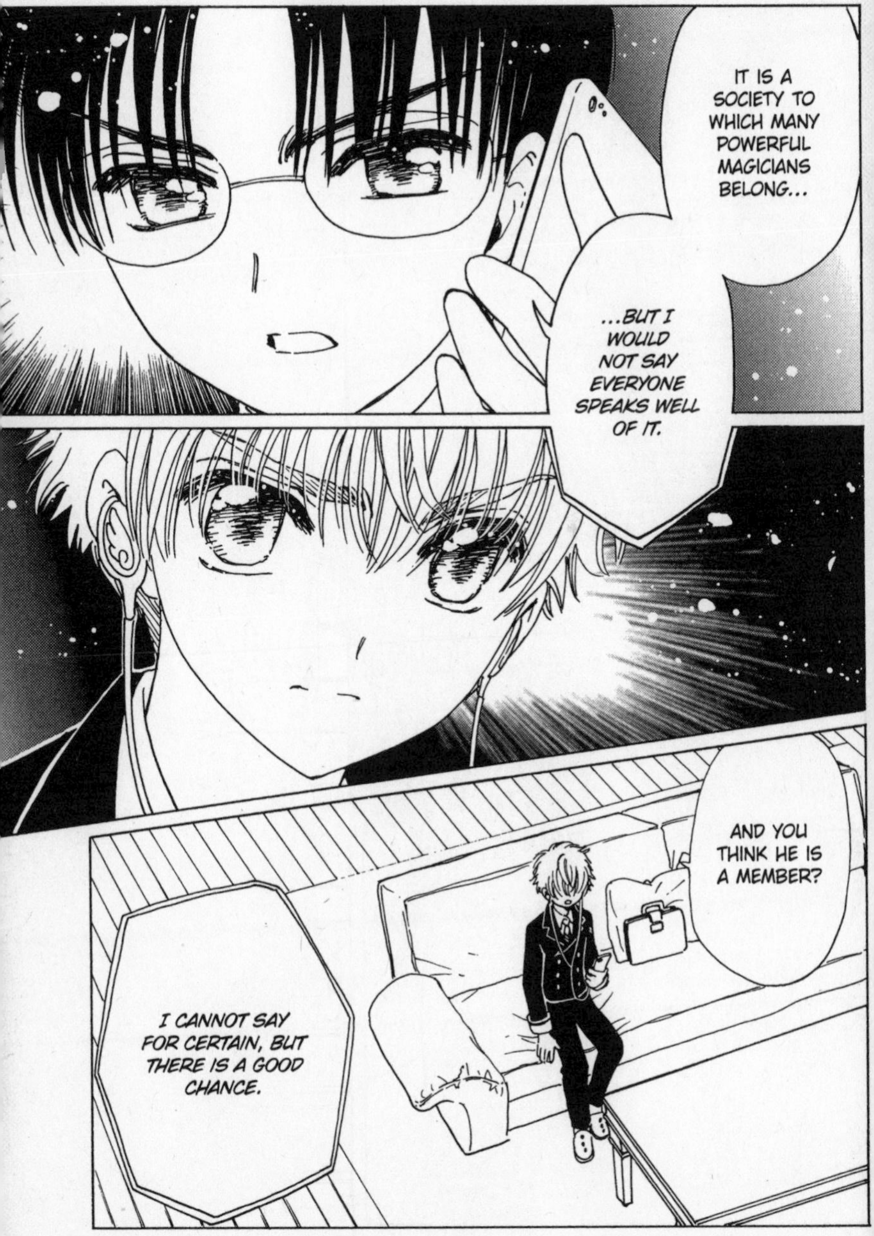
IT IS A SOCIETY TO WHICH MANY POWERFUL MAGICIANS BELONG...
...BUT I WOULD NOT SAY EVERYONE SPEAKS WELL OF IT.
AND YOU THINK HE IS A MEMBER?
I CANNOT SAY FOR CERTAIN, BUT THERE IS A GOOD CHANCE.

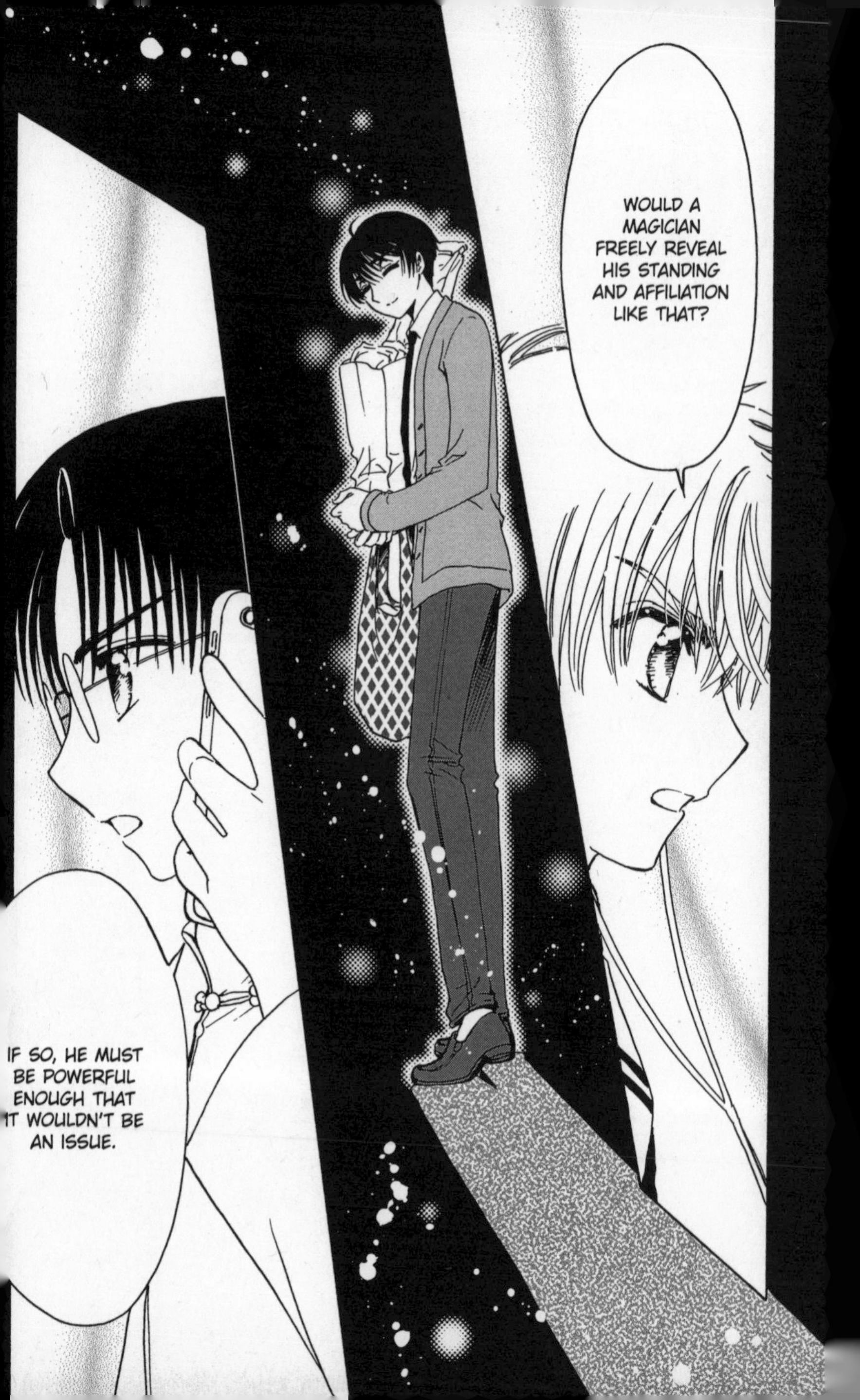
WOULD A MAGICIAN FREELY REVEAL HIS STANDING AND AFFILIATION LIKE THAT?
IF SO, HE MUST BE POWERFUL ENOUGH THAT IT WOULDN'T BE AN ISSUE.

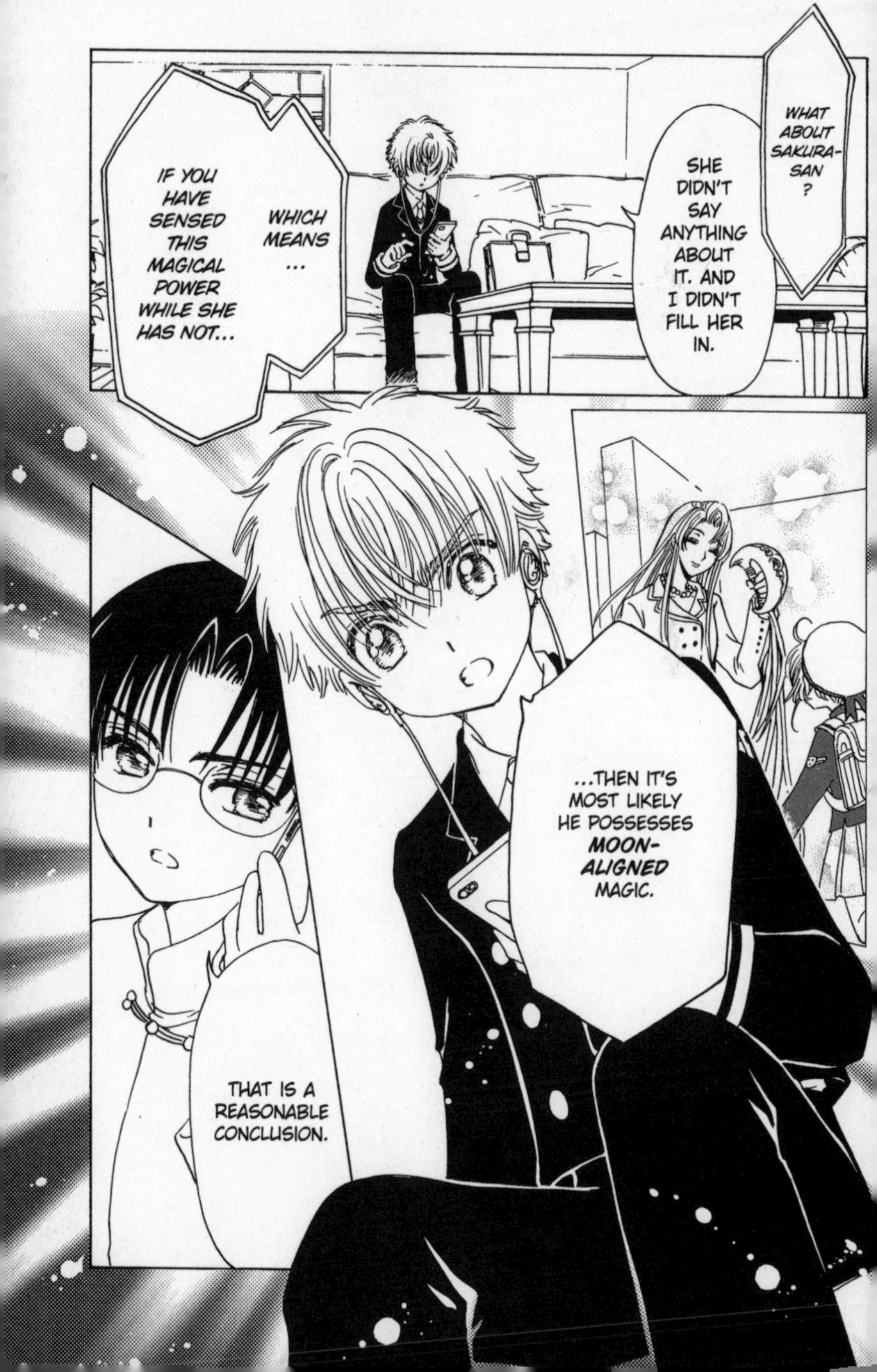

WHAT ABOUT SAKURA-SAN?
SHE DIDN'T SAY ANYTHING ABOUT IT. AND I DIDN'T FILL HER IN.
WHICH MEANS...
IF YOU HAVE SENSED THIS MAGICAL POWER WHILE SHE HAS NOT...
...THEN IT'S MOST LIKELY HE POSSESSES MOON-ALIGNED MAGIC.
THAT IS A REASONABLE CONCLUSION.

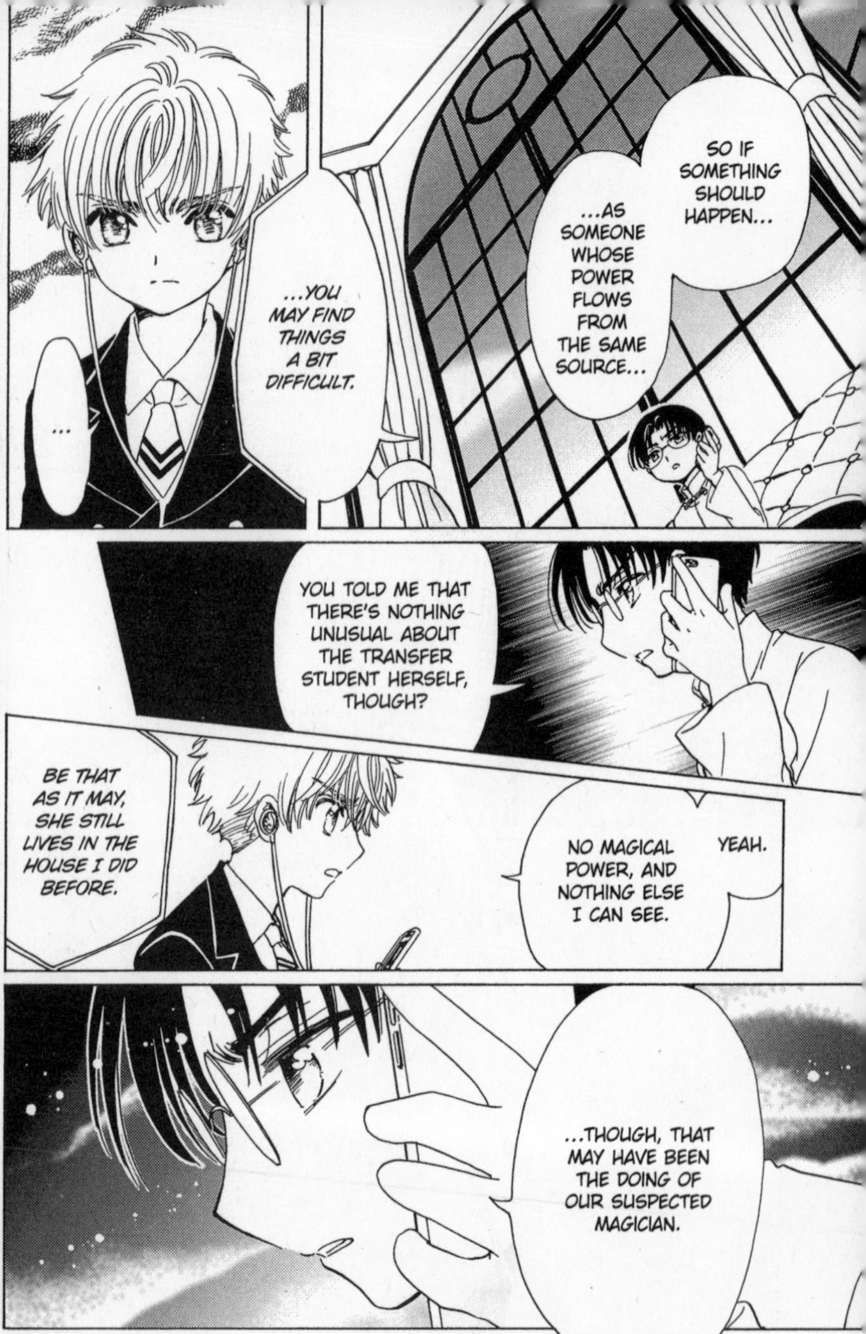
SO IF SOMETHING SHOULD HAPPEN...
...AS SOMEONE WHOSE POWER FLOWS FROM THE SAME SOURCE...
...YOU MAY FIND THINGS A BIT DIFFICULT.
...
YOU TOLD ME THAT THERE'S NOTHING UNUSUAL ABOUT THE TRANSFER STUDENT HERSELF, THOUGH?
YEAH.
NO MAGICAL POWER, AND NOTHING ELSE I CAN SEE.
BE THAT AS IT MAY, SHE STILL LIVES IN THE HOUSE I DID BEFORE.
...THOUGH, THAT MAY HAVE BEEN THE DOING OF OUR SUSPECTED MAGICIAN.

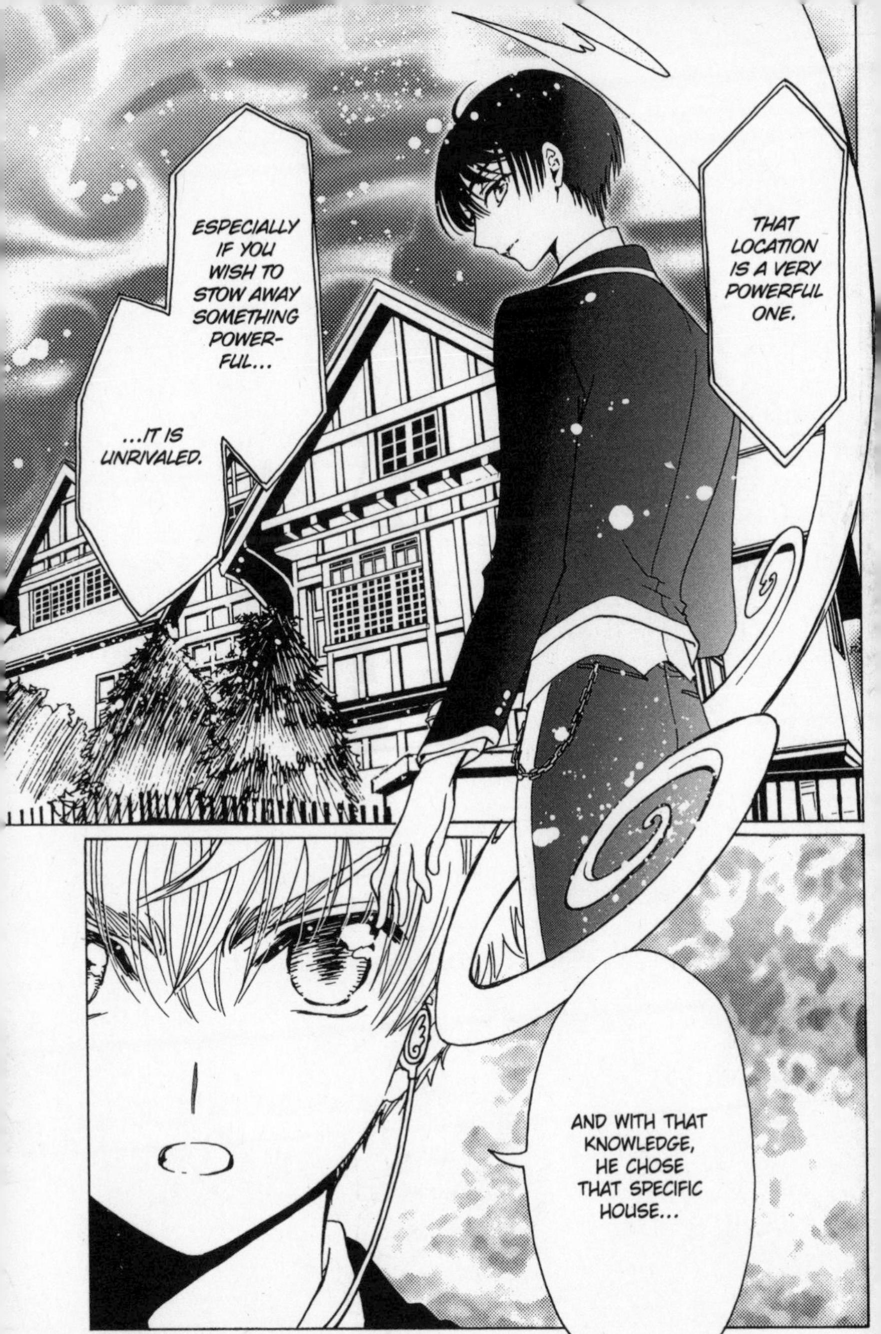
THAT LOCATION IS A VERY POWERFUL ONE.
ESPECIALLY IF YOU WISH TO STOW AWAY SOMETHING POWER-FUL...
...IT IS UNRIVALED.
AND WITH THAT KNOWLEDGE, HE CHOSE THAT SPECIFIC HOUSE...

✿ To be continued... ✿

Cardcaptor Sakura

CLEAR CARD

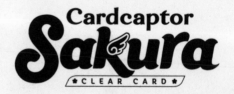

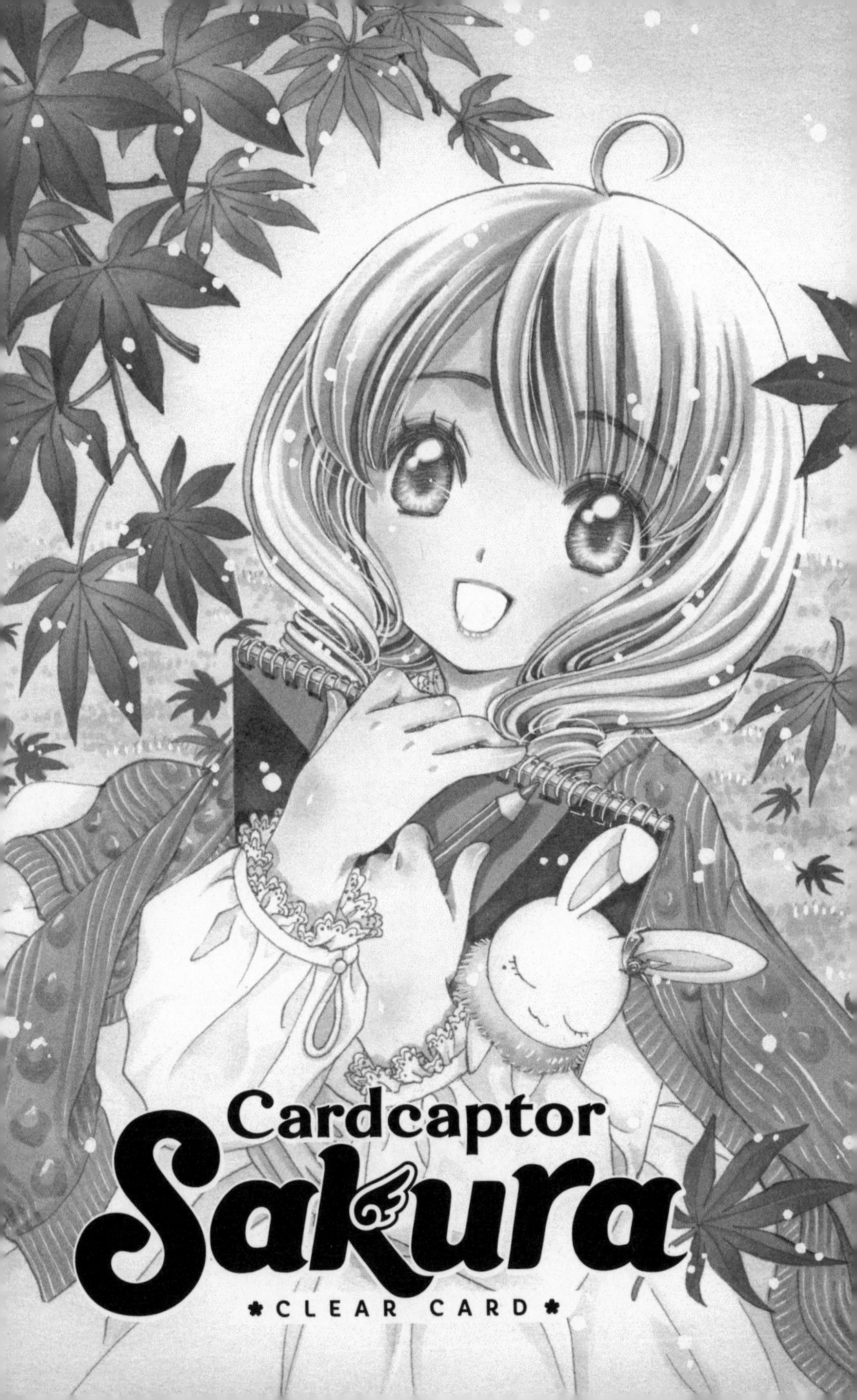
Cardcaptor
Sakura
CLEAR CARD

Cardcaptor Sakura
CLEAR CARD

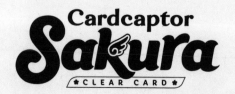

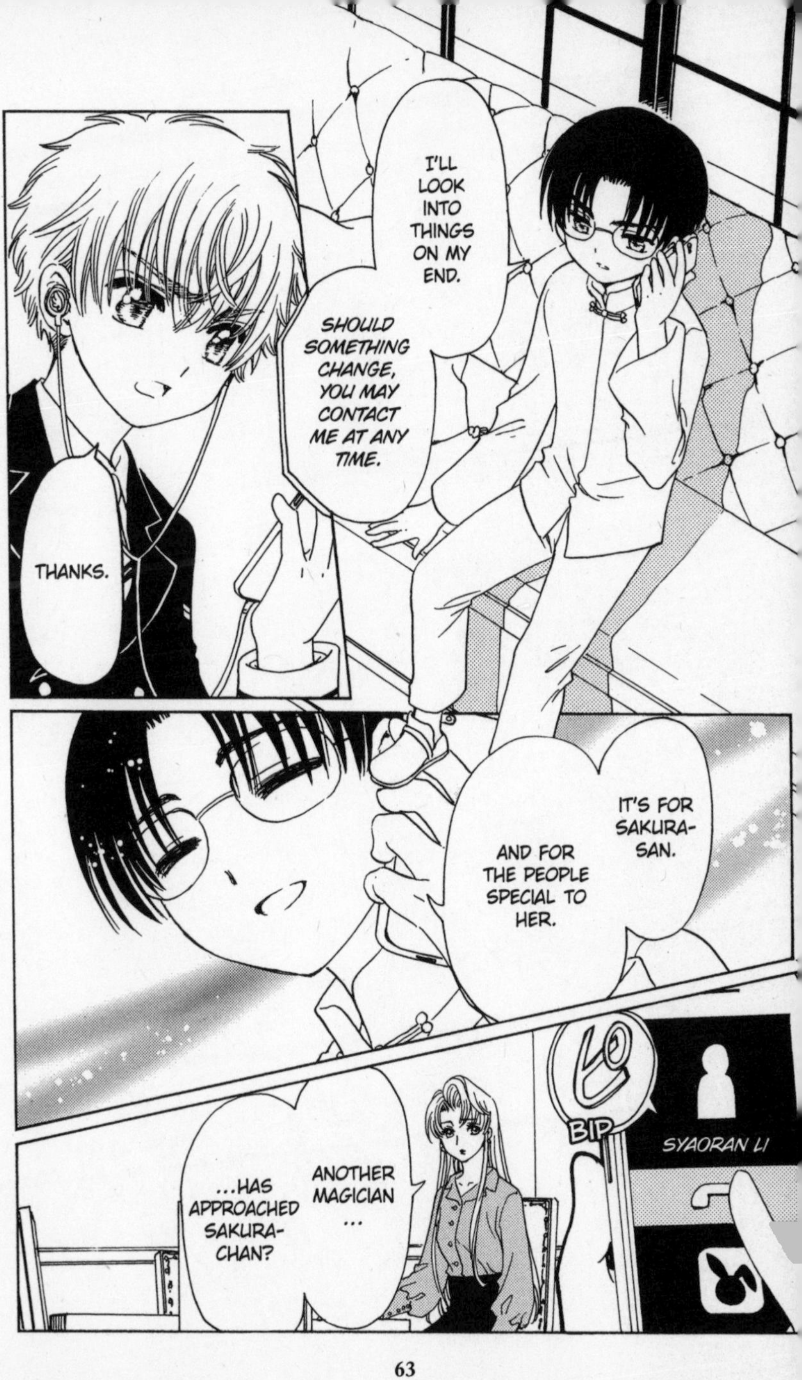
I'LL LOOK INTO THINGS ON MY END.
SHOULD SOMETHING CHANGE, YOU MAY CONTACT ME AT ANY TIME.
THANKS.
IT'S FOR SAKURA-SAN.
AND FOR THE PEOPLE SPECIAL TO HER.
BIP
SYAORAN LI
ANOTHER MAGICIAN ...
...HAS APPROACHED SAKURA-CHAN?

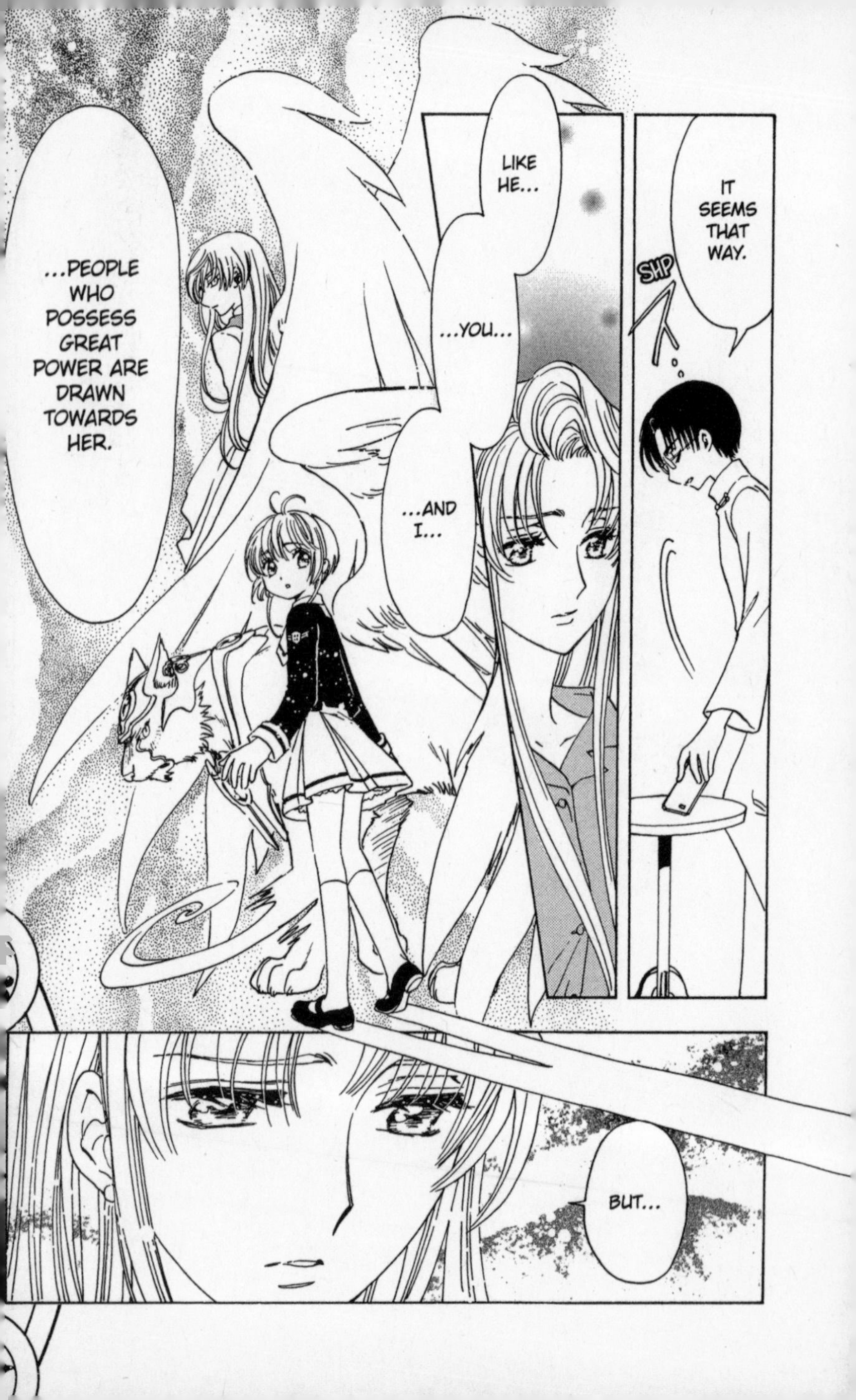
IT SEEMS THAT WAY.
SHP
LIKE HE...
...YOU...
...AND I...
...PEOPLE WHO POSSESS GREAT POWER ARE DRAWN TOWARDS HER.
BUT...

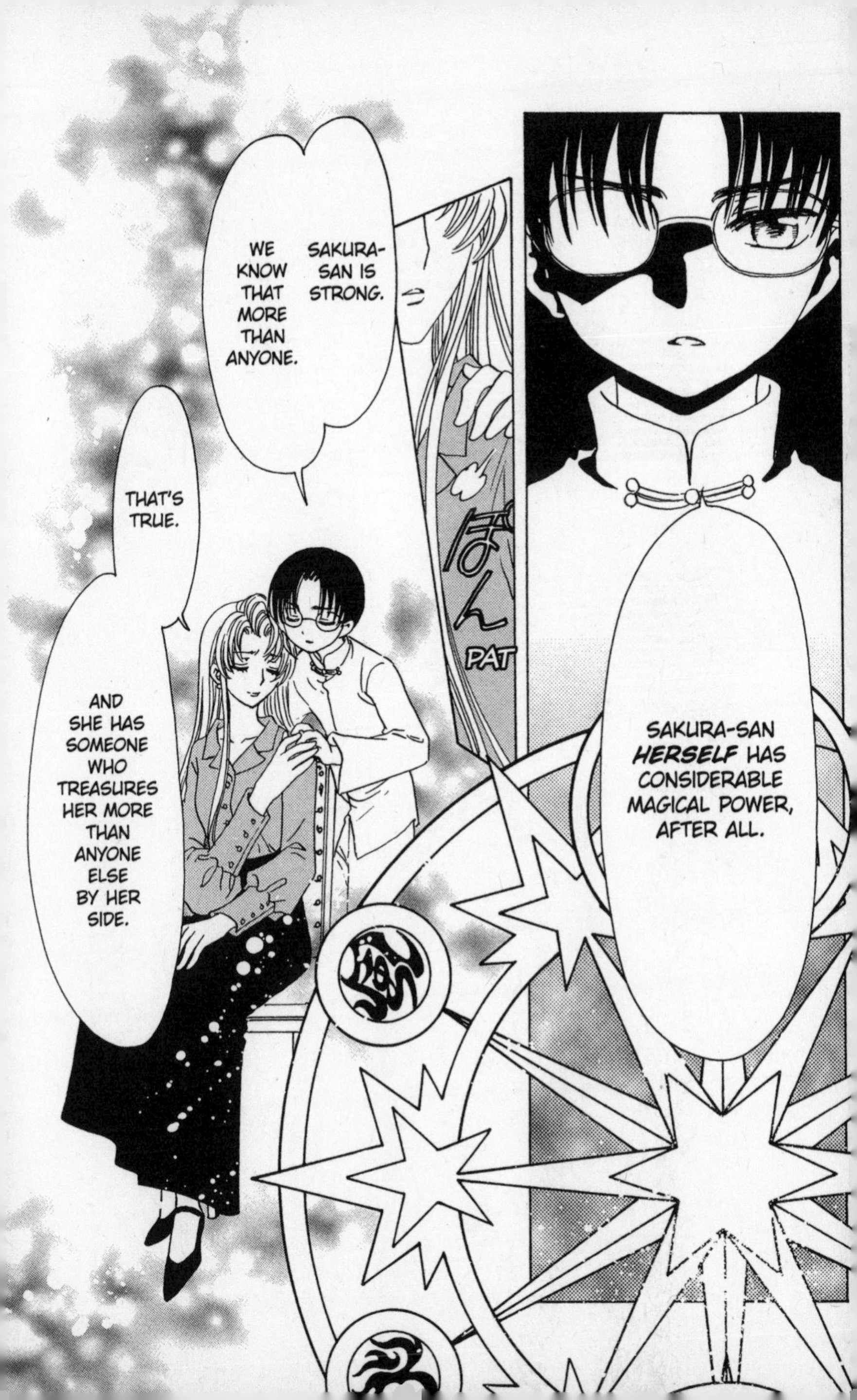
SAKURA-SAN *HERSELF* HAS CONSIDERABLE MAGICAL POWER, AFTER ALL.
SAKURA-SAN IS STRONG.
WE KNOW THAT MORE THAN ANYONE.
ぽん
PAT
THAT'S TRUE.
AND SHE HAS SOMEONE WHO TREASURES HER MORE THAN ANYONE ELSE BY HER SIDE.

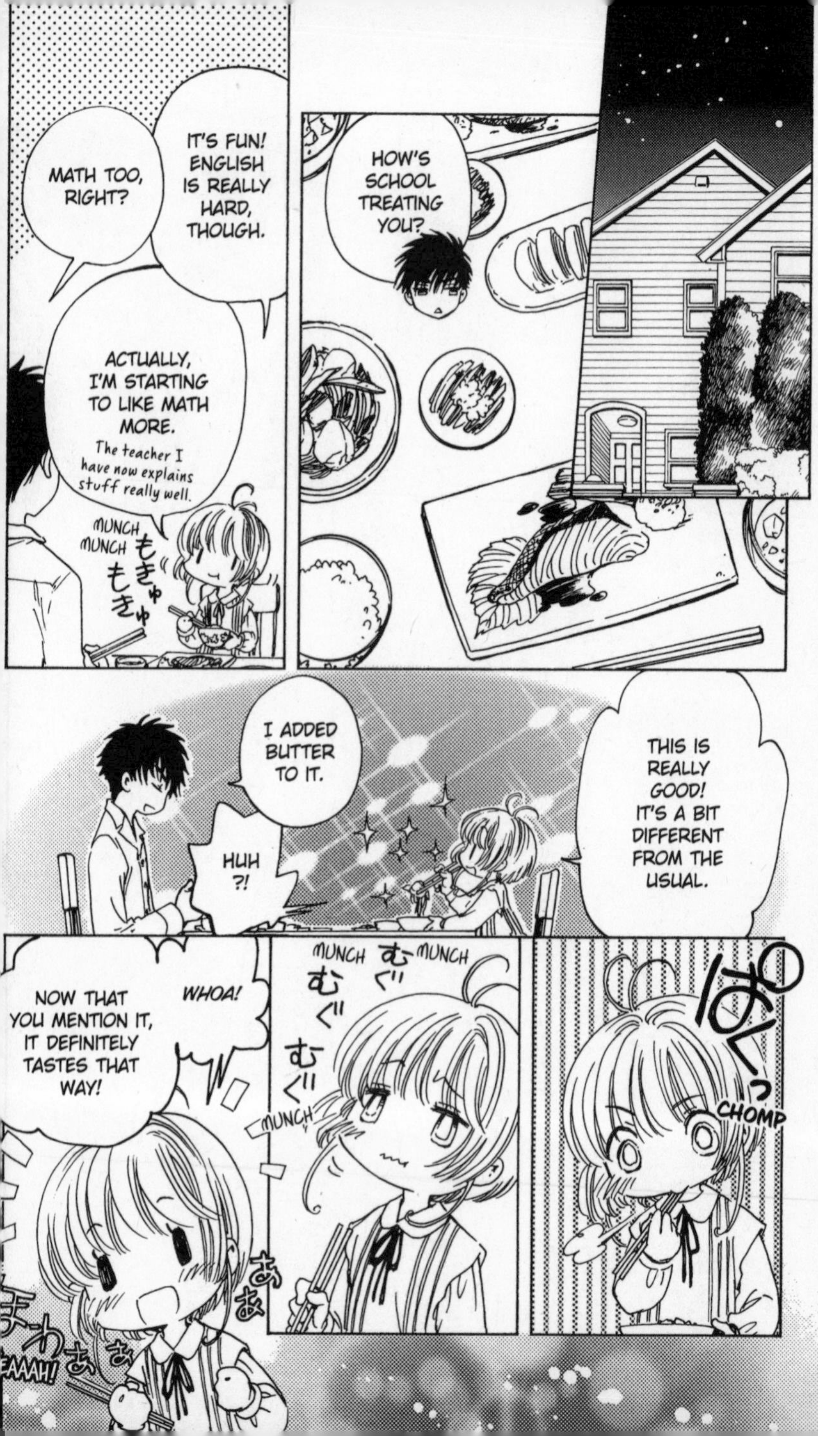

HOW'S SCHOOL TREATING YOU?
IT'S FUN! ENGLISH IS REALLY HARD, THOUGH.
MATH TOO, RIGHT?
ACTUALLY, I'M STARTING TO LIKE MATH MORE.
The teacher I have now explains stuff really well.
MUNCH MUNCH
もきゅもきゅ
THIS IS REALLY GOOD! IT'S A BIT DIFFERENT FROM THE USUAL.
I ADDED BUTTER TO IT.
HUH ?!
ぱくっ
CHOMP
MUNCH MUNCH
むぐむぐむぐ
MUNCH
WHOA!
NOW THAT YOU MENTION IT, IT DEFINITELY TASTES THAT WAY!
ああ

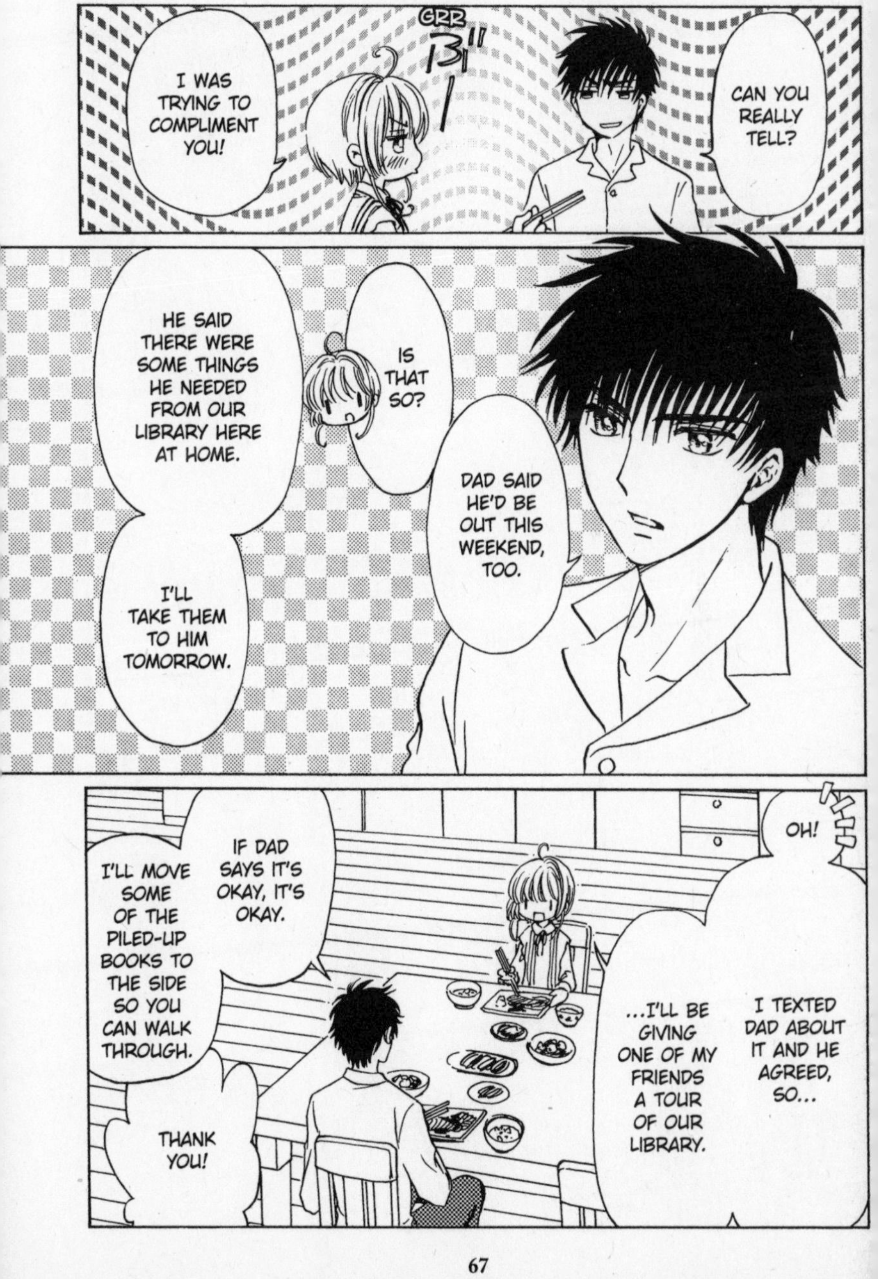
CAN YOU REALLY TELL?
GRR
I WAS TRYING TO COMPLIMENT YOU!
DAD SAID HE'D BE OUT THIS WEEKEND, TOO.
IS THAT SO?
HE SAID THERE WERE SOME THINGS HE NEEDED FROM OUR LIBRARY HERE AT HOME.
I'LL TAKE THEM TO HIM TOMORROW.
OH!
I TEXTED DAD ABOUT IT AND HE AGREED, SO...
...I'LL BE GIVING ONE OF MY FRIENDS A TOUR OF OUR LIBRARY.
IF DAD SAYS IT'S OKAY, IT'S OKAY.
I'LL MOVE SOME OF THE PILED-UP BOOKS TO THE SIDE SO YOU CAN WALK THROUGH.
THANK YOU!

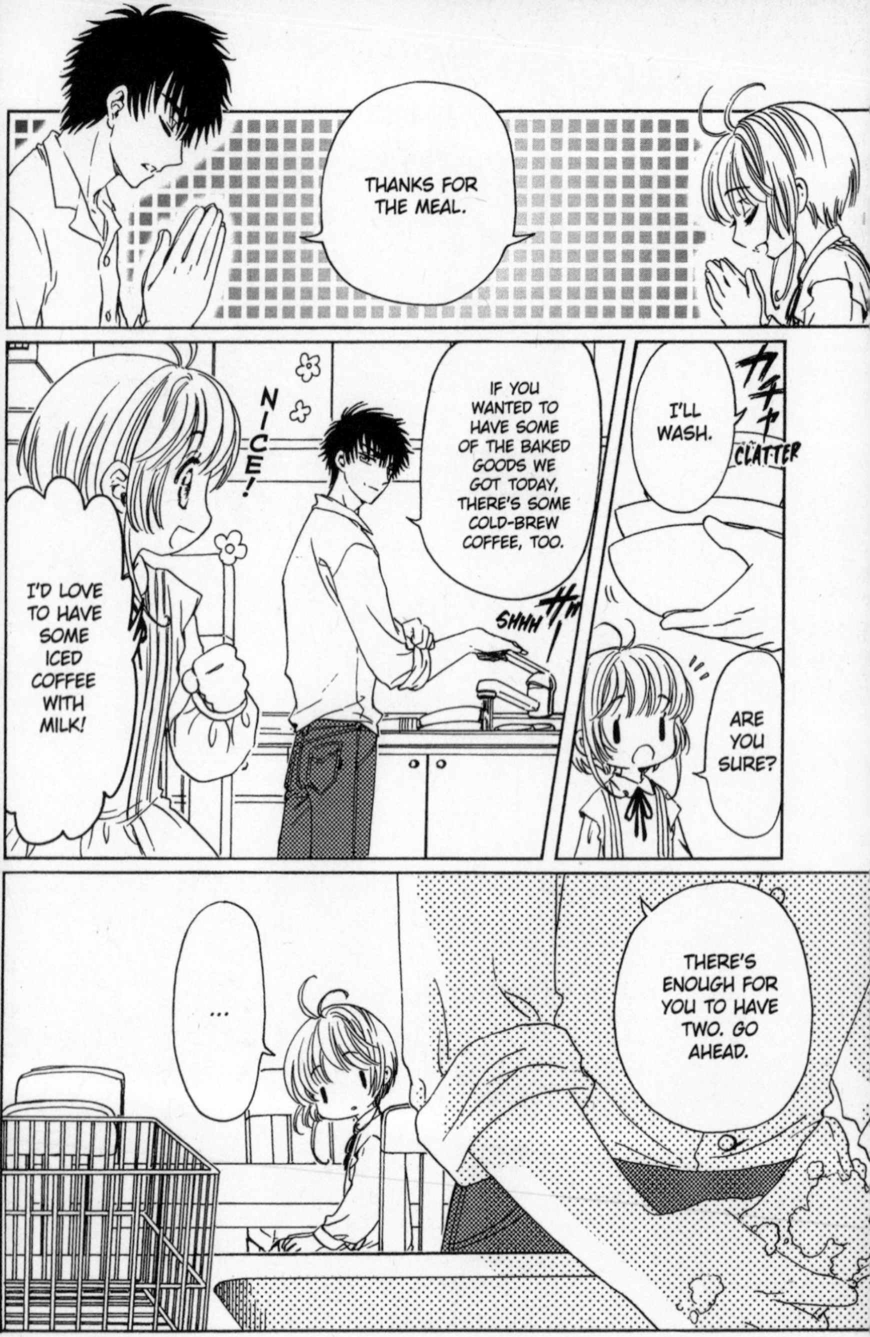
THANKS FOR THE MEAL.
カチャ
CLATTER
I'LL WASH.
ARE YOU SURE?
IF YOU WANTED TO HAVE SOME OF THE BAKED GOODS WE GOT TODAY, THERE'S SOME COLD-BREW COFFEE, TOO.
SHHH
NICE!
I'D LOVE TO HAVE SOME ICED COFFEE WITH MILK!
THERE'S ENOUGH FOR YOU TO HAVE TWO. GO AHEAD.
...

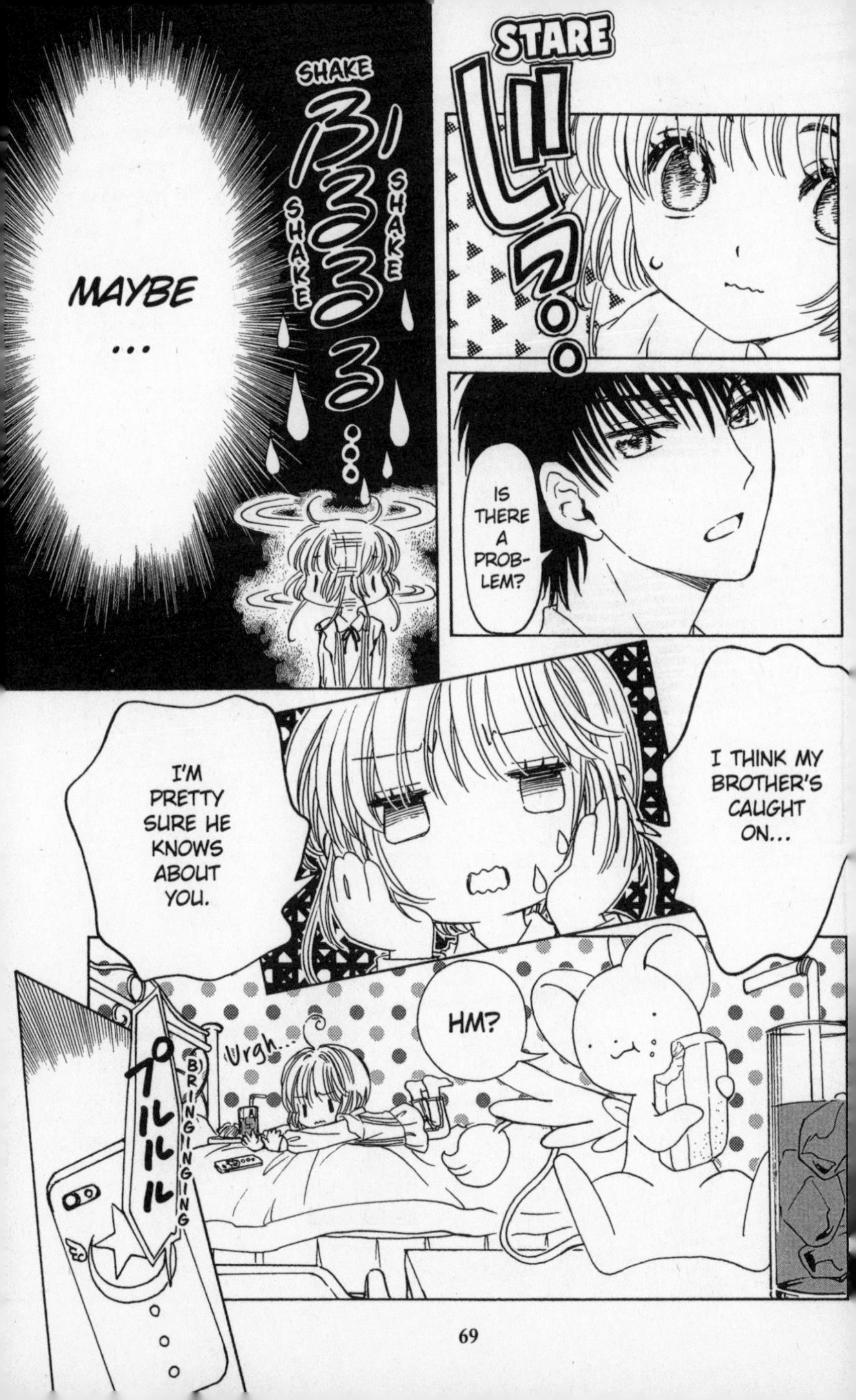
STARE
IS THERE A PROBLEM?
SHAKE
SHAKE SHAKE
MAYBE...
I THINK MY BROTHER'S CAUGHT ON...
I'M PRETTY SURE HE KNOWS ABOUT YOU.
HM?
Urgh...
BRINGINGINGING

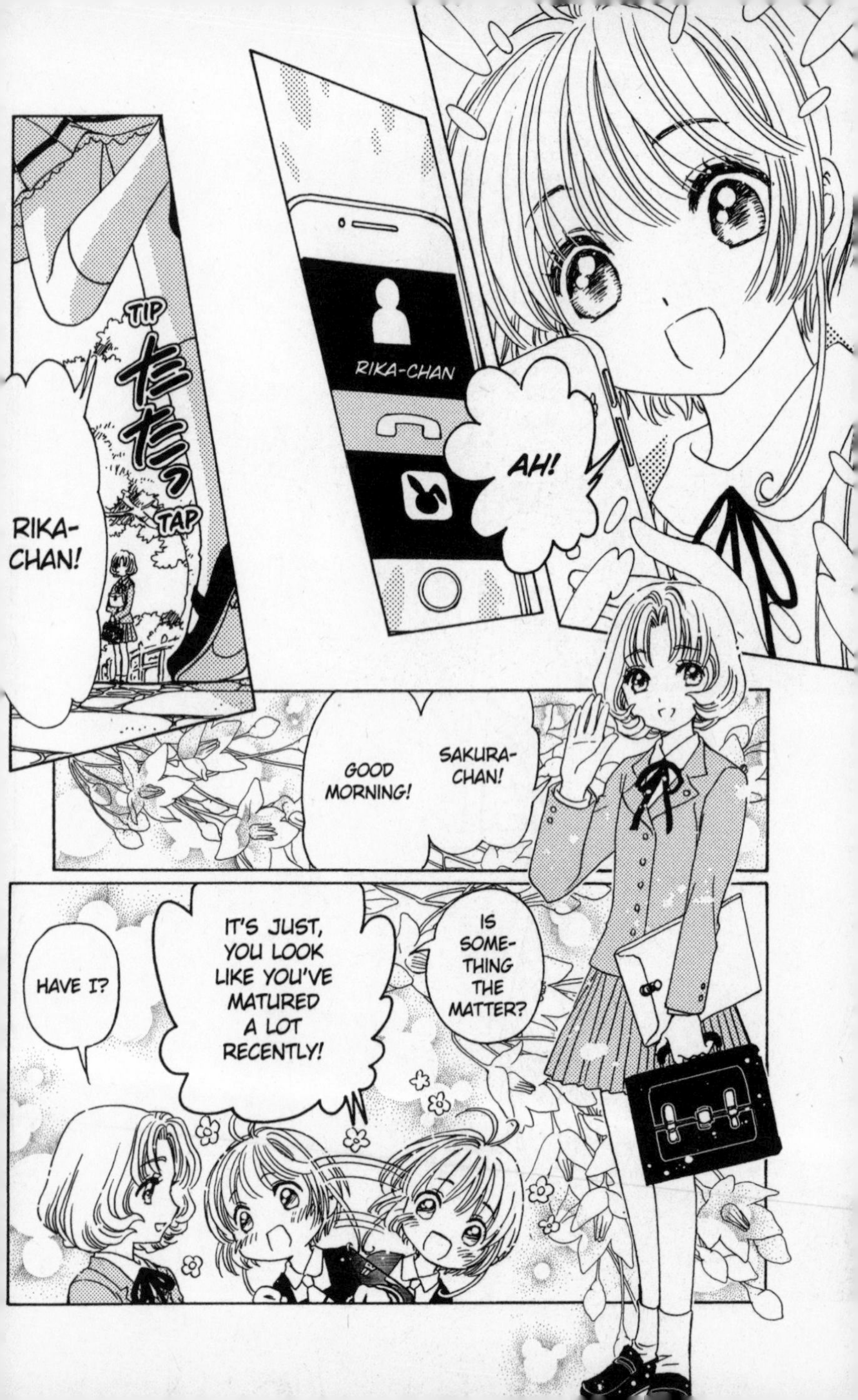
AH!
RIKA-CHAN
TIP
たたっ
TAP
RIKA-CHAN!
SAKURA-CHAN!
GOOD MORNING!
IS SOMETHING THE MATTER?
IT'S JUST, YOU LOOK LIKE YOU'VE MATURED A LOT RECENTLY!
HAVE I?

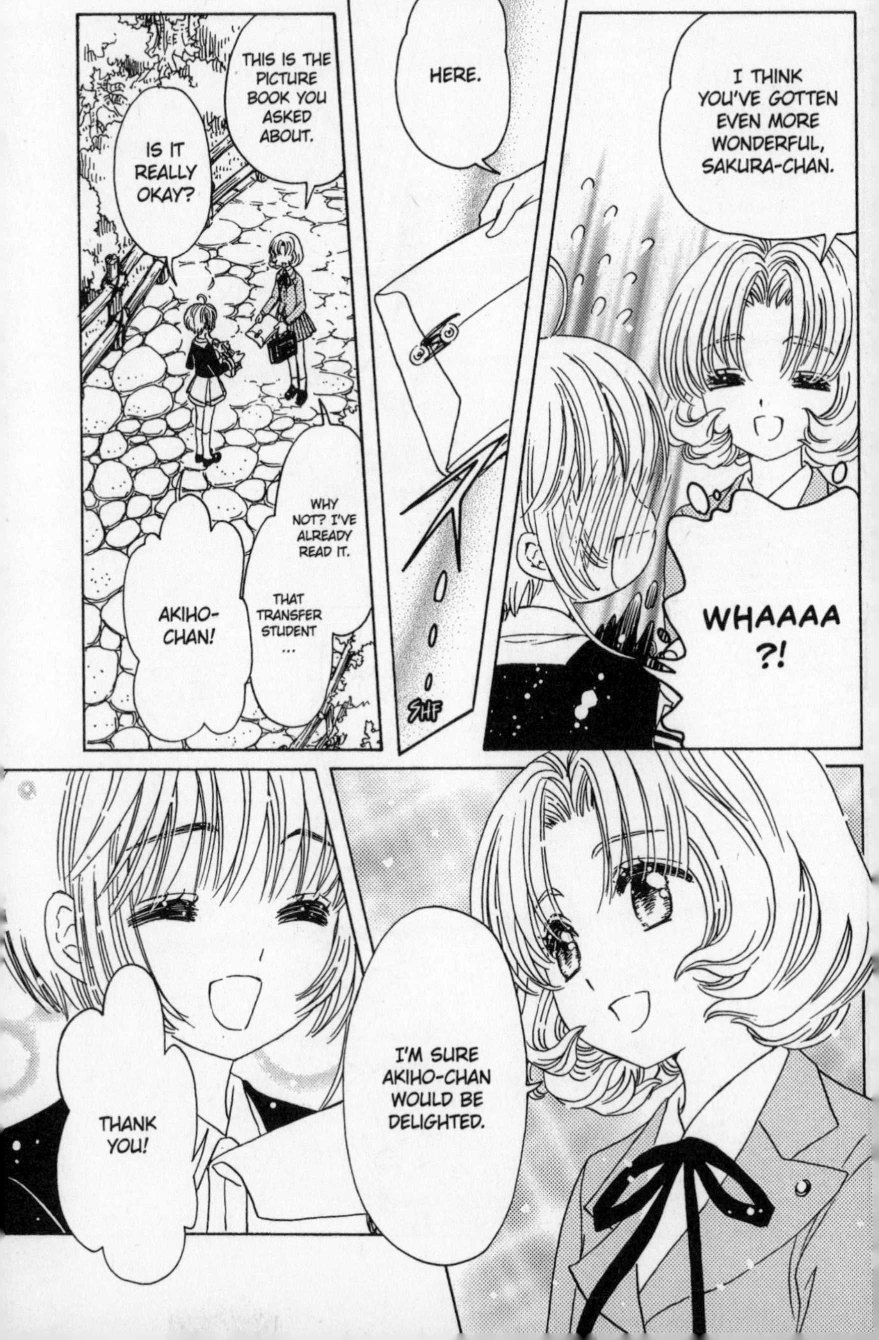
I THINK YOU'VE GOTTEN EVEN MORE WONDERFUL, SAKURA-CHAN.
WHAAAA ?!
HERE.
SHF
THIS IS THE PICTURE BOOK YOU ASKED ABOUT.
IS IT REALLY OKAY?
WHY NOT? I'VE ALREADY READ IT.
THAT TRANSFER STUDENT ...
AKIHO-CHAN!
I'M SURE AKIHO-CHAN WOULD BE DELIGHTED.
THANK YOU!

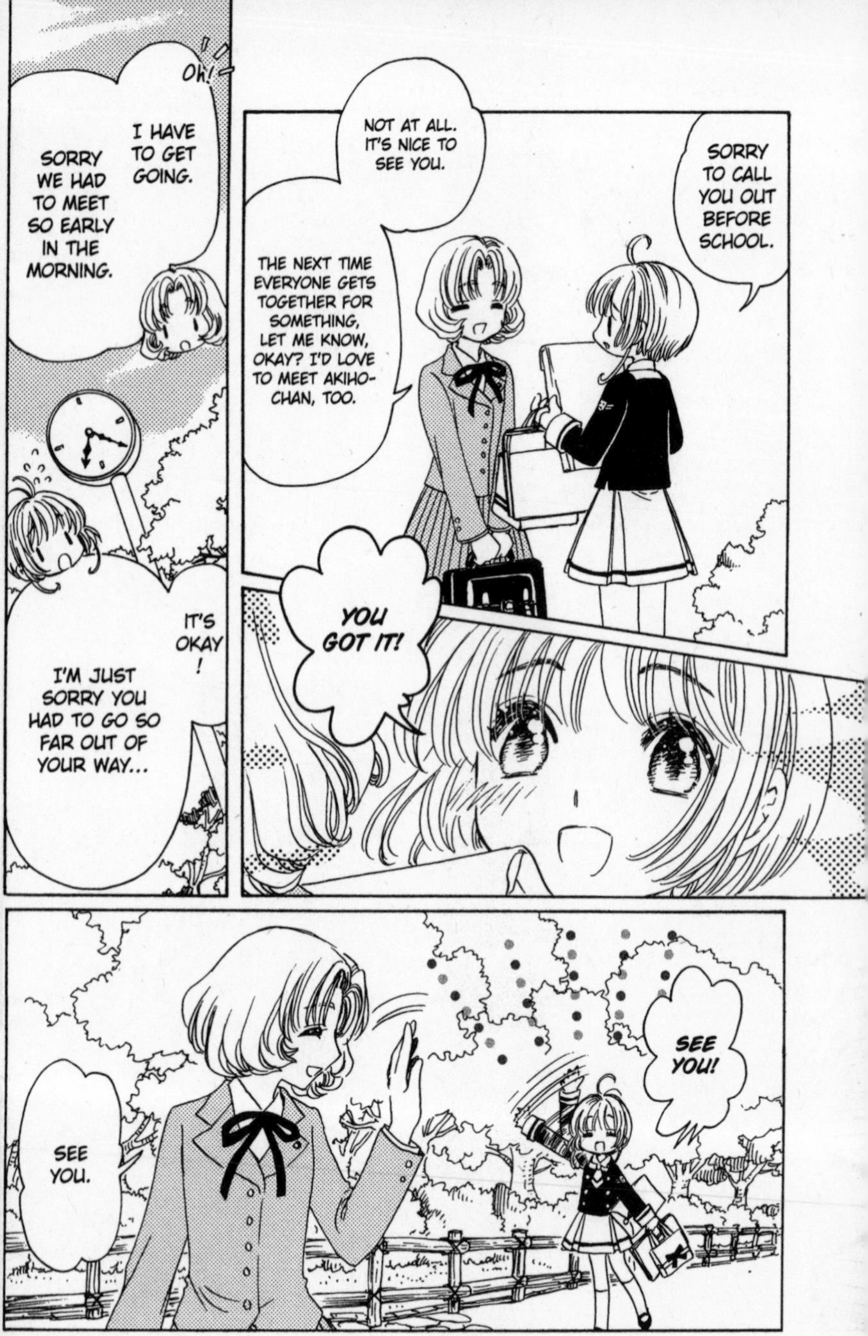
SORRY TO CALL YOU OUT BEFORE SCHOOL.
NOT AT ALL. IT'S NICE TO SEE YOU.
THE NEXT TIME EVERYONE GETS TOGETHER FOR SOMETHING, LET ME KNOW, OKAY? I'D LOVE TO MEET AKIHO-CHAN, TOO.
YOU GOT IT!
Oh!
I HAVE TO GET GOING.
SORRY WE HAD TO MEET SO EARLY IN THE MORNING.
IT'S OKAY!
I'M JUST SORRY YOU HAD TO GO SO FAR OUT OF YOUR WAY...
SEE YOU!
SEE YOU.

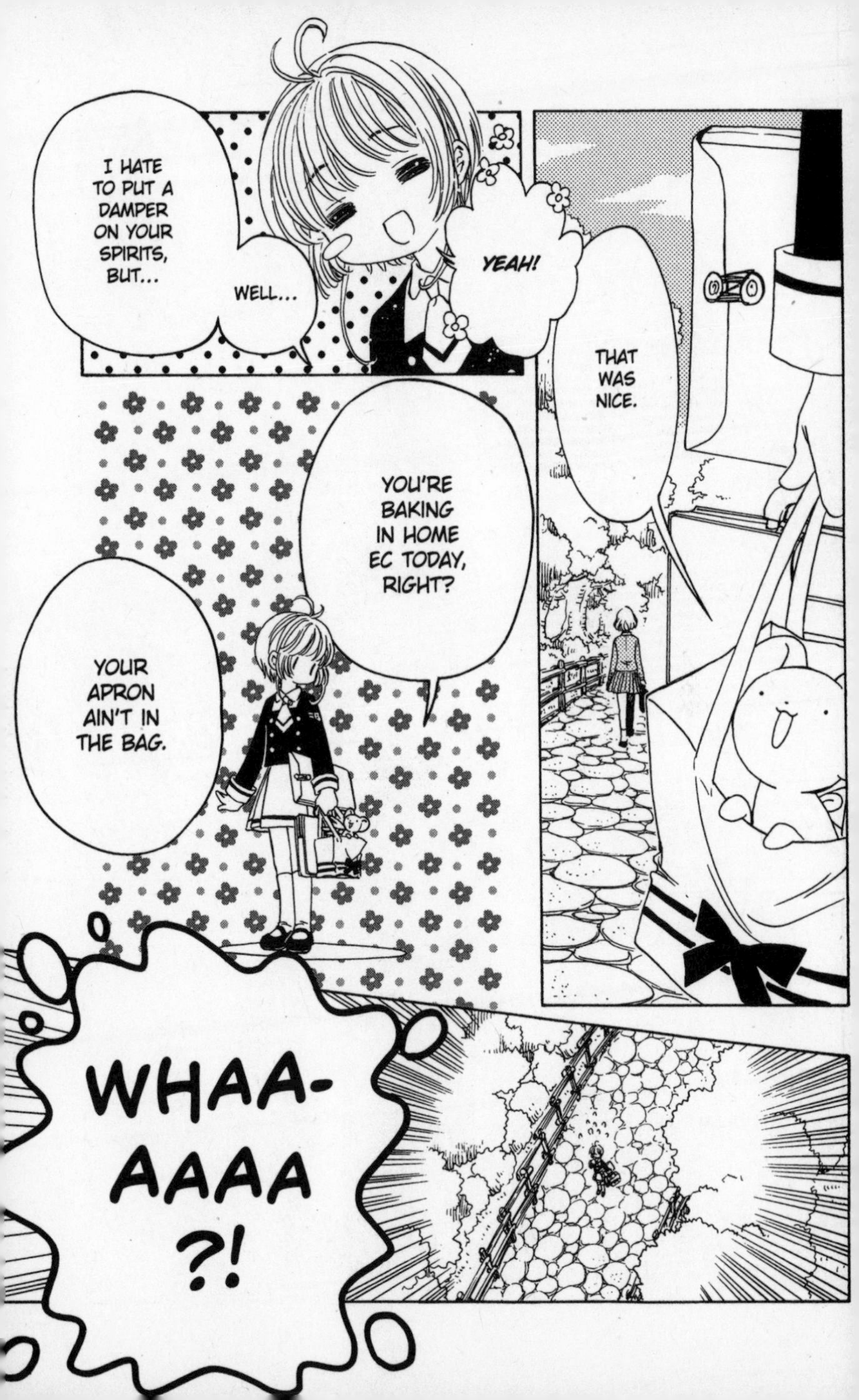
THAT WAS NICE.
YEAH!
WELL...
I HATE TO PUT A DAMPER ON YOUR SPIRITS, BUT...
YOU'RE BAKING IN HOME EC TODAY, RIGHT?
YOUR APRON AIN'T IN THE BAG.
WHAA-AAAA?!

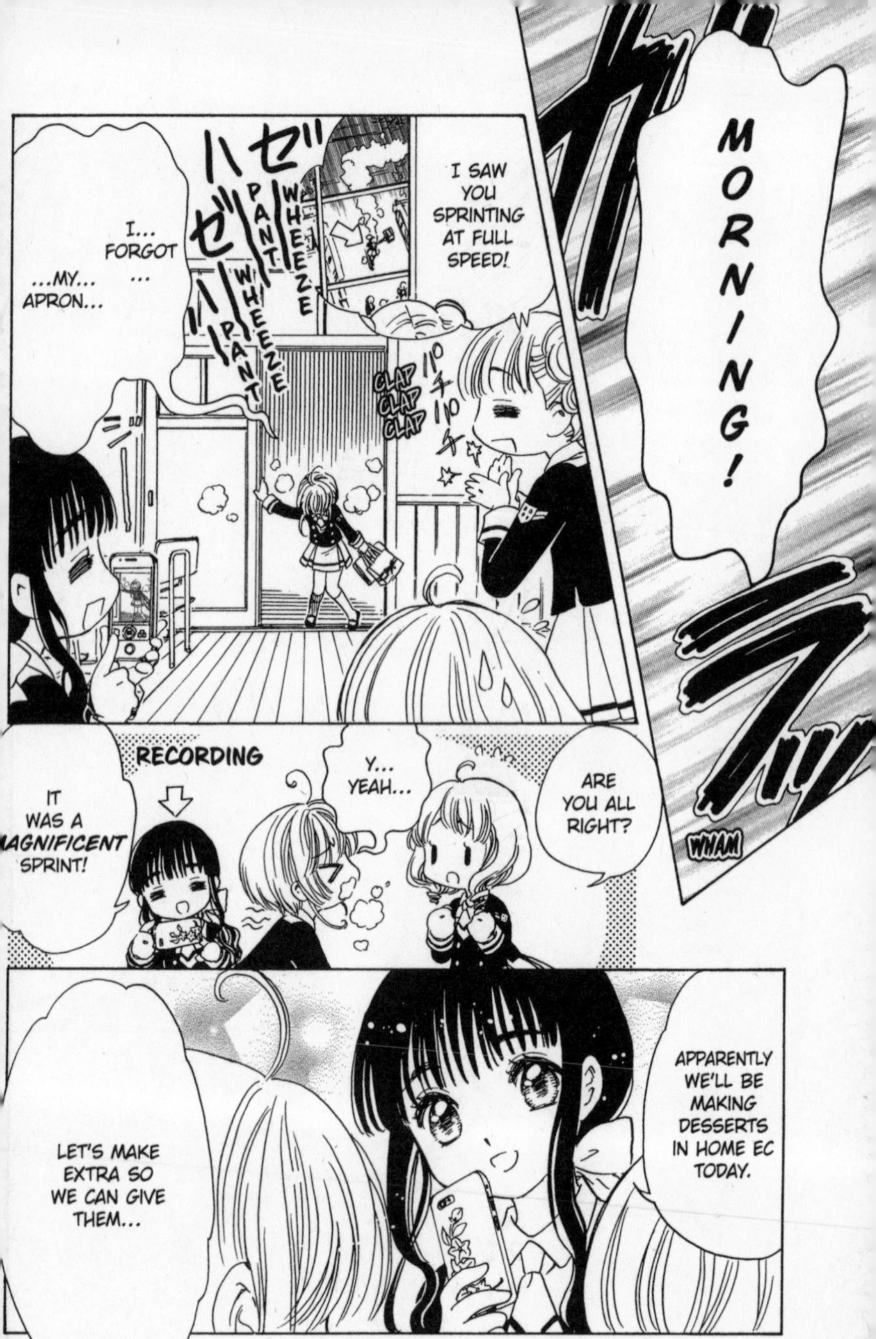
MORNING!
WHAM
I SAW YOU SPRINTING AT FULL SPEED!
PANT PANT
WHEEZE WHEEZE
CLAP CLAP CLAP
I... FORGOT ...
...MY... APRON...
ARE YOU ALL RIGHT?
Y... YEAH...
RECORDING
IT WAS A AGNIFICENT SPRINT!
APPARENTLY WE'LL BE MAKING DESSERTS IN HOME EC TODAY.
LET'S MAKE EXTRA SO WE CAN GIVE THEM...

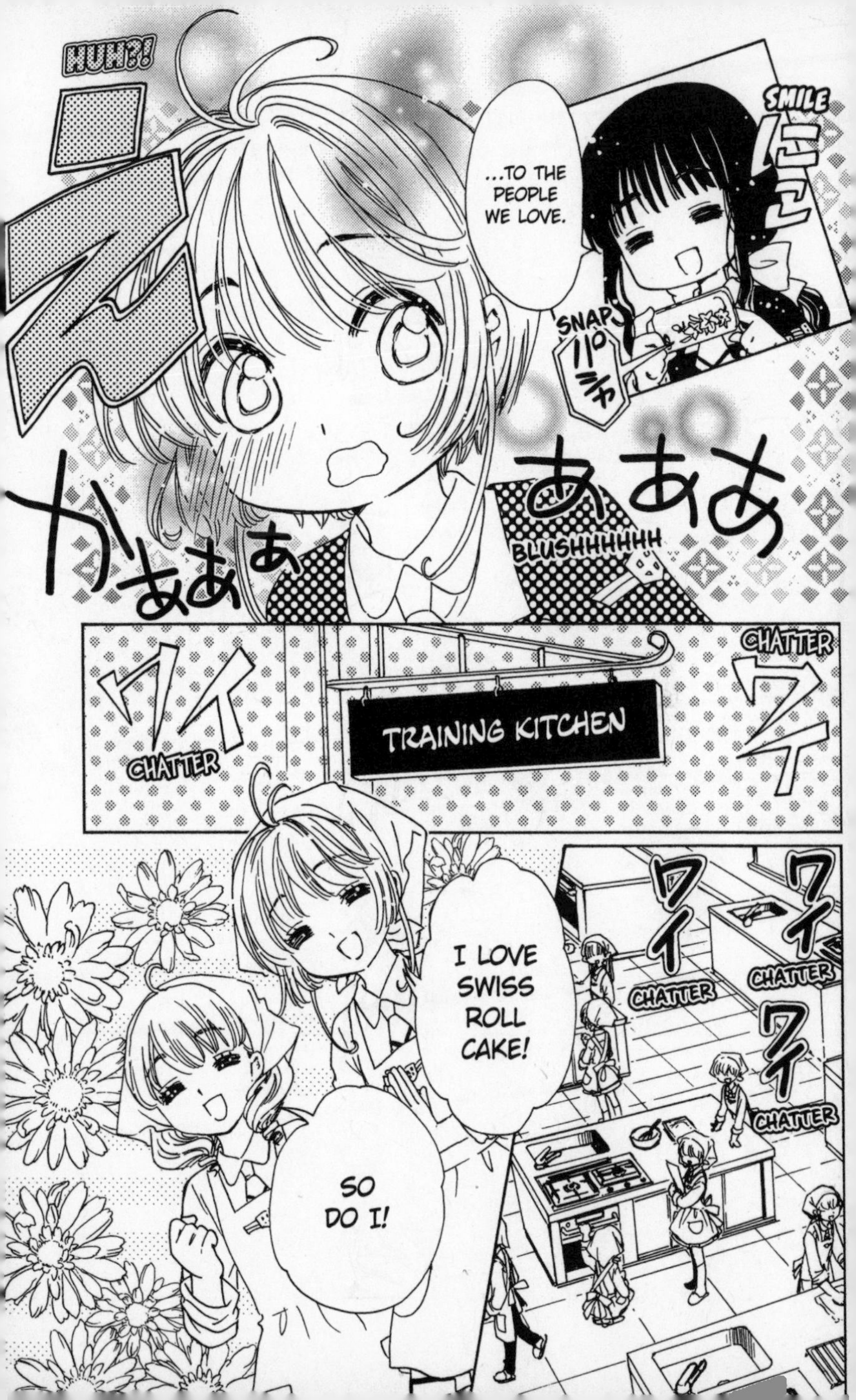
SMILE
...TO THE PEOPLE WE LOVE.
SNAP
HUH?!
BLUSHHHHHH
CHATTER
TRAINING KITCHEN
CHATTER
CHATTER
CHATTER
CHATTER
I LOVE SWISS ROLL CAKE!
SO DO I!

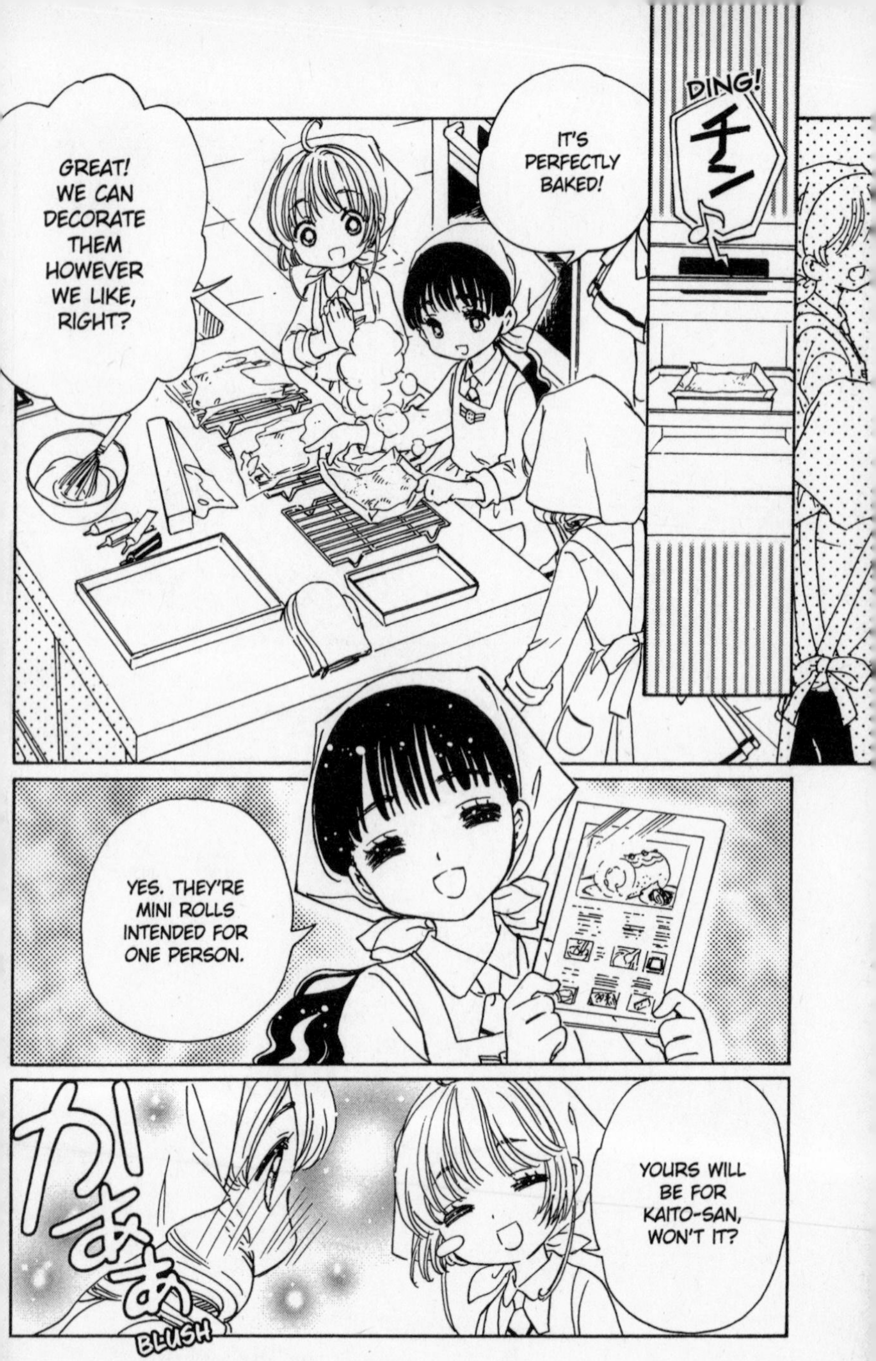

DING!
チン
IT'S PERFECTLY BAKED!
GREAT! WE CAN DECORATE THEM HOWEVER WE LIKE, RIGHT?
YES. THEY'RE MINI ROLLS INTENDED FOR ONE PERSON.
YOURS WILL BE FOR KAITO-SAN, WON'T IT?
かぁぁ
BLUSH

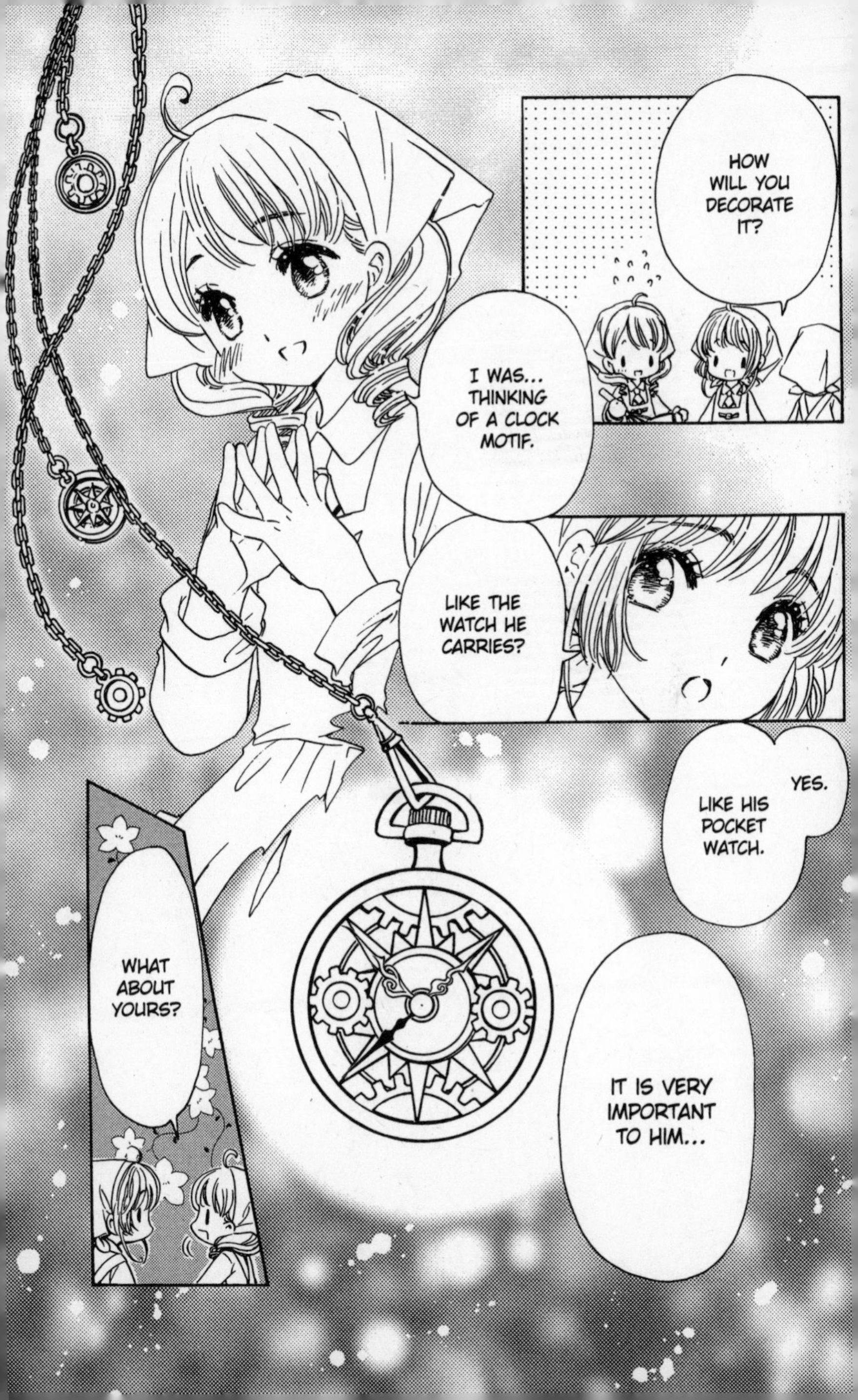
HOW WILL YOU DECORATE IT?
I WAS... THINKING OF A CLOCK MOTIF.
LIKE THE WATCH HE CARRIES?
YES.
LIKE HIS POCKET WATCH.
IT IS VERY IMPORTANT TO HIM...
WHAT ABOUT YOURS?

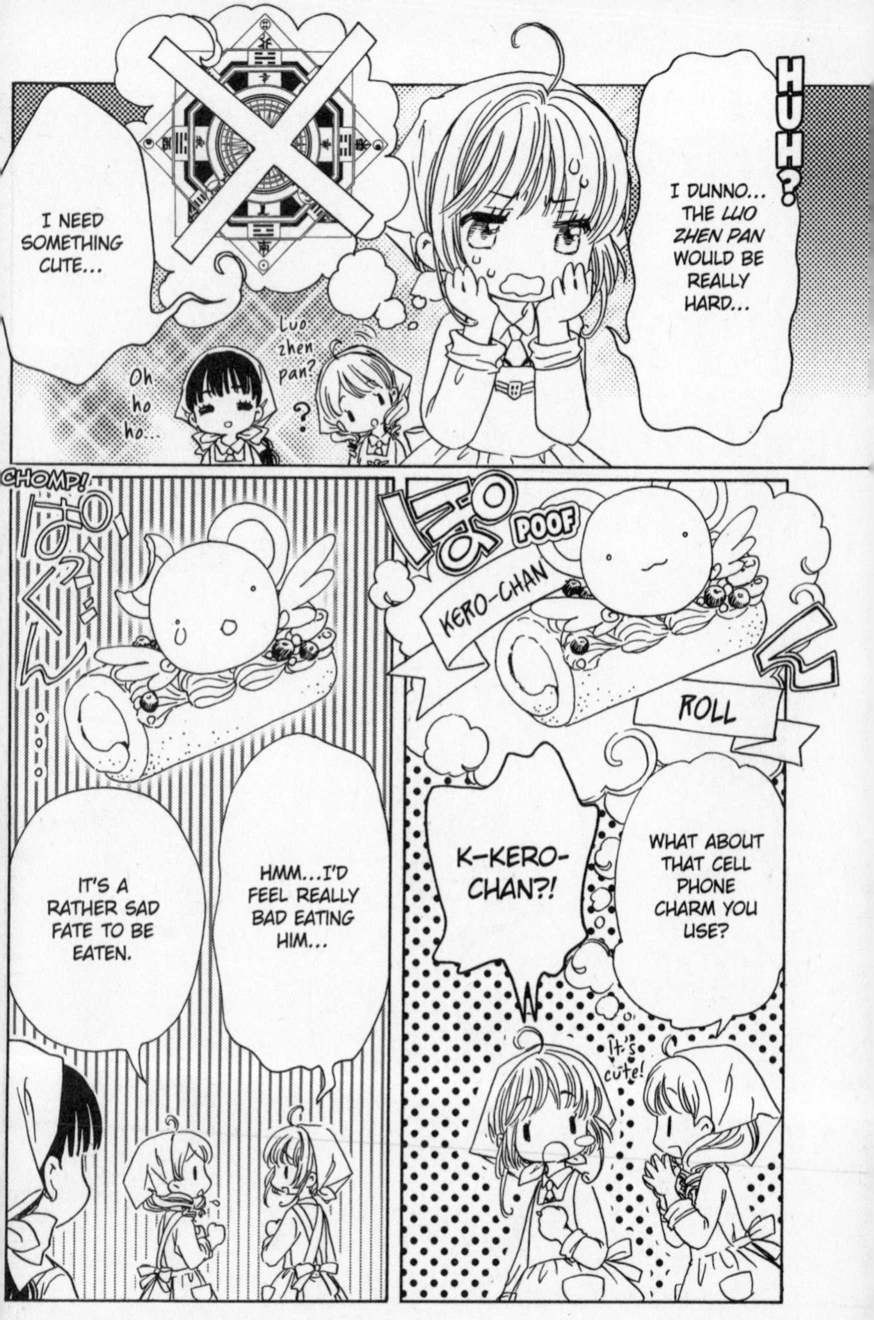
HUH?
I DUNNO... THE LUO ZHEN PAN WOULD BE REALLY HARD...
Luo zhen pan?
?
I NEED SOMETHING CUTE...
Oh ho ho...
ぽん
POOF
KERO-CHAN
ROLL
WHAT ABOUT THAT CELL PHONE CHARM YOU USE?
K-KERO-CHAN?!
It's cute!
CHOMP!
HMM...I'D FEEL REALLY BAD EATING HIM...
IT'S A RATHER SAD FATE TO BE EATEN.

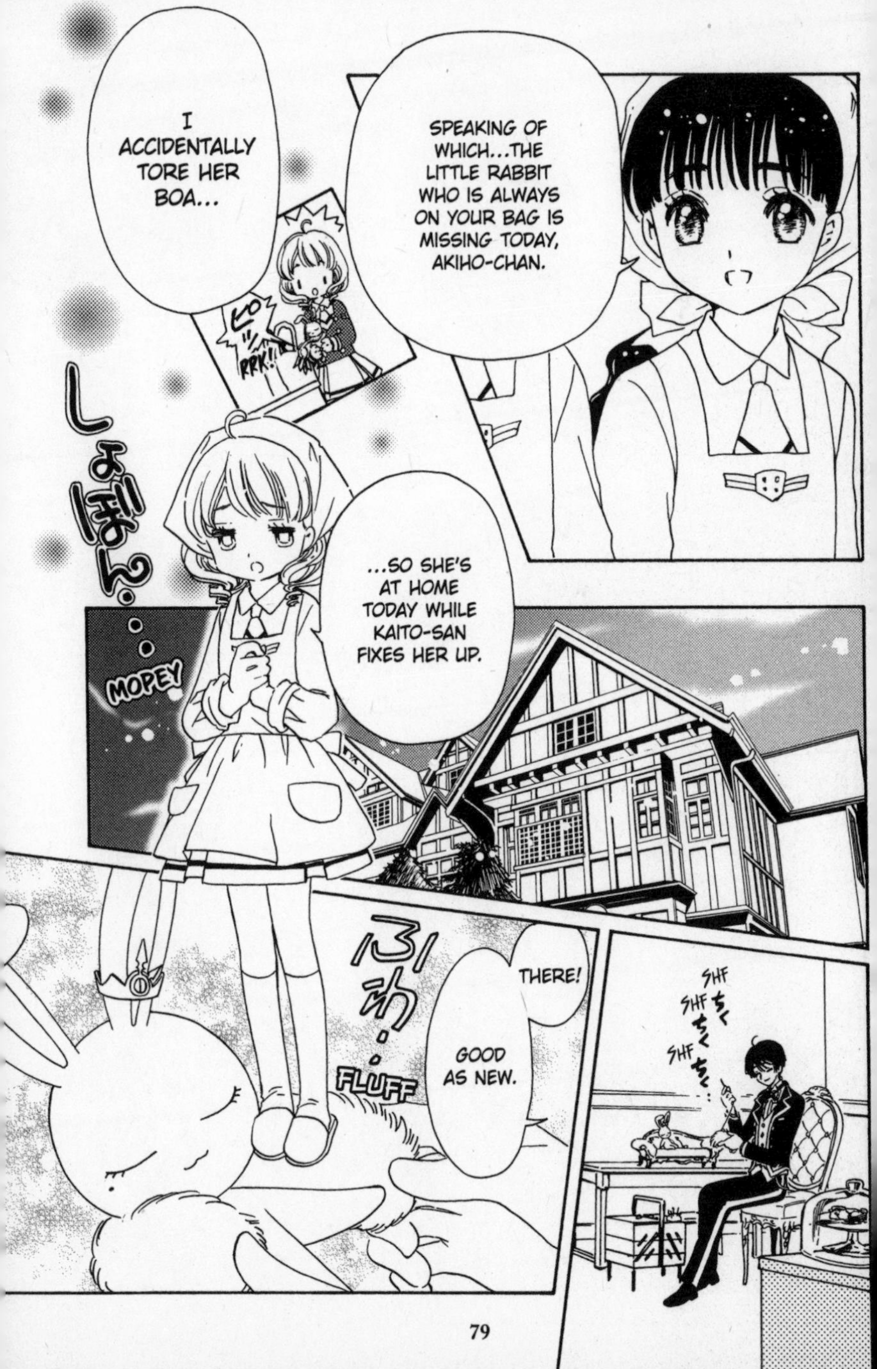
SPEAKING OF WHICH...THE LITTLE RABBIT WHO IS ALWAYS ON YOUR BAG IS MISSING TODAY, AKIHO-CHAN.
I ACCIDENTALLY TORE HER BOA...
ピッ
RRK!!
しょぼん…
MOPEY
...SO SHE'S AT HOME TODAY WHILE KAITO-SAN FIXES HER UP.
SHF ちく
SHF ちく
SHF ちく
THERE!
GOOD AS NEW.
ふわ…
FLUFF

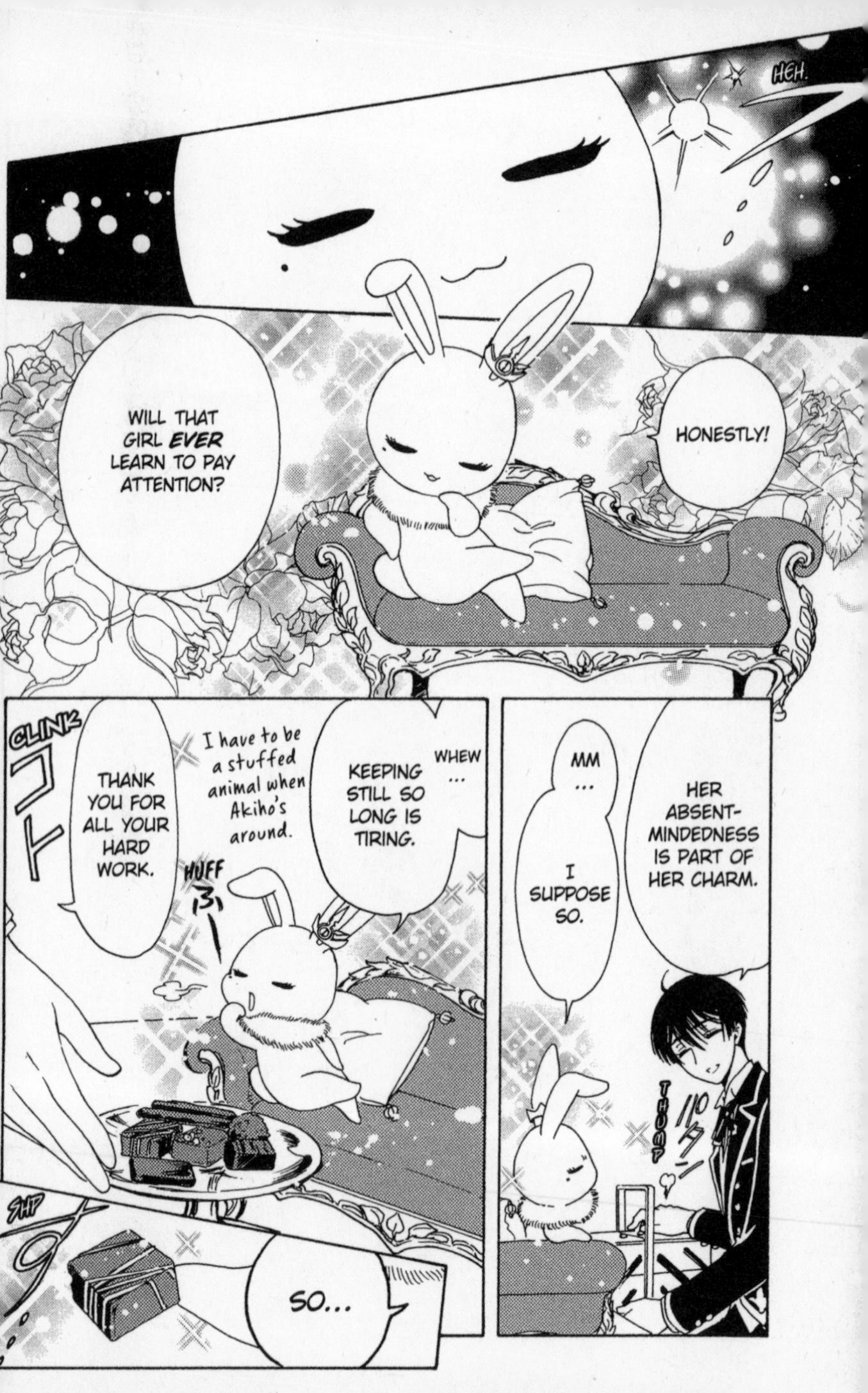
HEH.
HONESTLY!
WILL THAT GIRL EVER LEARN TO PAY ATTENTION?
HER ABSENT-MINDEDNESS IS PART OF HER CHARM.
MM... I SUPPOSE SO.
THUMP
WHEW...
KEEPING STILL SO LONG IS TIRING.
I have to be a stuffed animal when Akiho's around.
HUFF
CLINK
THANK YOU FOR ALL YOUR HARD WORK.
SHP
SO...

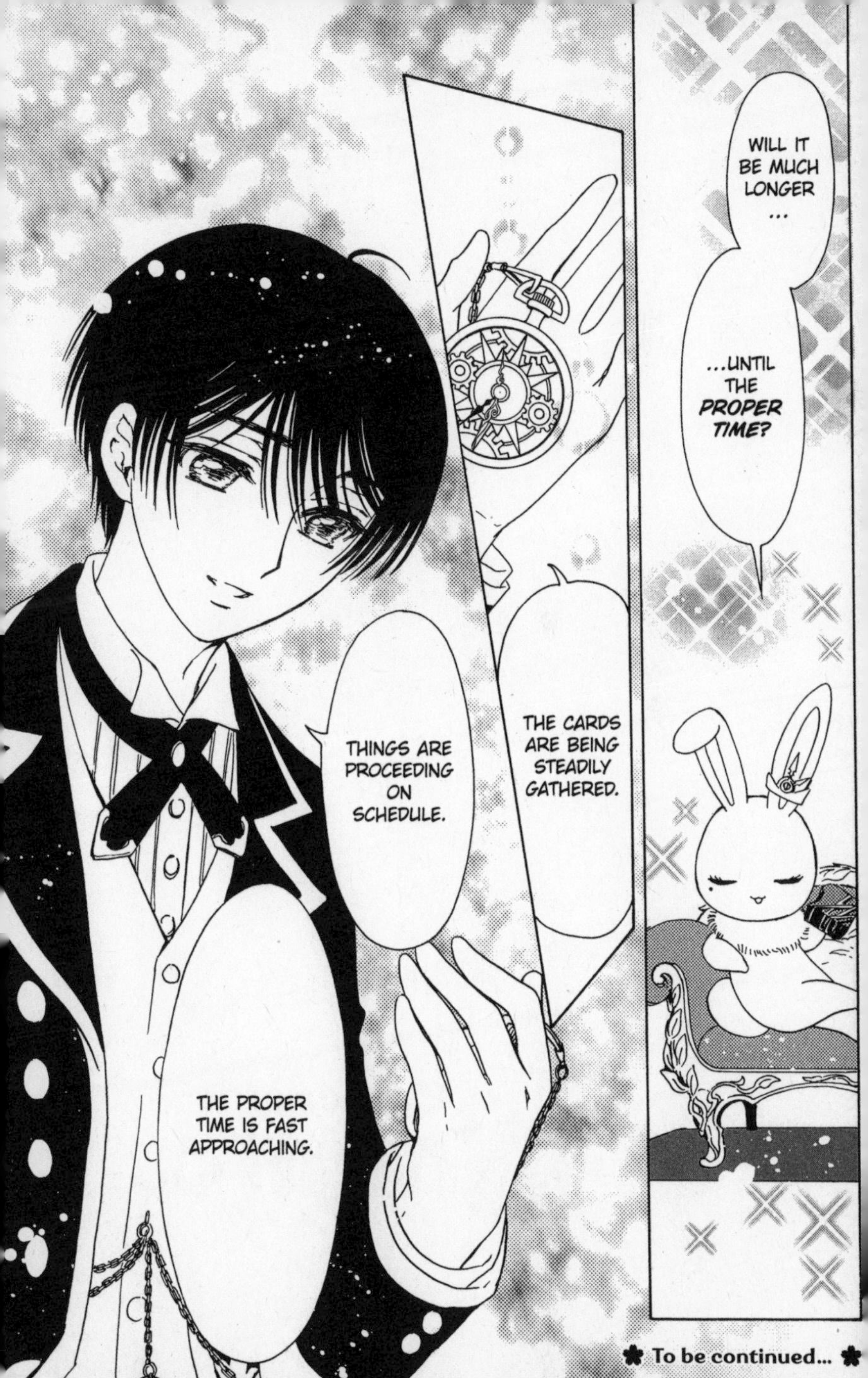
WILL IT BE MUCH LONGER ...
...UNTIL THE *PROPER TIME?*
THE CARDS ARE BEING STEADILY GATHERED.
THINGS ARE PROCEEDING ON SCHEDULE.
THE PROPER TIME IS FAST APPROACHING.

To be continued...

Cardcaptor Sakura

CLEAR CARD

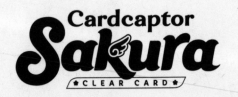

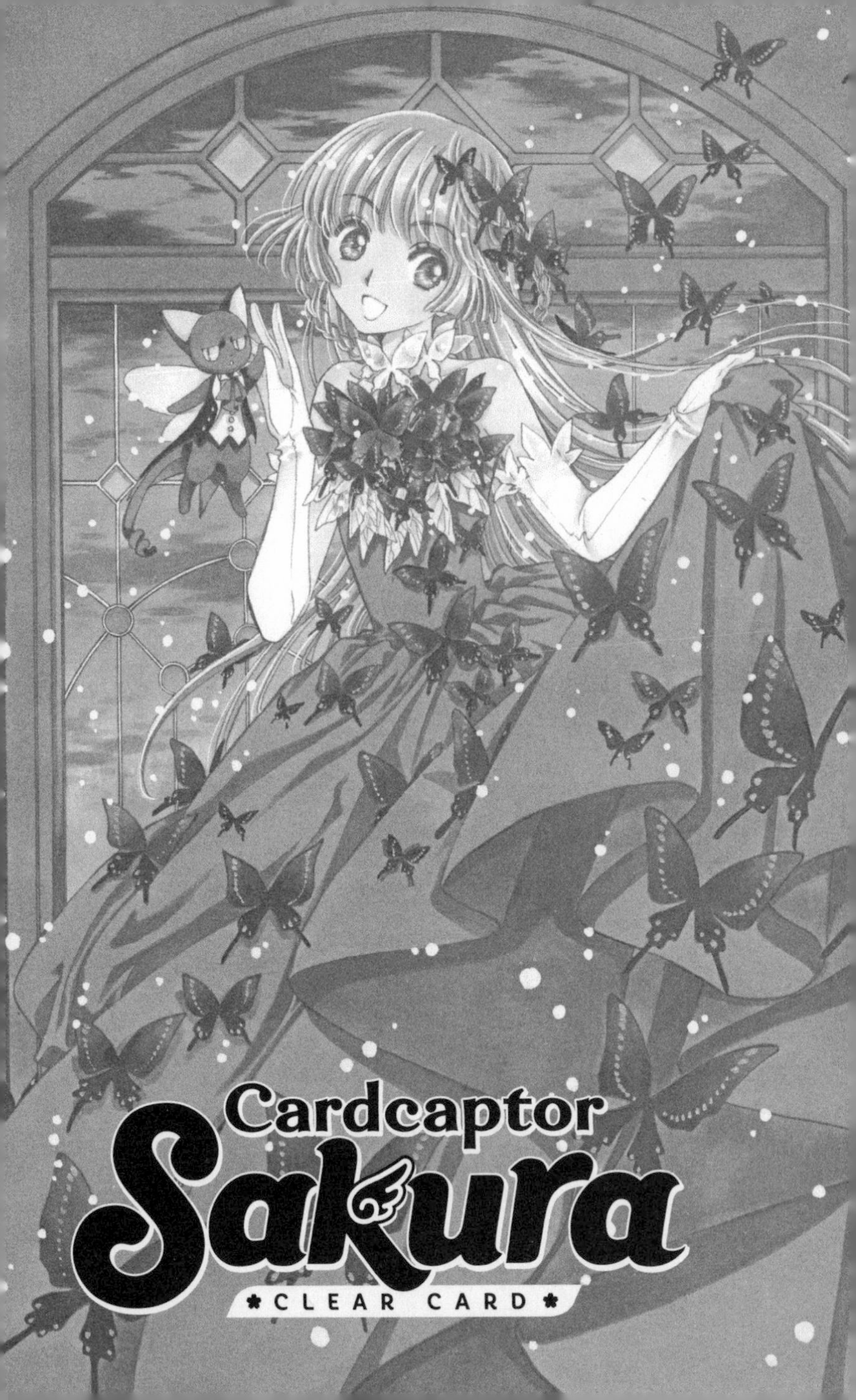
Cardcaptor
Sakura
CLEAR CARD

Cardcaptor Sakura
CLEAR CARD

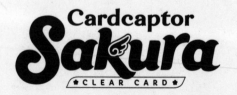

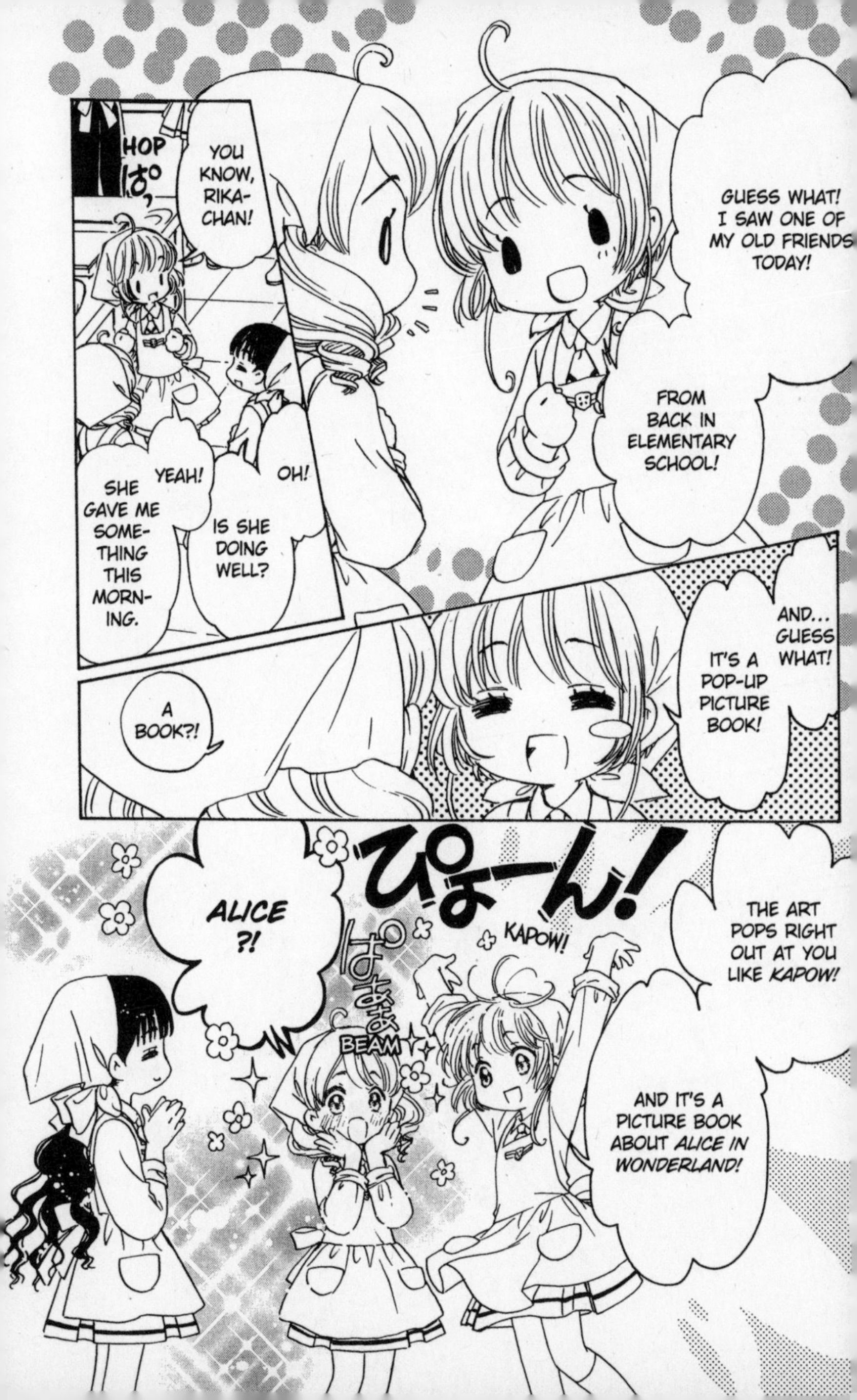
GUESS WHAT! I SAW ONE OF MY OLD FRIENDS TODAY!
FROM BACK IN ELEMENTARY SCHOOL!
HOP
ぱっ
YOU KNOW, RIKA-CHAN!
OH!
IS SHE DOING WELL?
YEAH!
SHE GAVE ME SOME-THING THIS MORN-ING.
AND... GUESS WHAT!
IT'S A POP-UP PICTURE BOOK!
A BOOK?!
THE ART POPS RIGHT OUT AT YOU LIKE KAPOW!
ぴょーん!
KAPOW!
AND IT'S A PICTURE BOOK ABOUT ALICE IN WONDERLAND!
ぱぁぁ
BEAM
ALICE?!

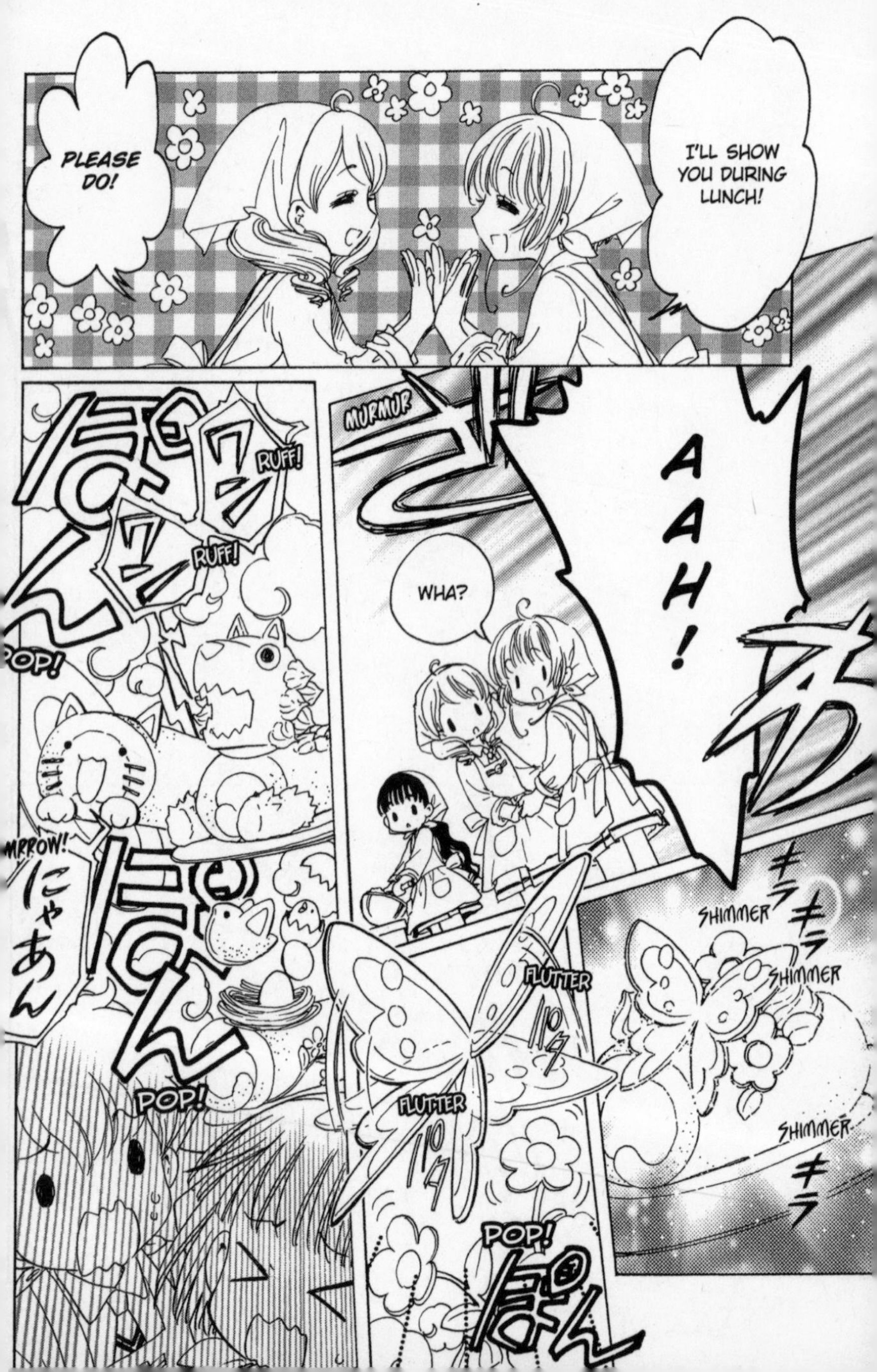
I'LL SHOW YOU DURING LUNCH!
PLEASE DO!
AAH!
MURMUR
WHA?
RUFF!
RUFF!
POP!
MRROW!
にゃあん
POP!
SHIMMER
SHIMMER
SHIMMER
FLUTTER
FLUTTER
POP!

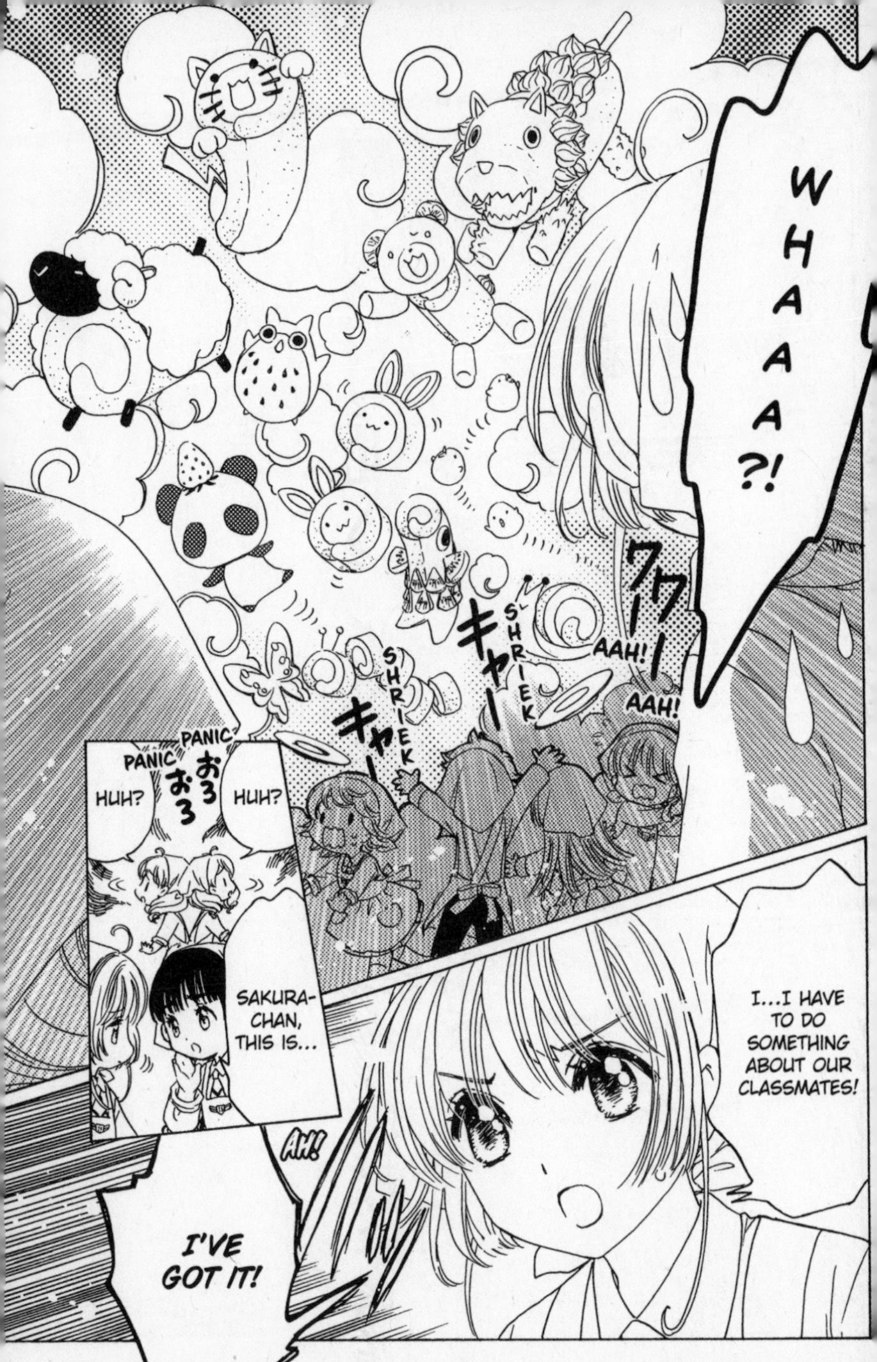
WHAAAA?!
ワァー
AAH! AAH!
キャー SHRIEK
キャー SHRIEK
PANIC PANIC おろおろ
HUH?
HUH?
SAKURA-CHAN, THIS IS...
I...I HAVE TO DO SOMETHING ABOUT OUR CLASSMATES!
AH!
I'VE GOT IT!

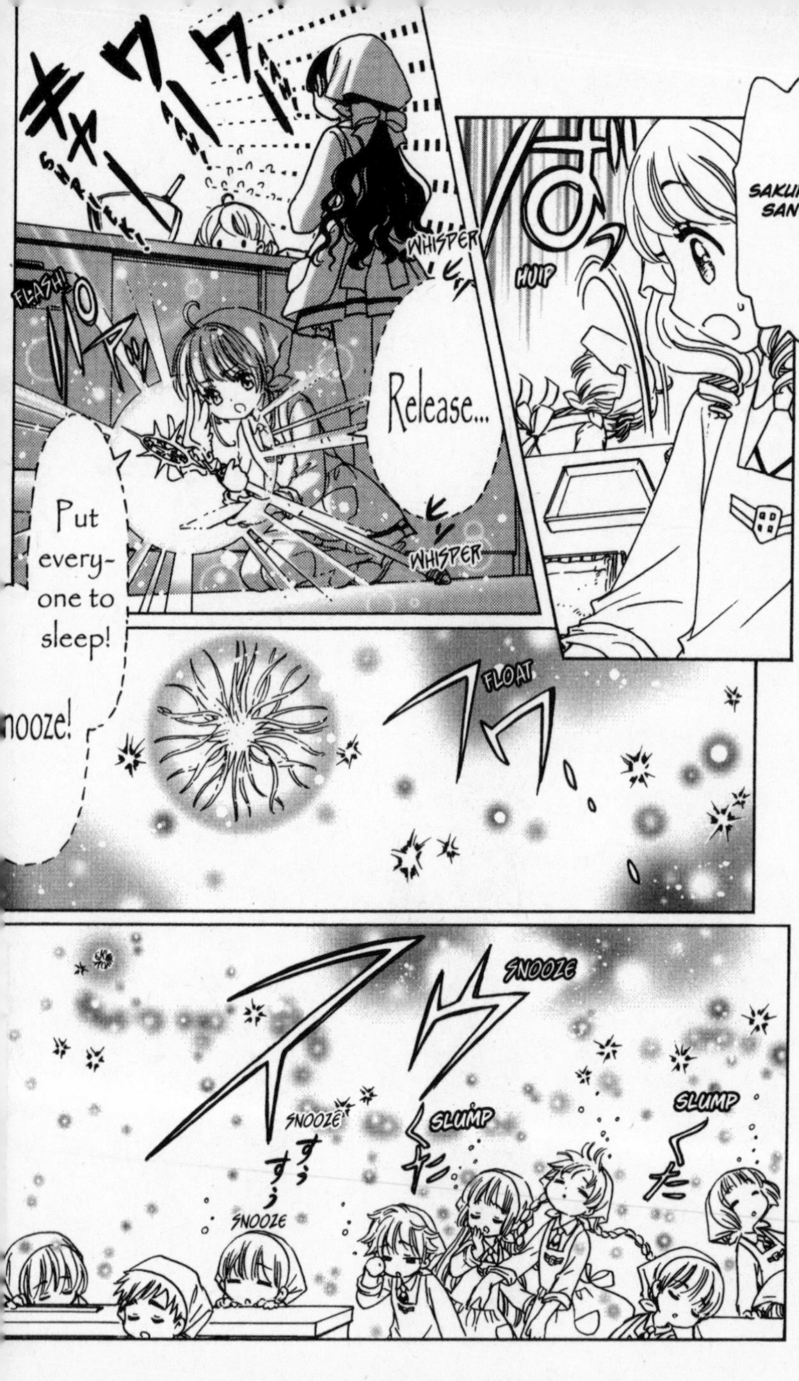
HUIP
SAKURA-SAN?!
AAH!
AAH!
SIZZLE!
WHISPER
FLASH!
Release...
WHISPER
Put everyone to sleep!
Snooze!
FLOAT
SNOOZE
SLUMP
SNOOZE
SNOOZE
SLUMP

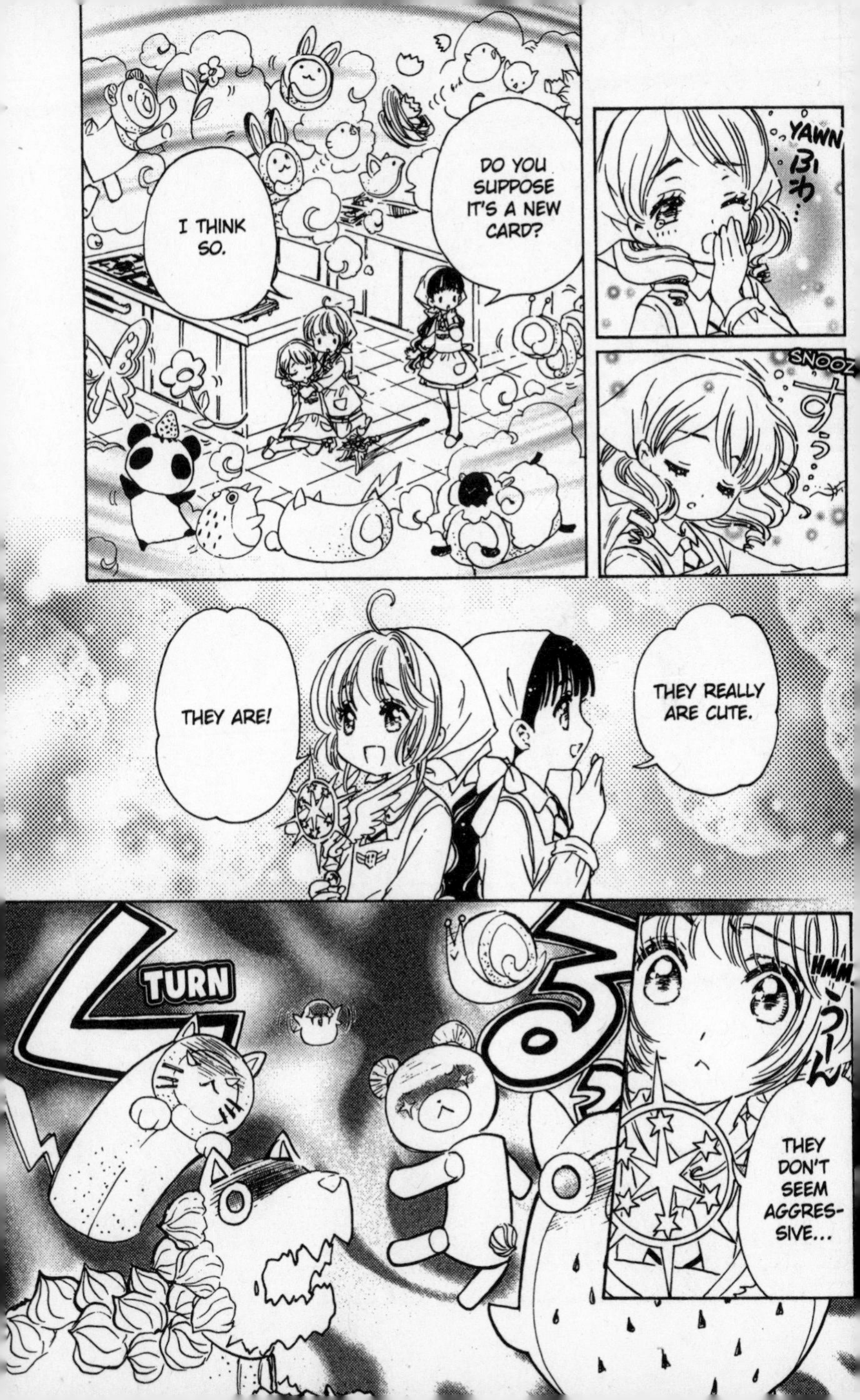
YAWN
ふわ…
SNOOZ
すぅ…
DO YOU SUPPOSE IT'S A NEW CARD?
I THINK SO.
THEY REALLY ARE CUTE.
THEY ARE!
HMM...
うーん
THEY DON'T SEEM AGGRES-SIVE...
TURN

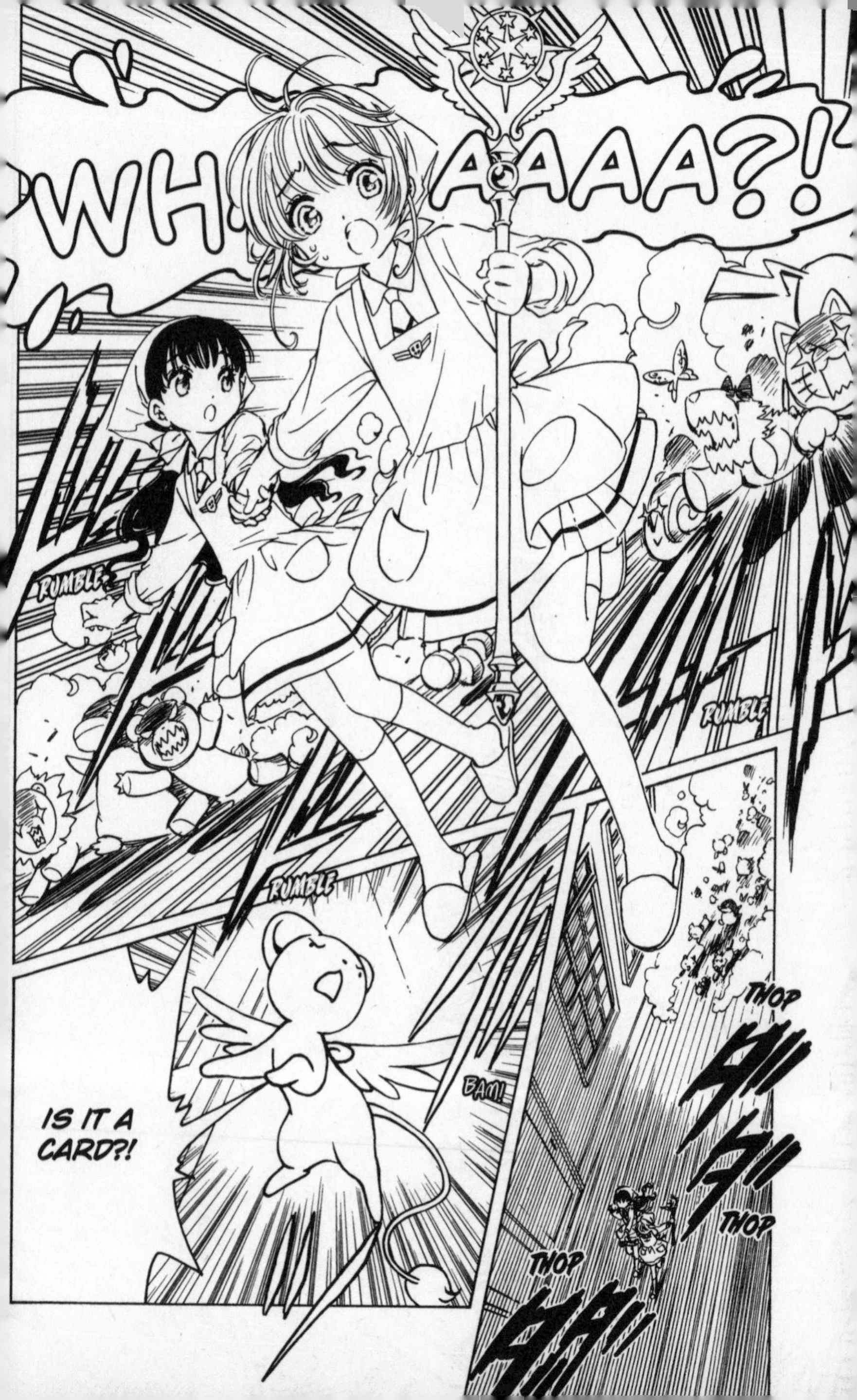
WHAAAAA?!
RUMBLE
RUMBLE
RUMBLE
THOP
THOP
THOP
BAM!
IS IT A CARD?!

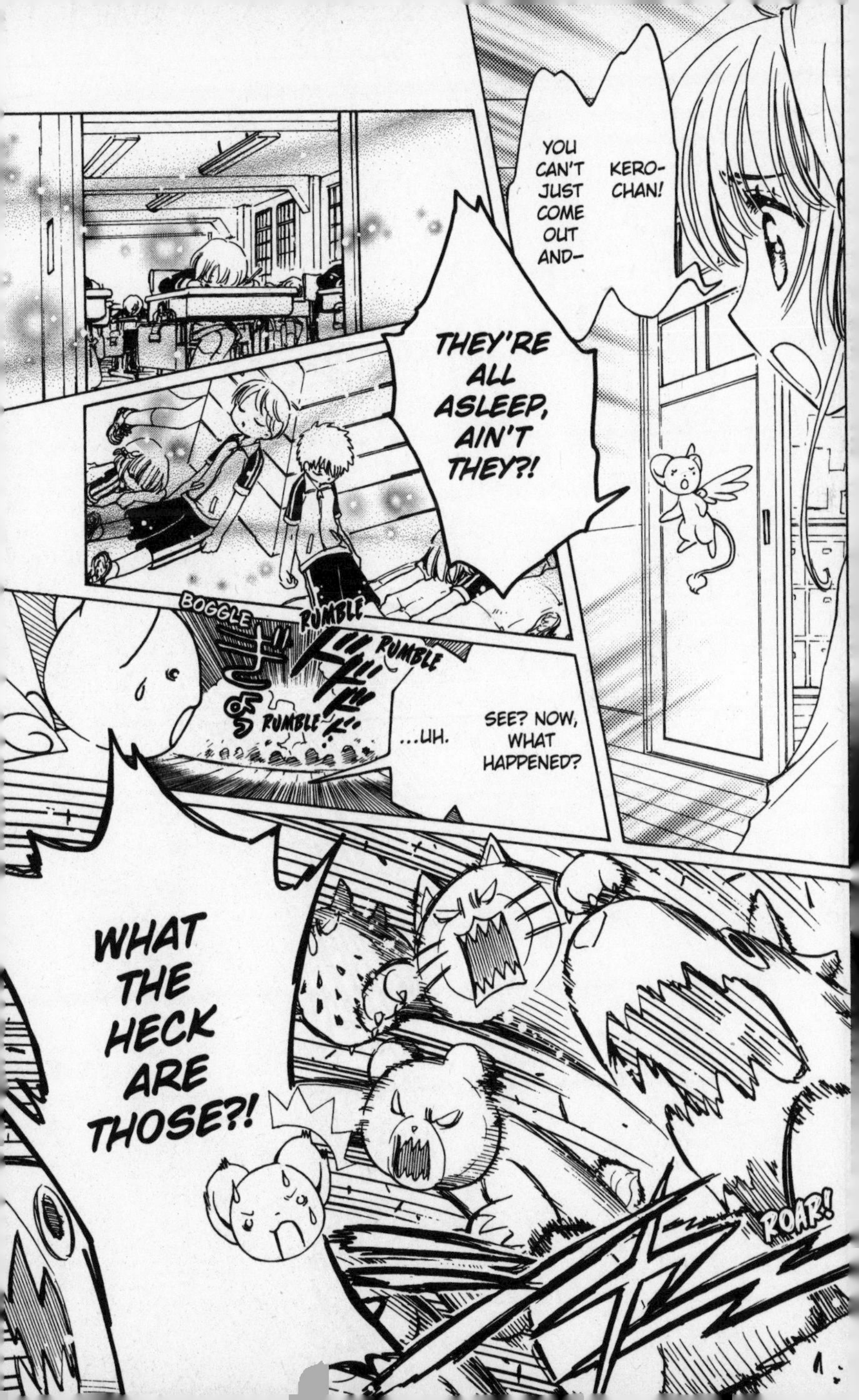
KERO-CHAN!
YOU CAN'T JUST COME OUT AND—
THEY'RE ALL ASLEEP, AIN'T THEY?!
SEE? NOW, WHAT HAPPENED?
...UH.
BOGGLE
RUMBLE
RUMBLE
RUMBLE
WHAT THE HECK ARE THOSE?!
ROAR!

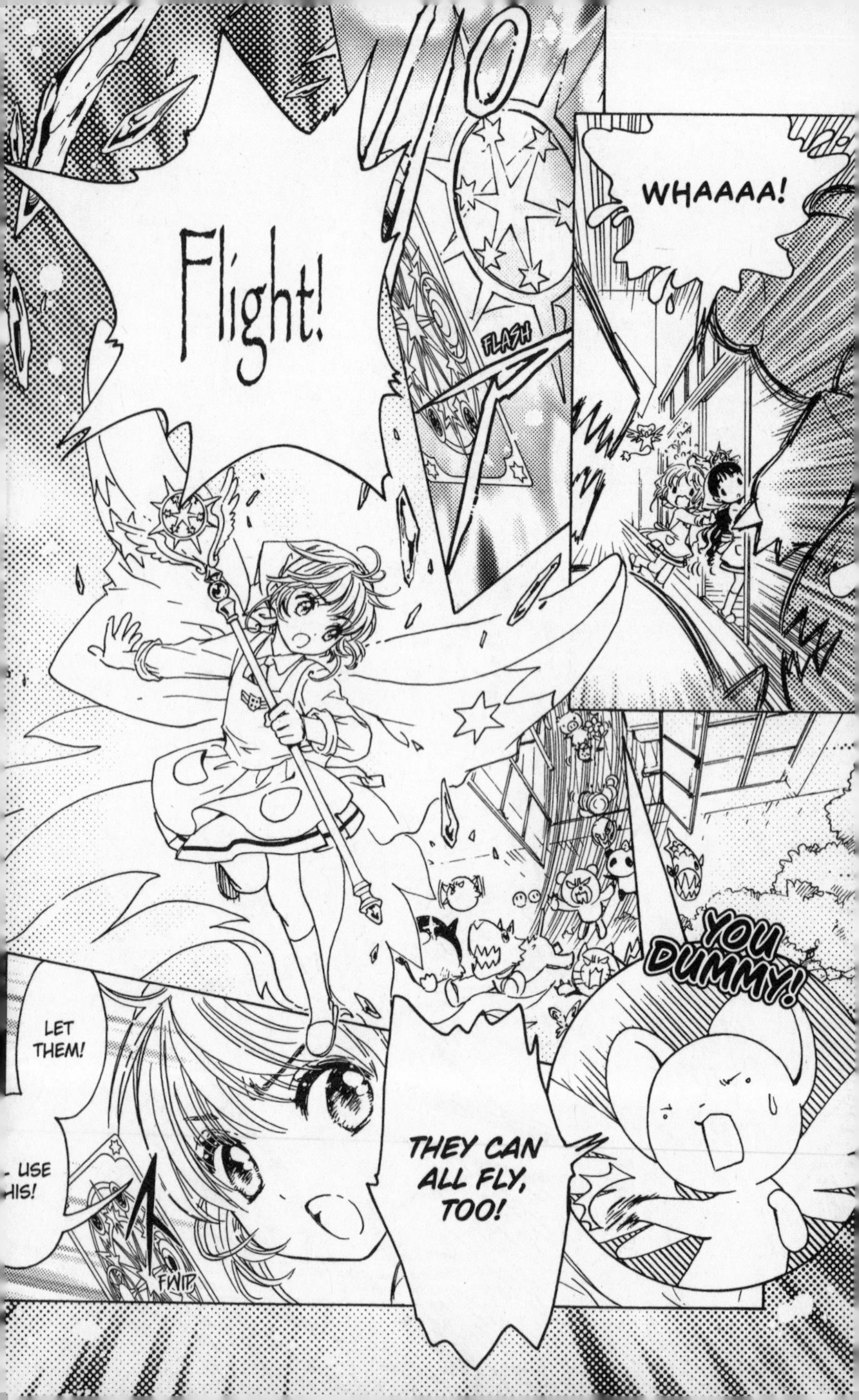
WHAAAA!
FLASH
Flight!
YOU DUMMY!
THEY CAN ALL FLY, TOO!
LET THEM!
USE HIS!
FWIP

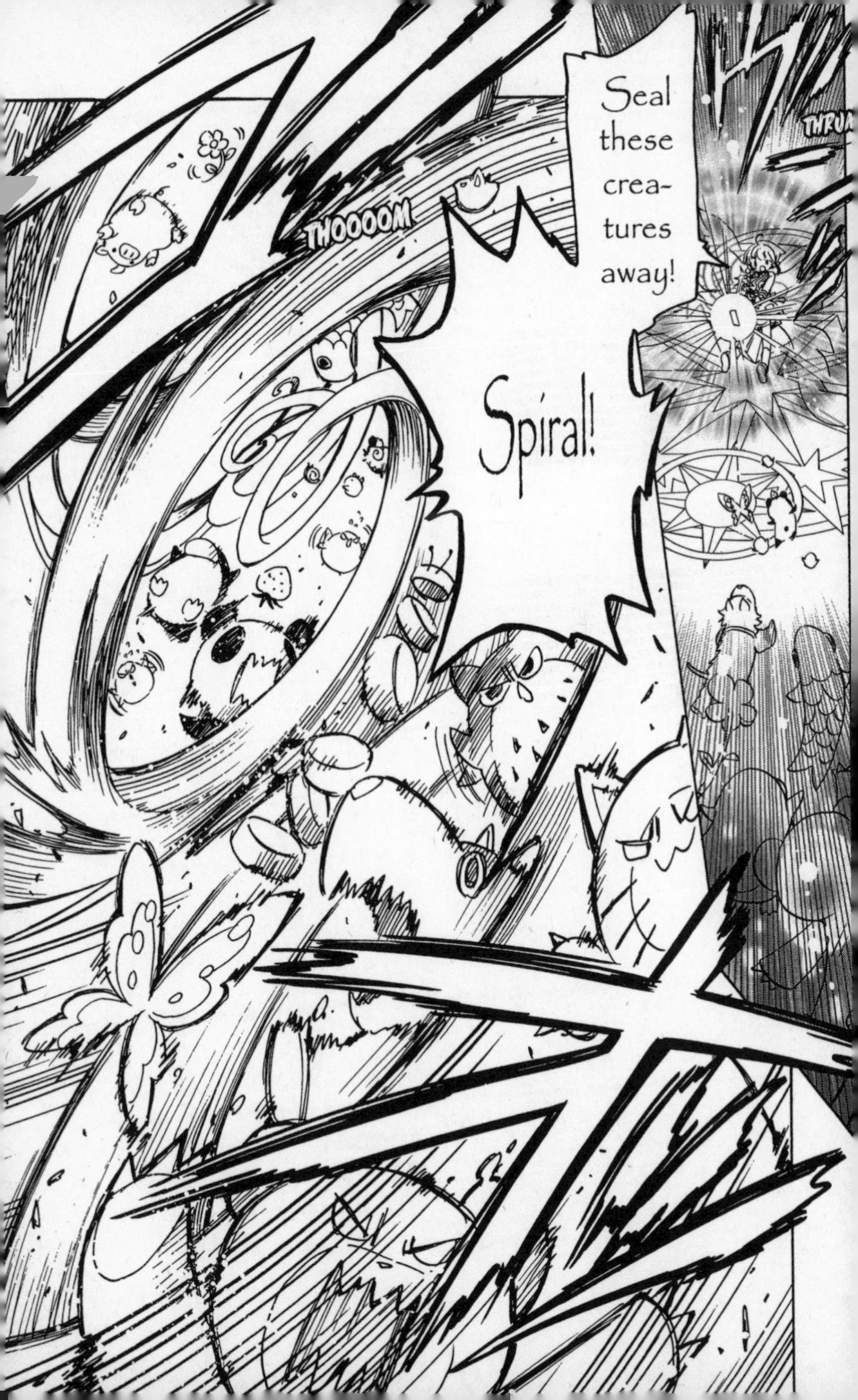
THRU
Seal these crea-tures away!
Spiral!
THOOOOM

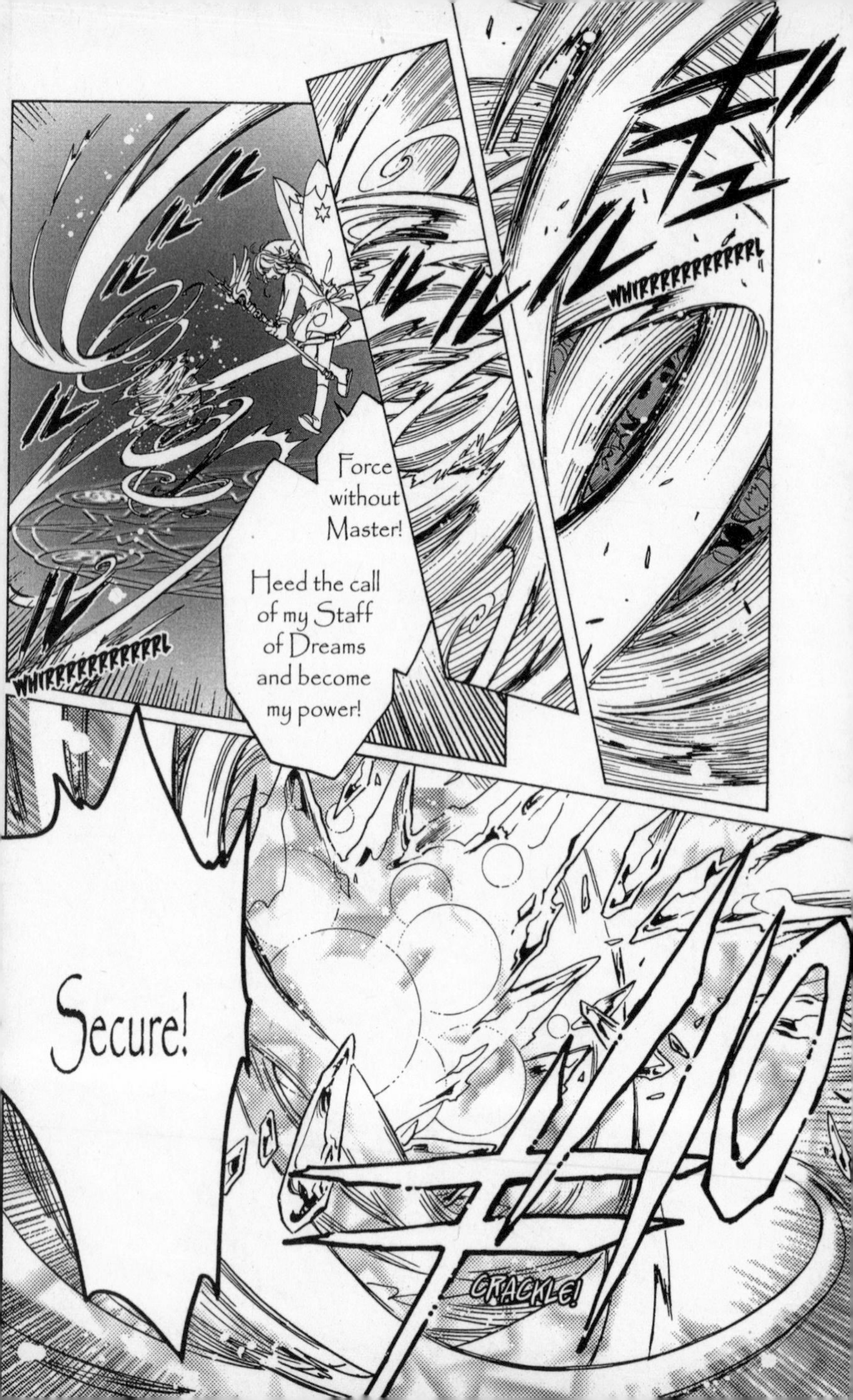
WHIRRRRRRRRRRRL
WHIRRRRRRRRRRRL
Force without Master!
Heed the call of my Staff of Dreams and become my power!
Secure!
CRACKLE!

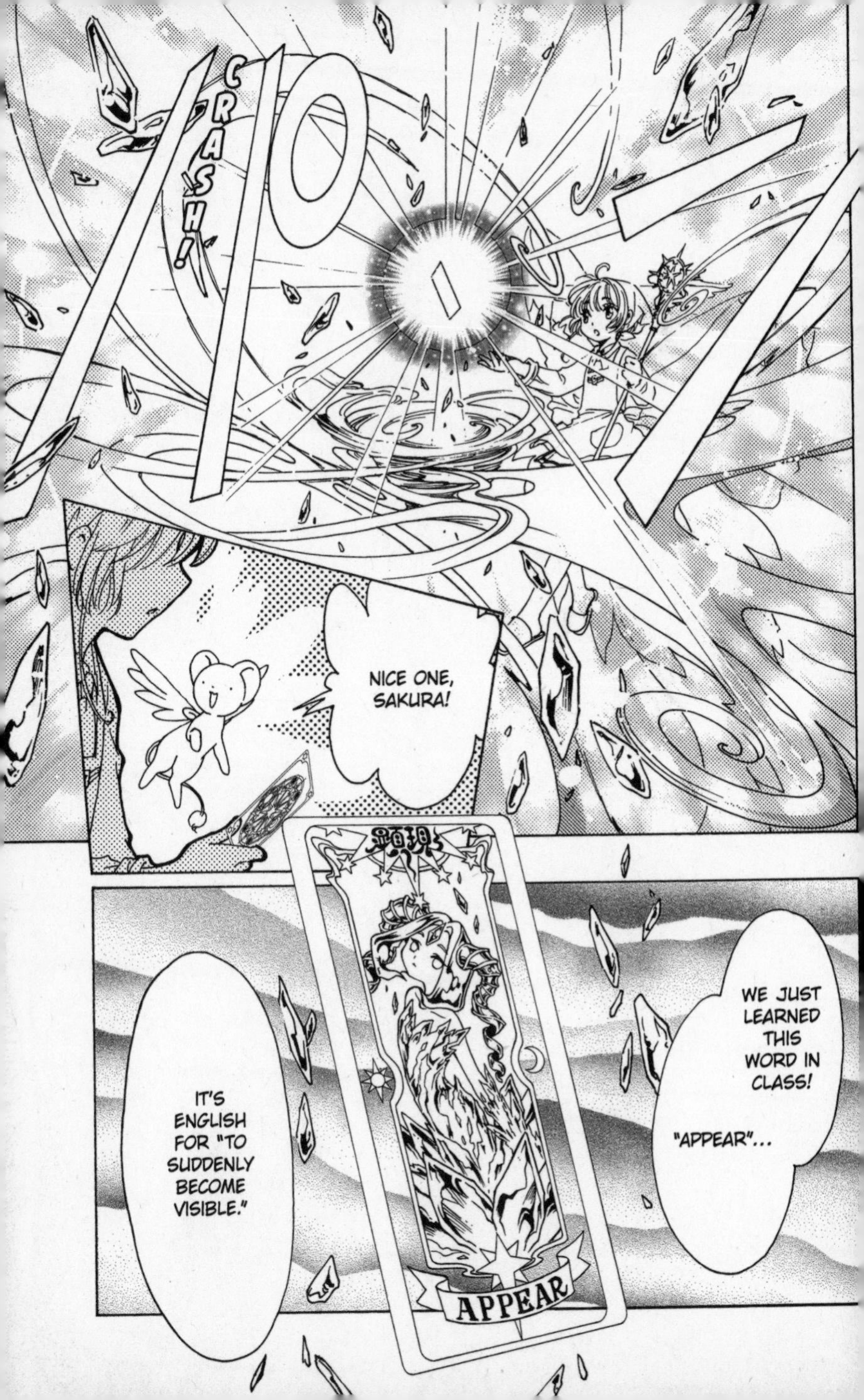
CRASH!
NICE ONE, SAKURA!
WE JUST LEARNED THIS WORD IN CLASS!
"APPEAR"...
APPEAR
IT'S ENGLISH FOR "TO SUDDENLY BECOME VISIBLE."

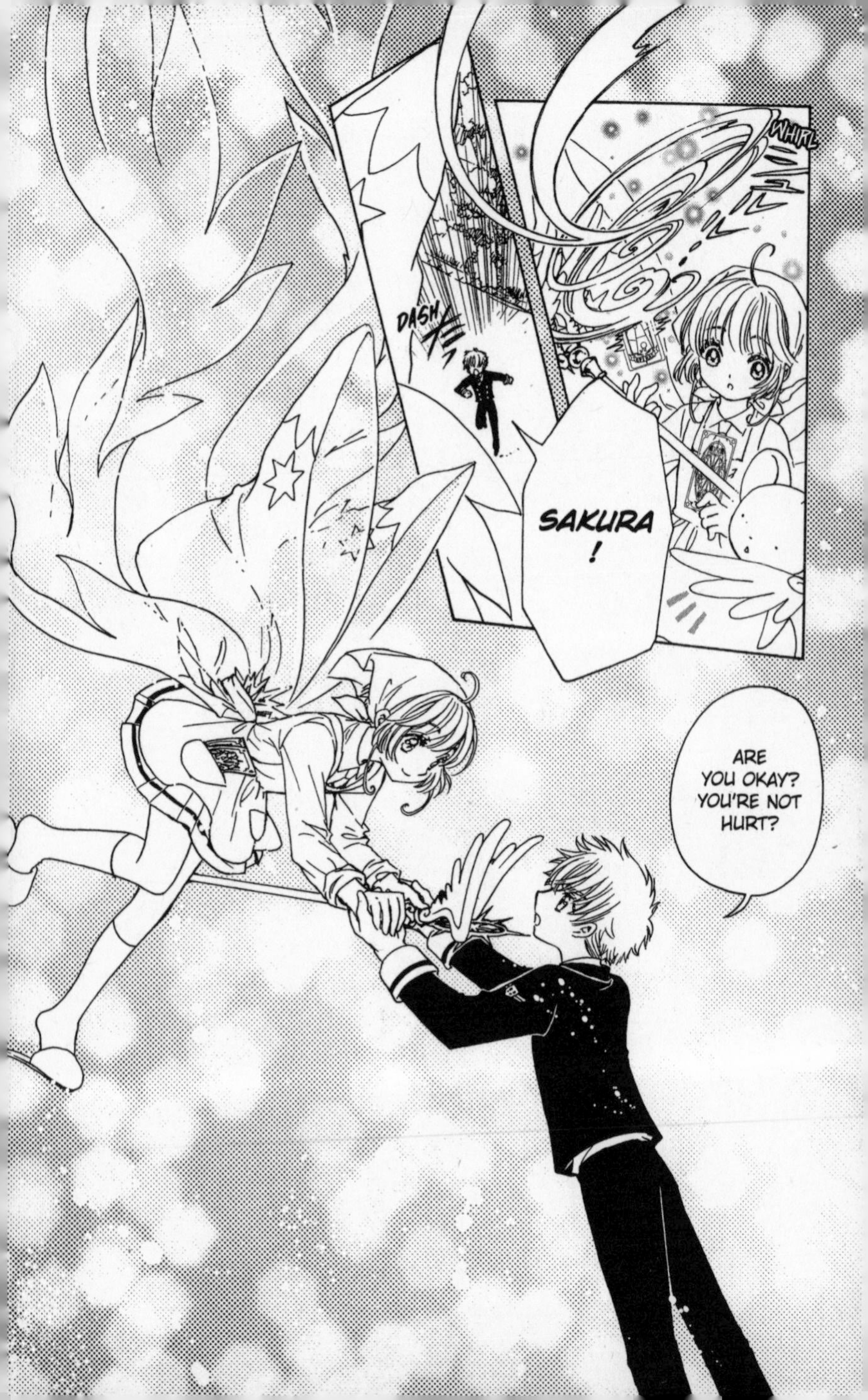
WHIRL
DASH
SAKURA!
ARE YOU OKAY? YOU'RE NOT HURT?

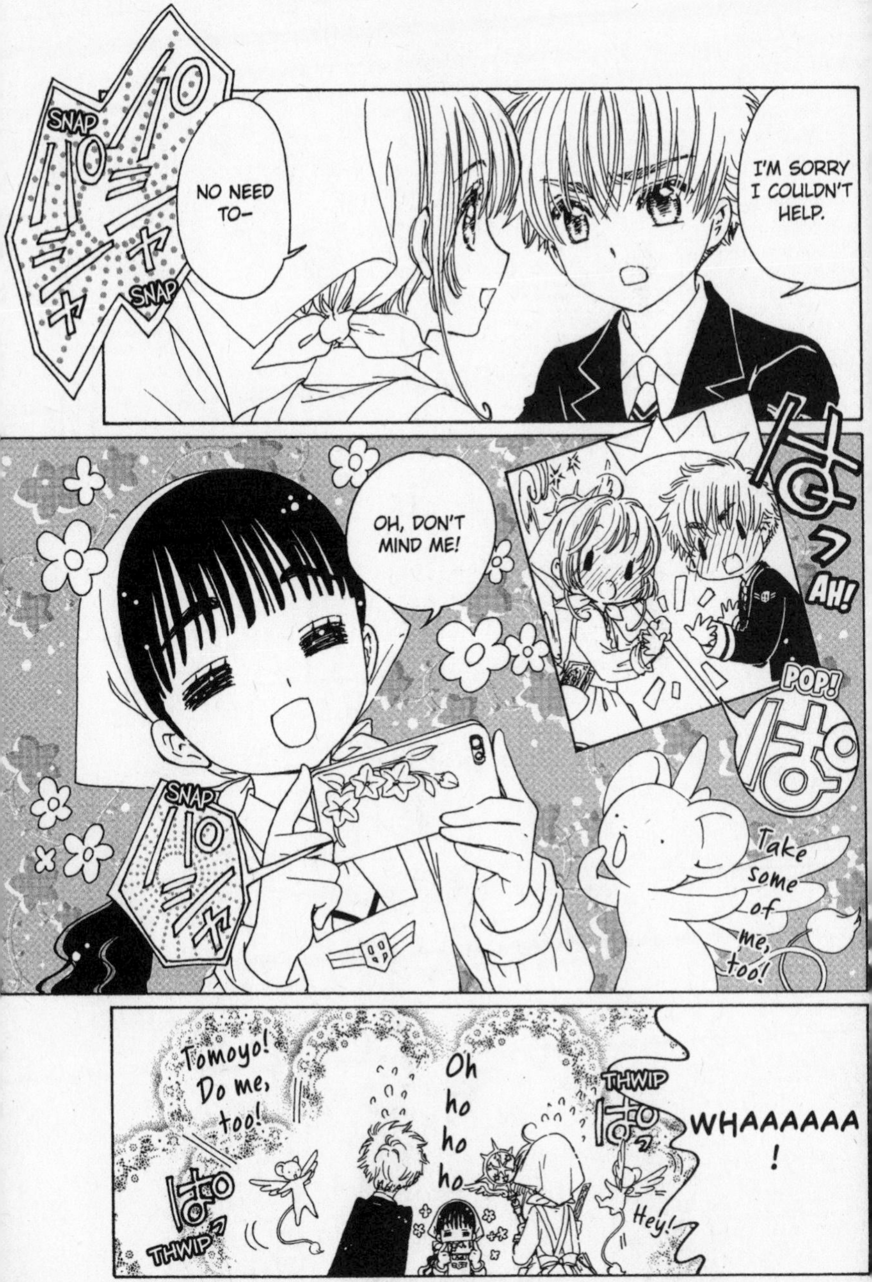

I'M SORRY I COULDN'T HELP.
NO NEED TO–
SNAP
パシャ
SNAP
パシャ
はっ
AH!
POP!
ぱっ
OH, DON'T MIND ME!
Take some of me, too!
SNAP
パシャ
WHAAAAAA!
THWIP
ぱっ
Hey!
Oh ho ho ho
Tomoyo! Do me, too!
ぱっ
THWIP

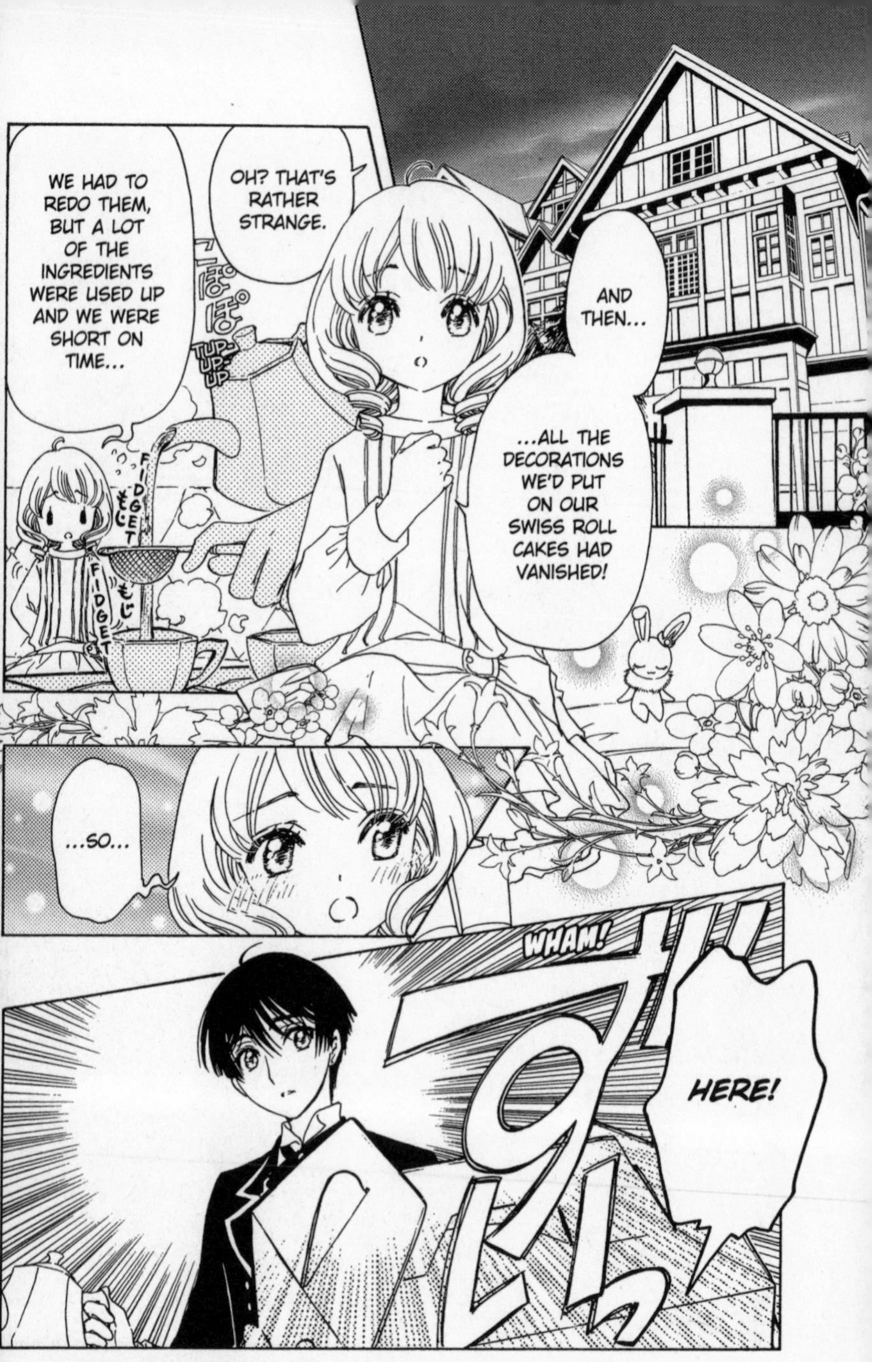
AND THEN...
...ALL THE DECORATIONS WE'D PUT ON OUR SWISS ROLL CAKES HAD VANISHED!
OH? THAT'S RATHER STRANGE.
ごぽぽ
TUP-UP-UP
WE HAD TO REDO THEM, BUT A LOT OF THE INGREDIENTS WERE USED UP AND WE WERE SHORT ON TIME...
もじ
FIDGET
もじ
FIDGET
...SO...
WHAM!
HERE!

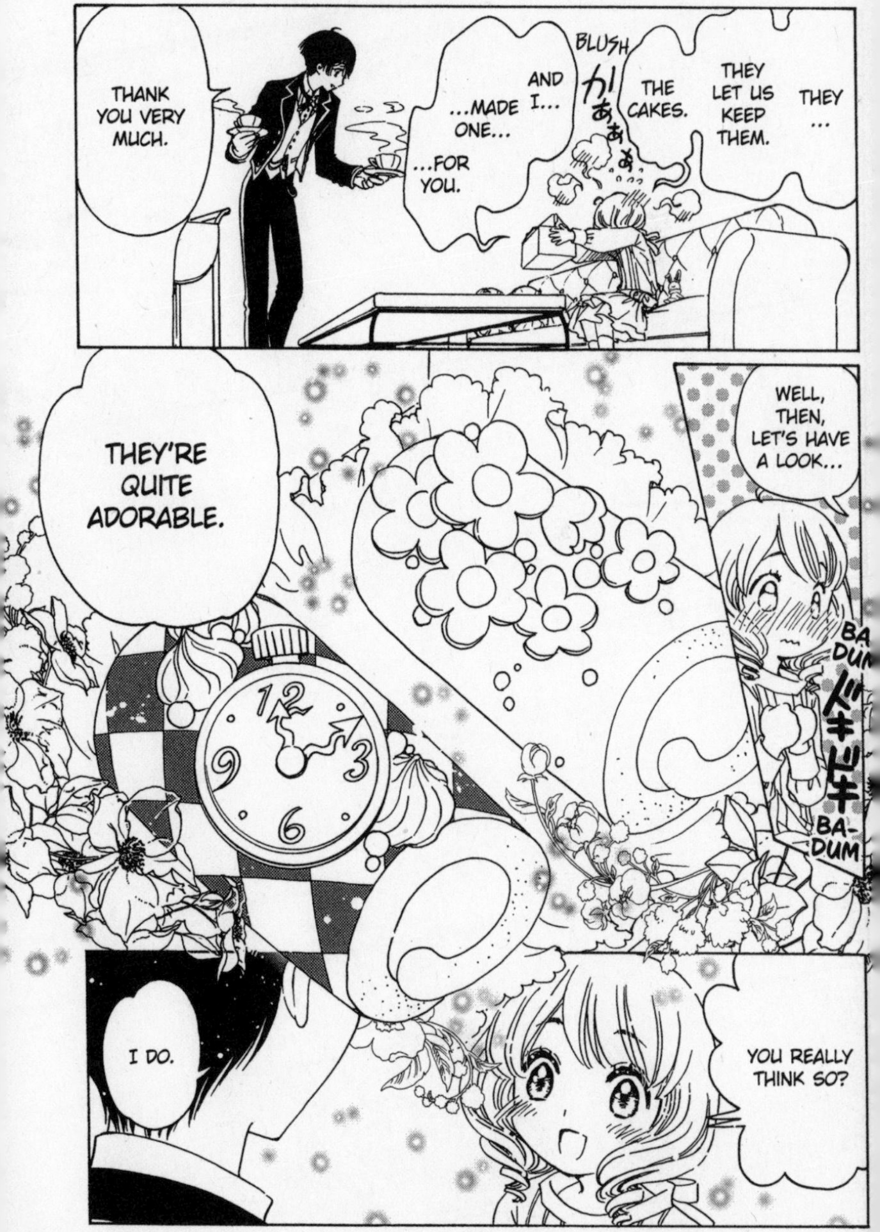
THEY ...
THEY LET US KEEP THEM.
THE CAKES.
BLUSH
かあああ
AND I...
...MADE ONE...
...FOR YOU.
THANK YOU VERY MUCH.
WELL, THEN, LET'S HAVE A LOOK...
BA-DUM
ドキドキ
BA-DUM
THEY'RE QUITE ADORABLE.
YOU REALLY THINK SO?
I DO.

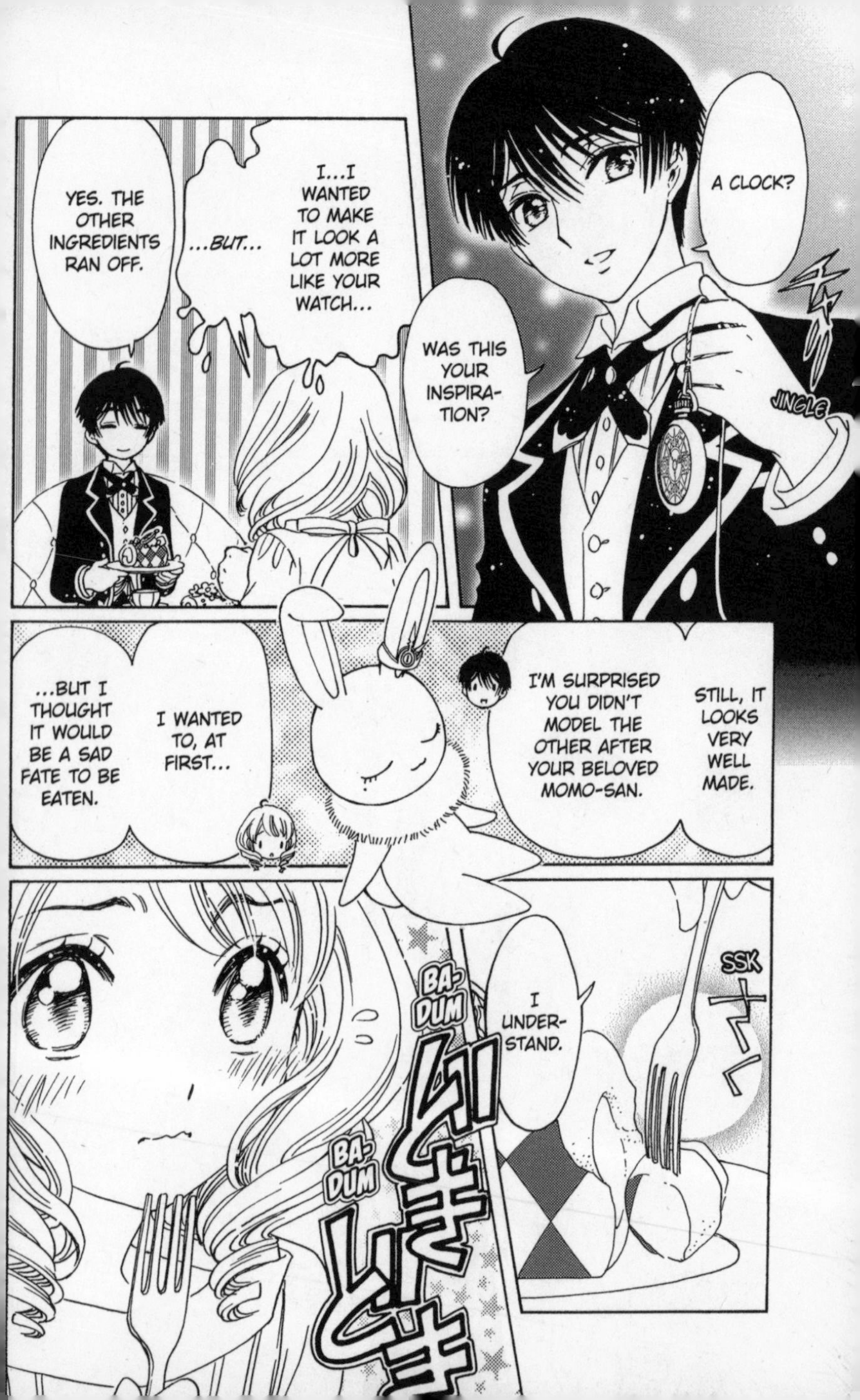
A CLOCK?
JINGLE
WAS THIS YOUR INSPIRATION?
I...I WANTED TO MAKE IT LOOK A LOT MORE LIKE YOUR WATCH...
...BUT...
YES. THE OTHER INGREDIENTS RAN OFF.
STILL, IT LOOKS VERY WELL MADE.
I'M SURPRISED YOU DIDN'T MODEL THE OTHER AFTER YOUR BELOVED MOMO-SAN.
I WANTED TO, AT FIRST...
...BUT I THOUGHT IT WOULD BE A SAD FATE TO BE EATEN.
SSK
I UNDERSTAND.
BA-DUM
BA-DUM

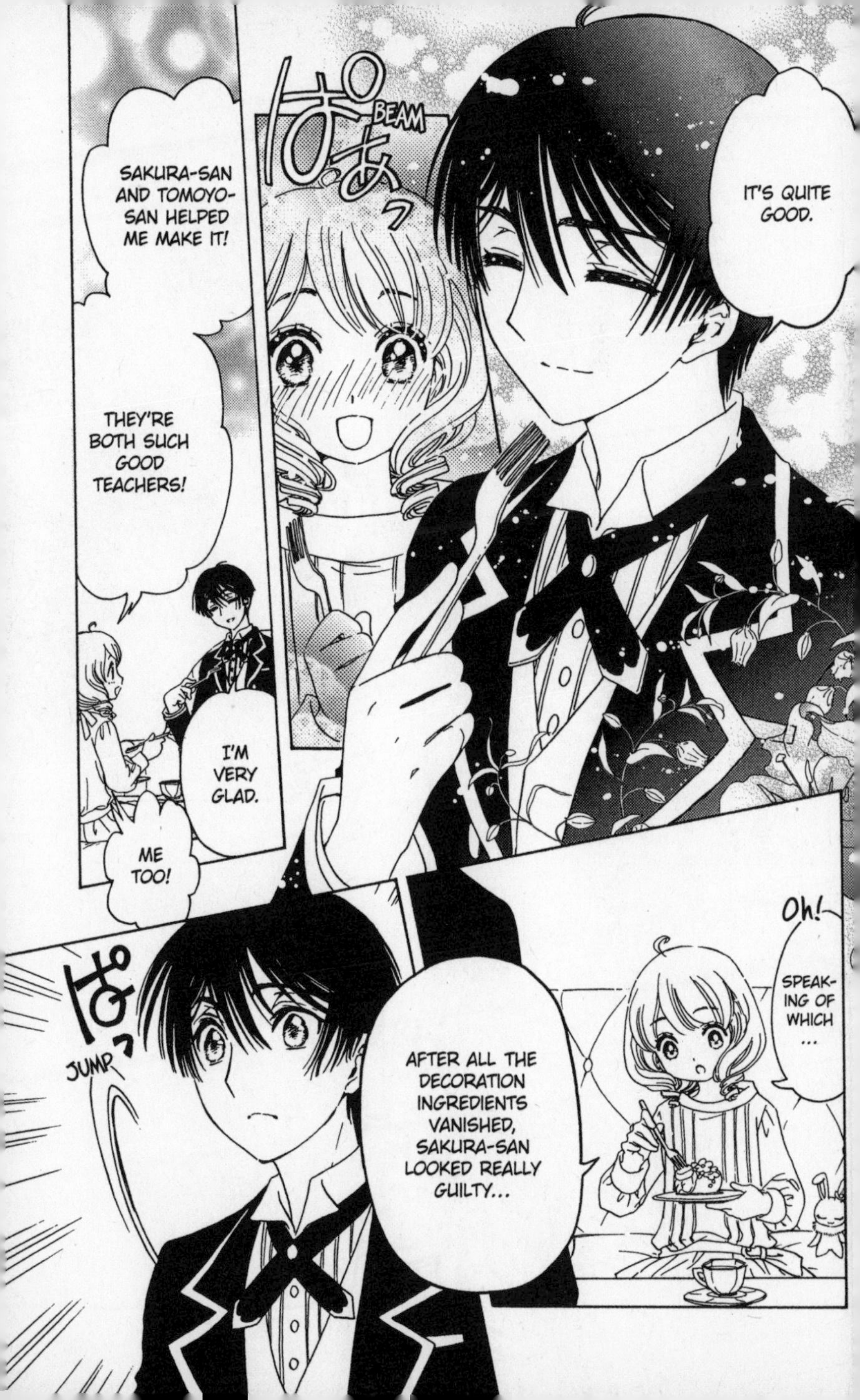
IT'S QUITE GOOD.
ぱあっ BEAM
SAKURA-SAN AND TOMOYO-SAN HELPED ME MAKE IT!
THEY'RE BOTH SUCH GOOD TEACHERS!
I'M VERY GLAD.
ME TOO!
Oh!
SPEAKING OF WHICH ...
AFTER ALL THE DECORATION INGREDIENTS VANISHED, SAKURA-SAN LOOKED REALLY GUILTY...
ぱっ JUMP

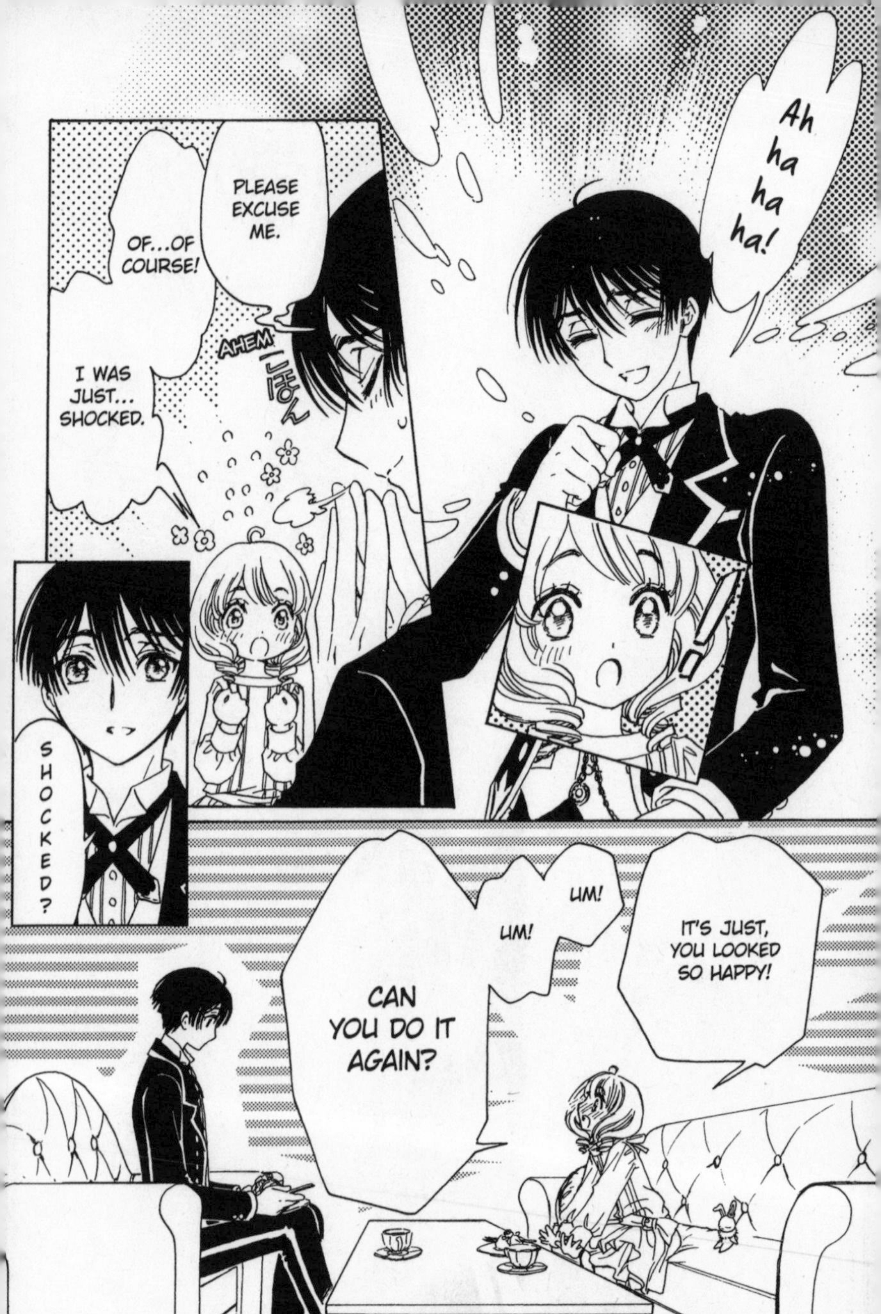
Ah ha ha ha!
PLEASE EXCUSE ME.
OF...OF COURSE!
AHEM
I WAS JUST... SHOCKED.
SHOCKED?
IT'S JUST, YOU LOOKED SO HAPPY!
UM!
UM!
CAN YOU DO IT AGAIN?

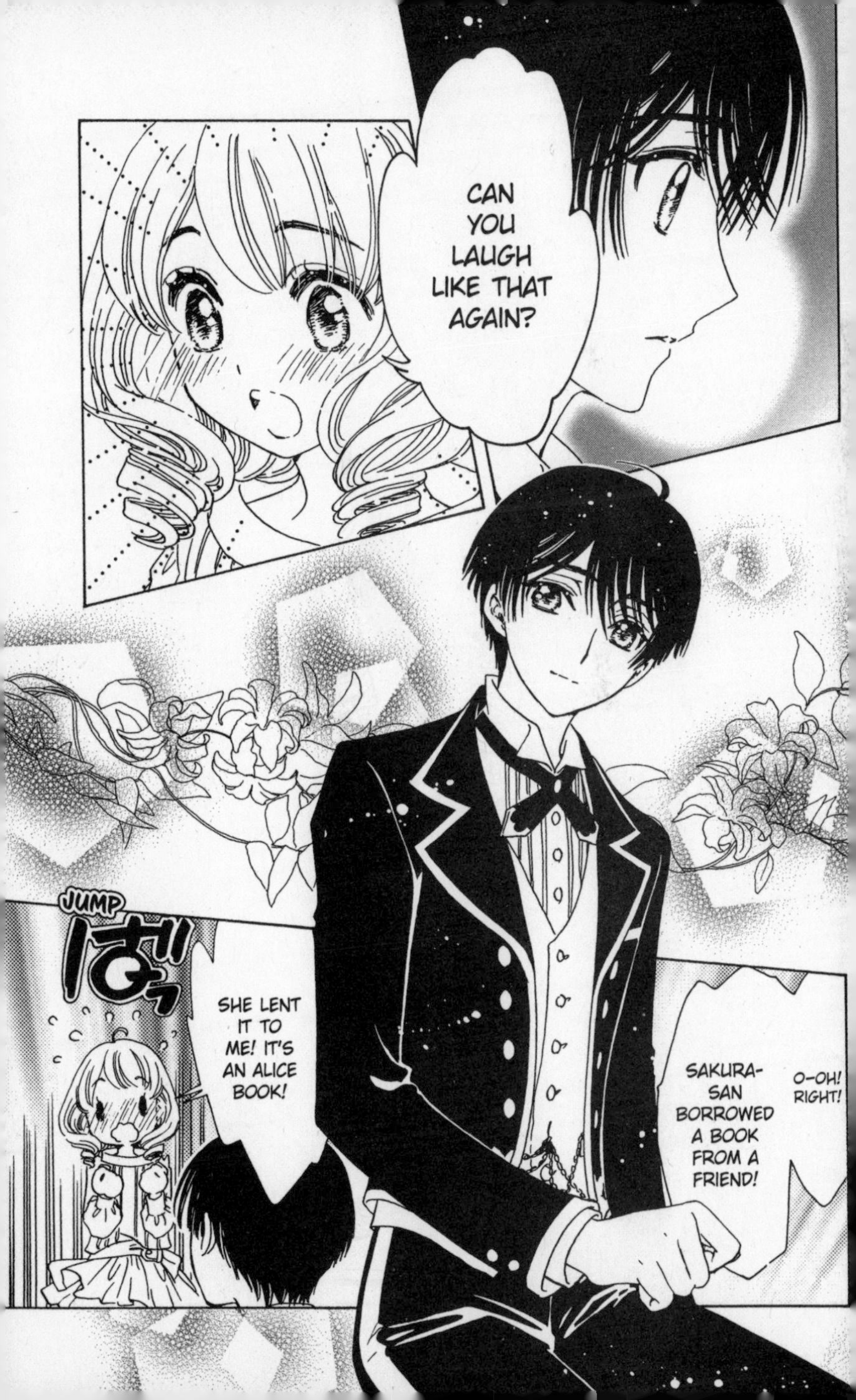
CAN YOU LAUGH LIKE THAT AGAIN?
O-OH! RIGHT!
SAKURA-SAN BORROWED A BOOK FROM A FRIEND!
JUMP
SHE LENT IT TO ME! IT'S AN ALICE BOOK!

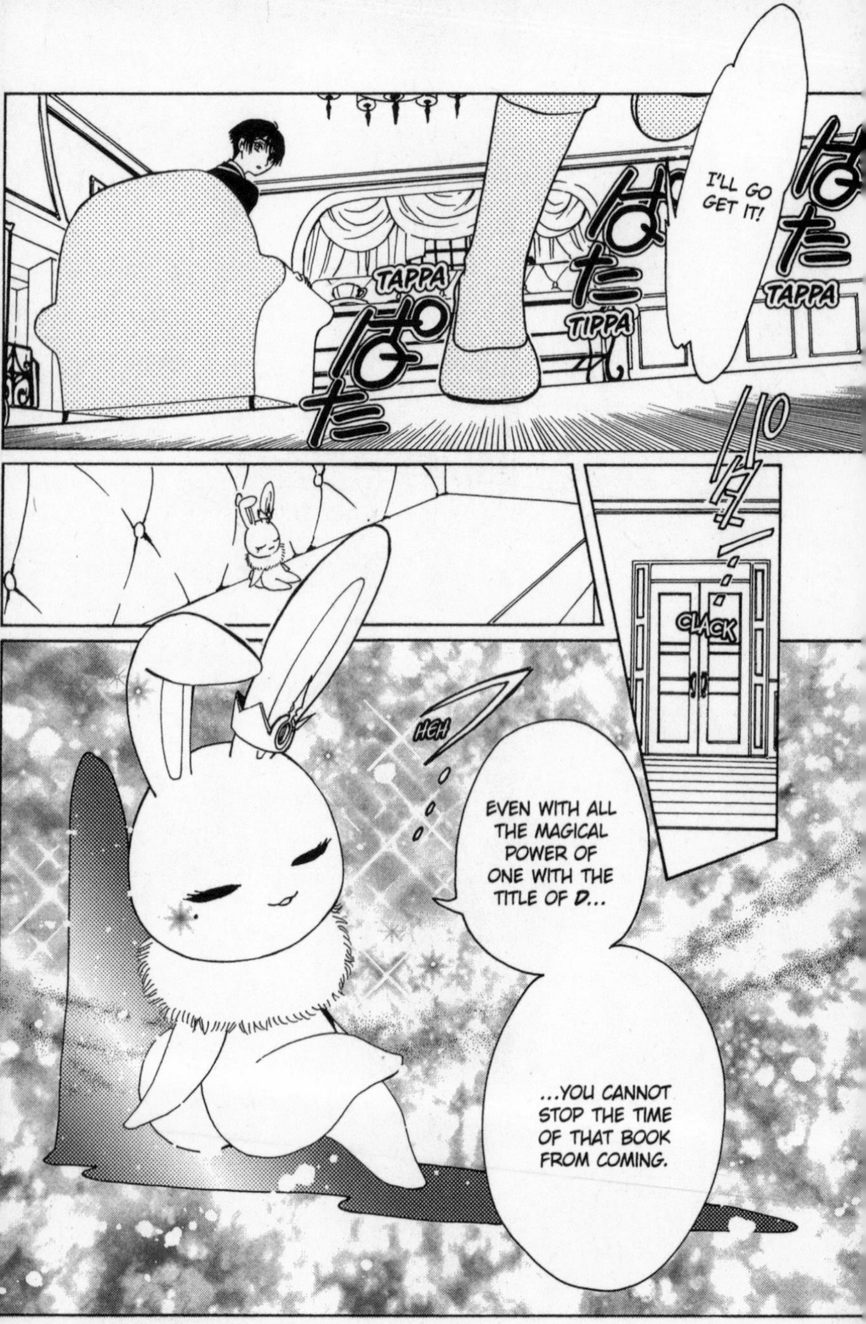
I'LL GO GET IT!
TAPPA
TIPPA
TAPPA
CLACK
HEH
EVEN WITH ALL THE MAGICAL POWER OF ONE WITH THE TITLE OF D...
...YOU CANNOT STOP THE TIME OF THAT BOOK FROM COMING.

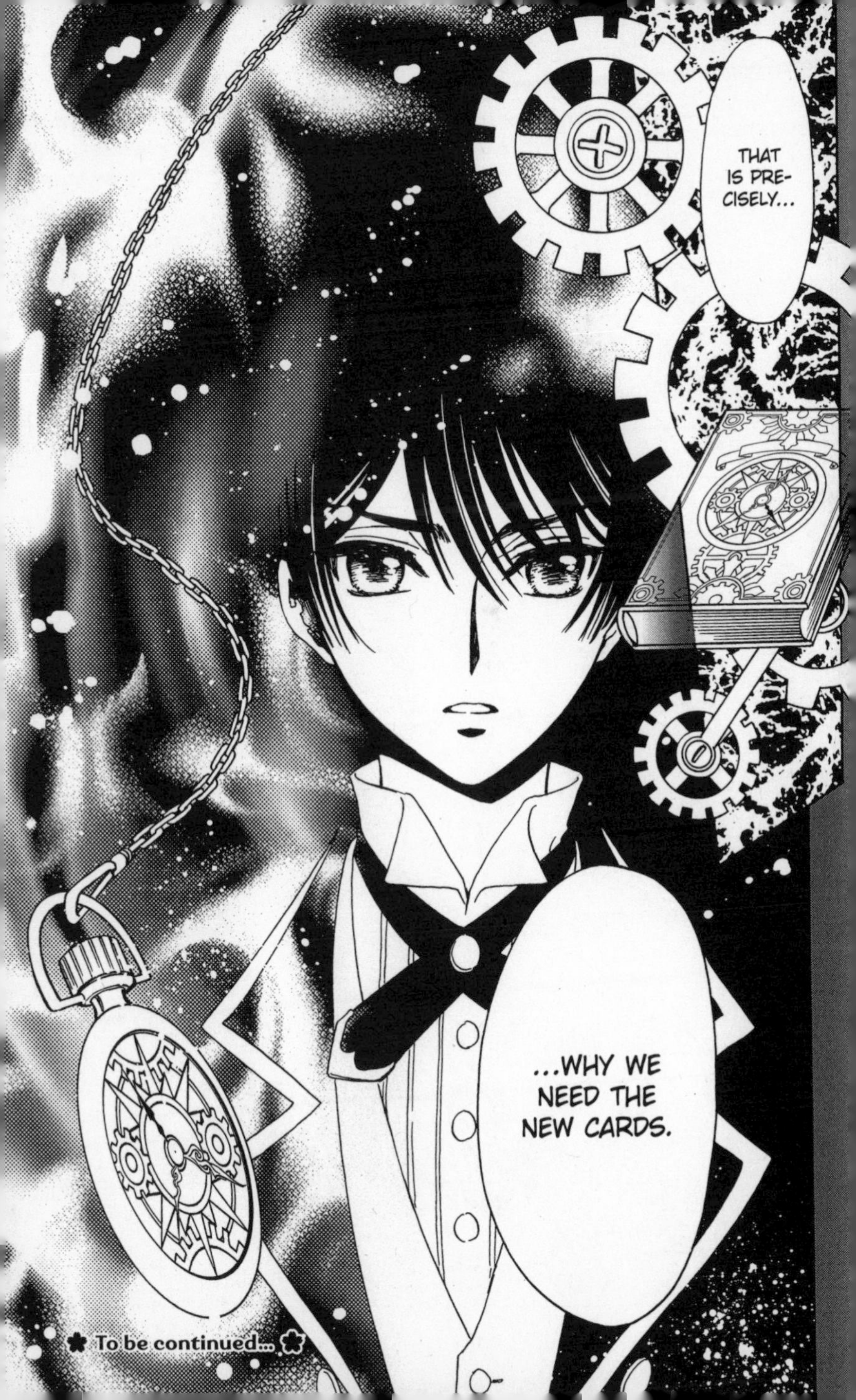
THAT IS PRE-CISELY...
...WHY WE NEED THE NEW CARDS.
To be continued...

Cardcaptor Sakura
CLEAR CARD

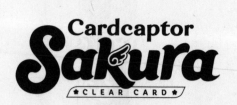

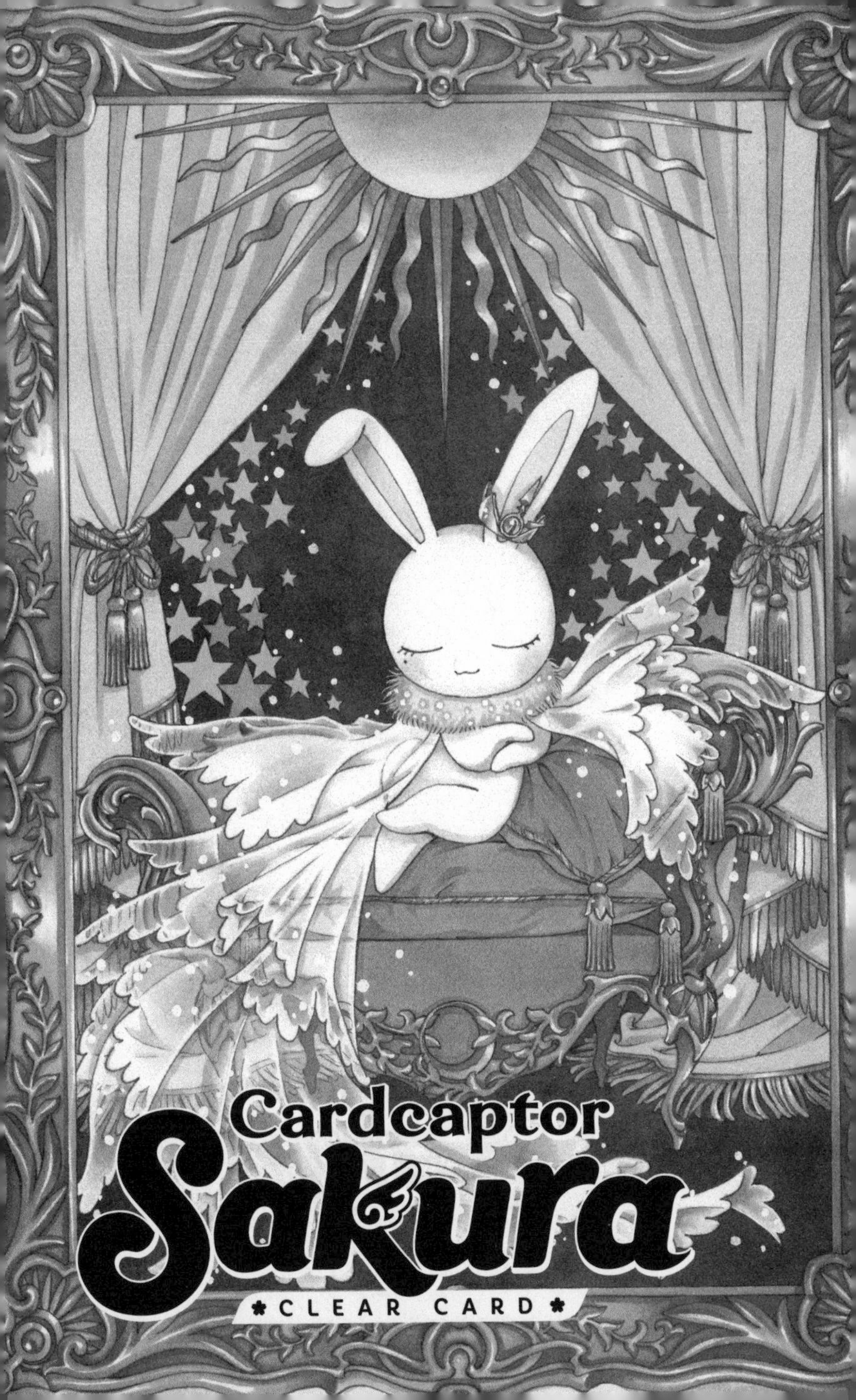
Cardcaptor
Sakura
CLEAR CARD

Cardcaptor Sakura

CLEAR CARD

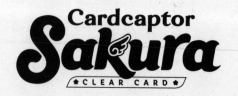

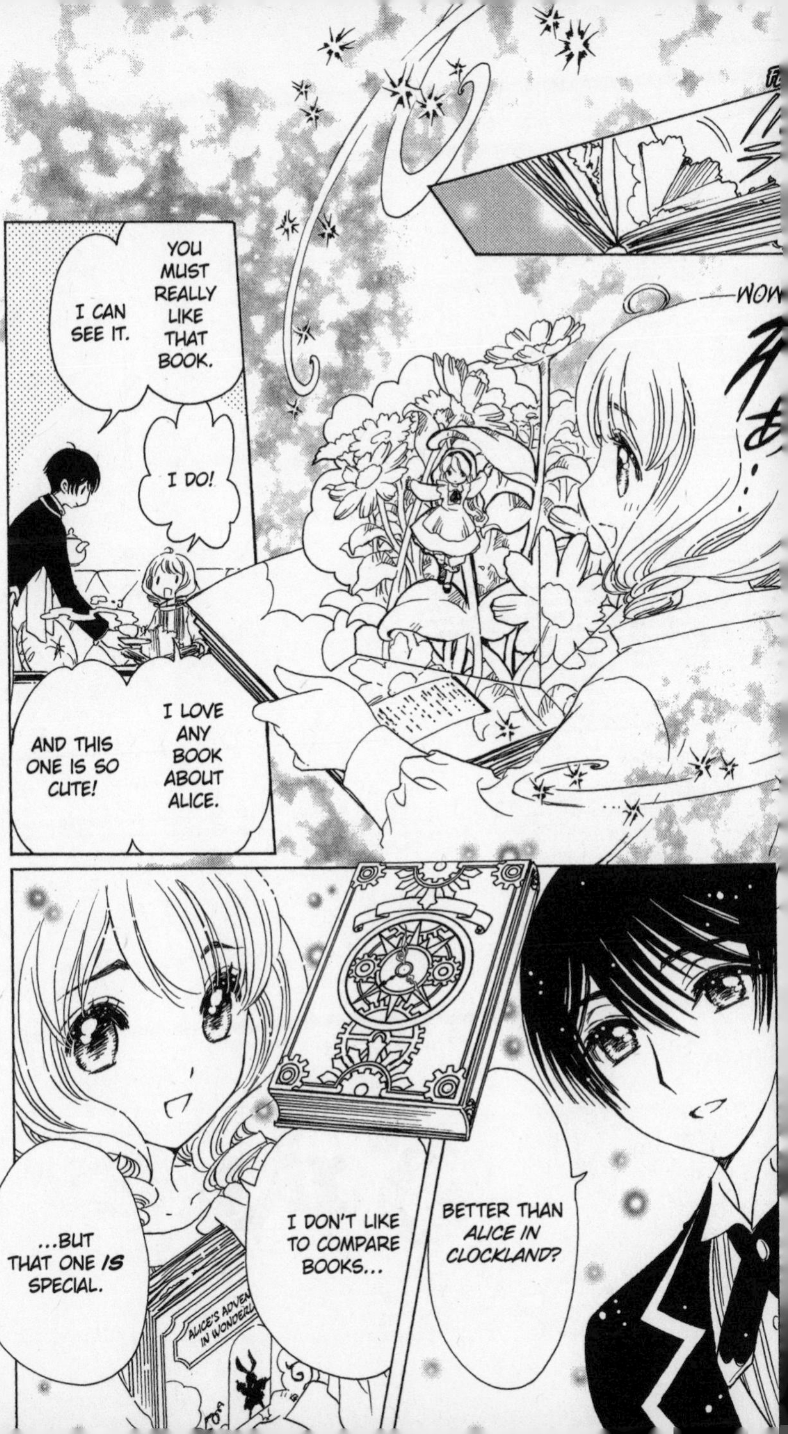

WOW
YOU MUST REALLY LIKE THAT BOOK.
I CAN SEE IT.
I DO!
I LOVE ANY BOOK ABOUT ALICE.
AND THIS ONE IS SO CUTE!
BETTER THAN *ALICE IN CLOCKLAND?*
I DON'T LIKE TO COMPARE BOOKS...
...BUT THAT ONE *IS* SPECIAL.

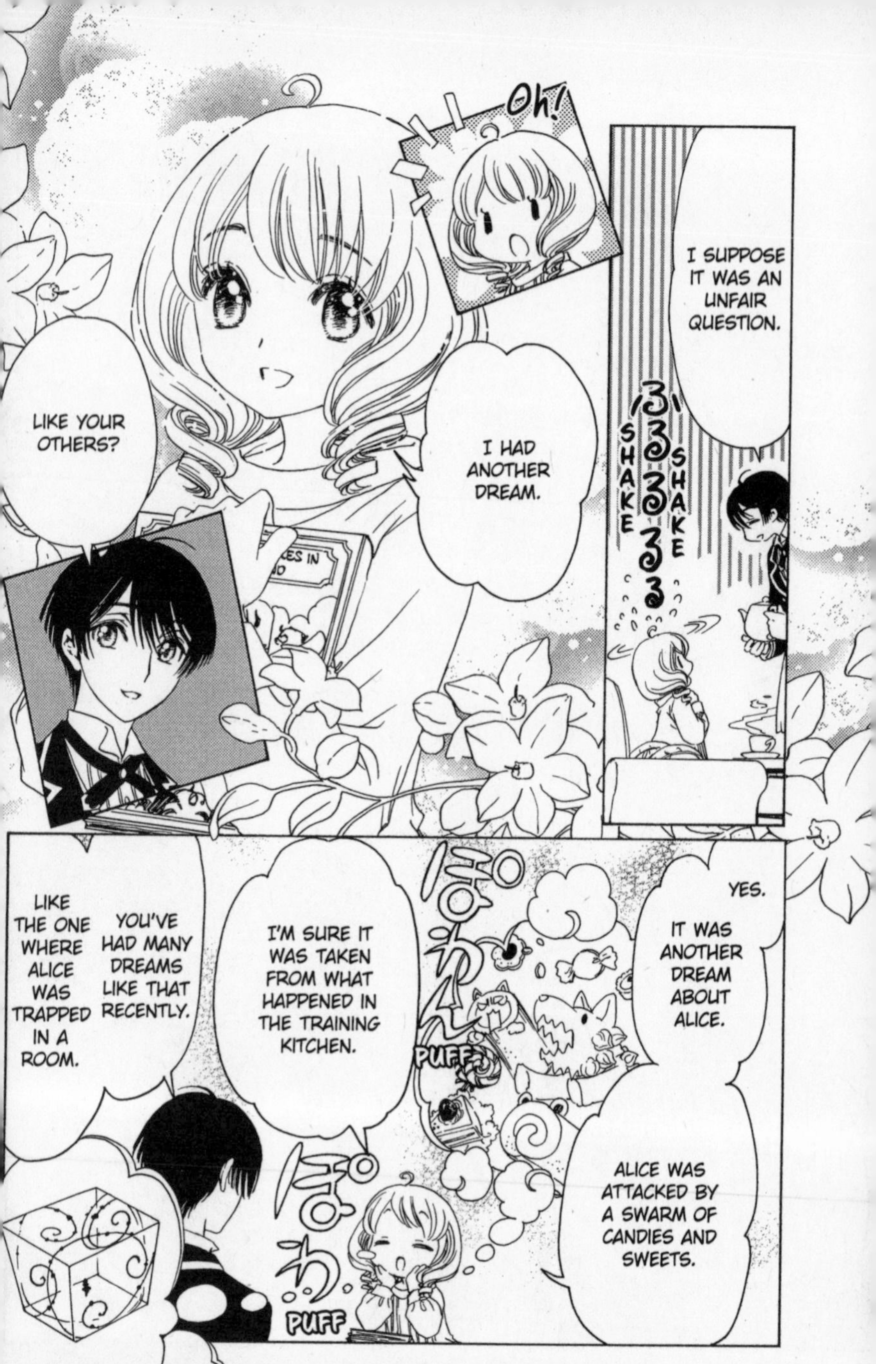
I SUPPOSE IT WAS AN UNFAIR QUESTION.
SHAKE
SHAKE
Oh!
I HAD ANOTHER DREAM.
LIKE YOUR OTHERS?
YES.
IT WAS ANOTHER DREAM ABOUT ALICE.
ALICE WAS ATTACKED BY A SWARM OF CANDIES AND SWEETS.
PUFF
PUFF
I'M SURE IT WAS TAKEN FROM WHAT HAPPENED IN THE TRAINING KITCHEN.
YOU'VE HAD MANY DREAMS LIKE THAT RECENTLY.
LIKE THE ONE WHERE ALICE WAS TRAPPED IN A ROOM.

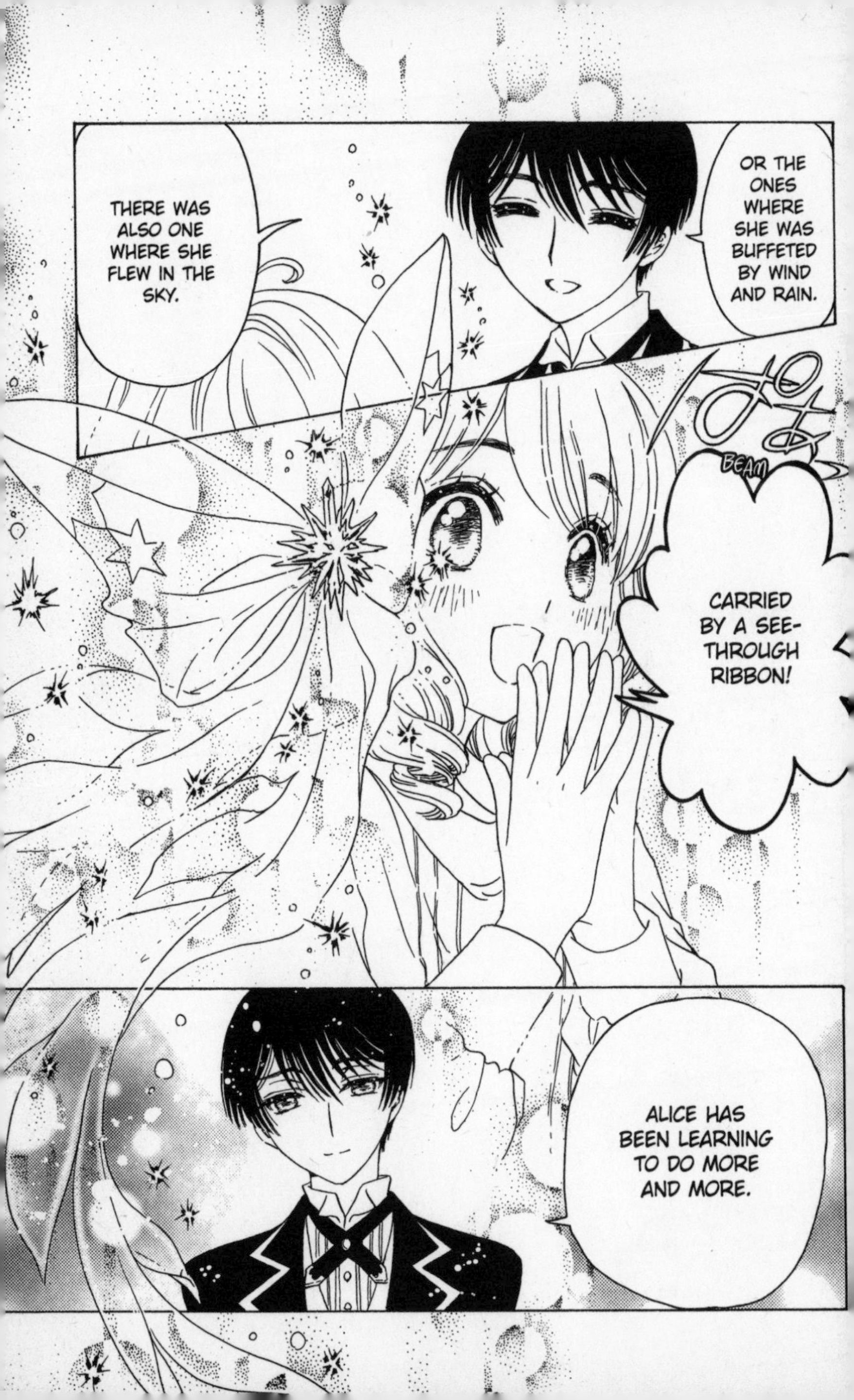
OR THE ONES WHERE SHE WAS BUFFETED BY WIND AND RAIN.
THERE WAS ALSO ONE WHERE SHE FLEW IN THE SKY.
BEAM
CARRIED BY A SEE-THROUGH RIBBON!
ALICE HAS BEEN LEARNING TO DO MORE AND MORE.

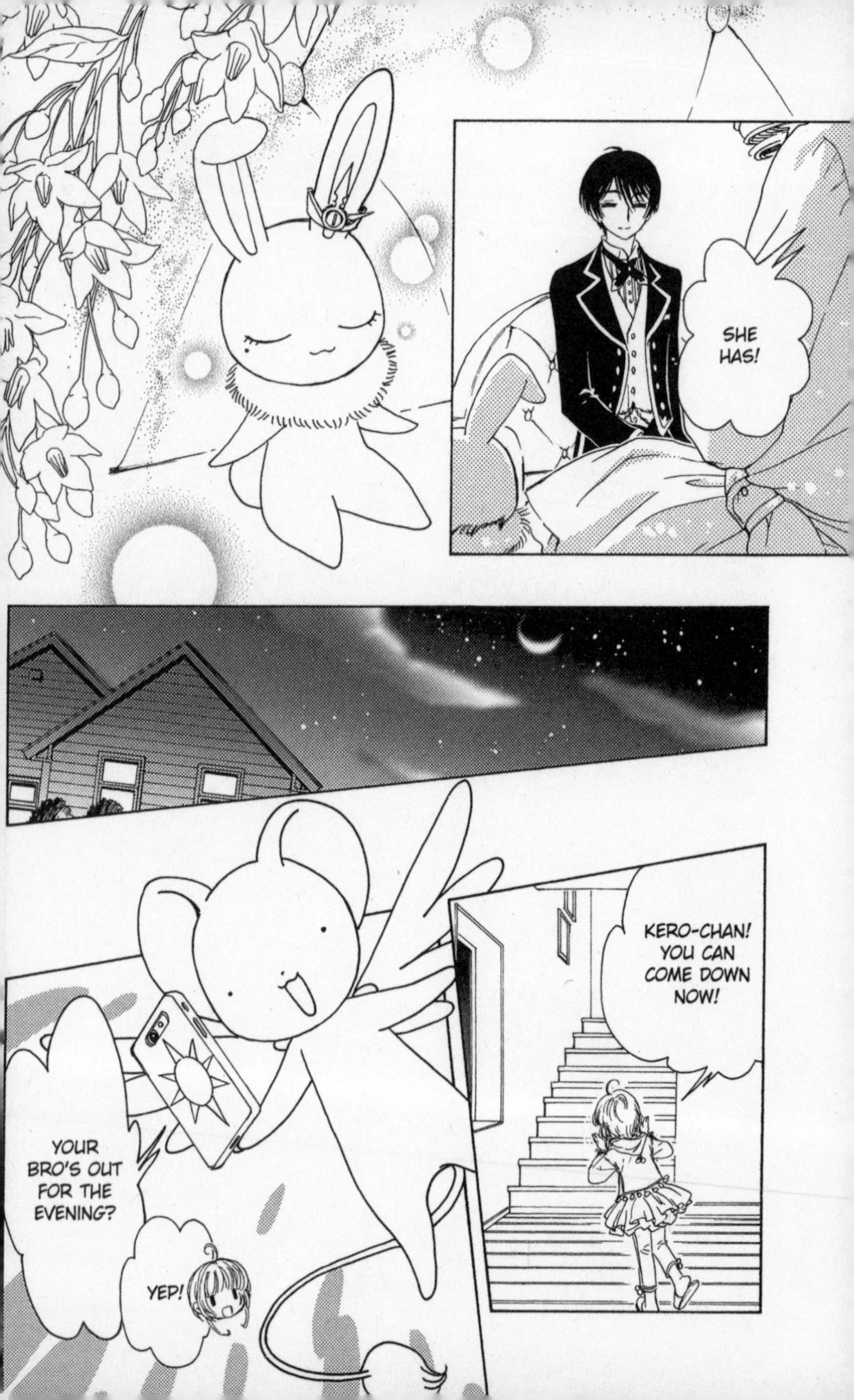
SHE HAS!
KERO-CHAN! YOU CAN COME DOWN NOW!
YOUR BRO'S OUT FOR THE EVENING?
YEP!

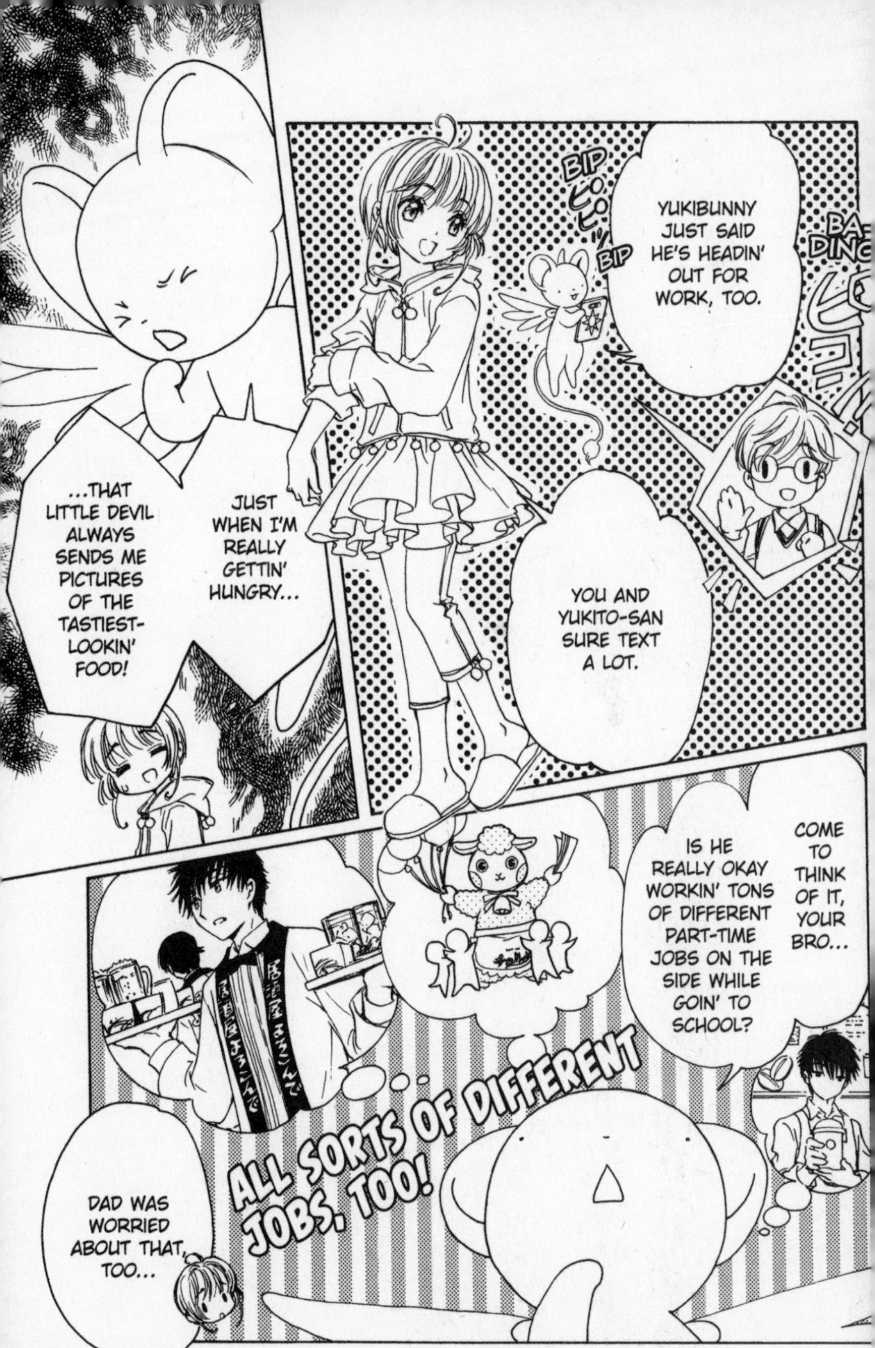
BIP BIP BIP
YUKIBUNNY JUST SAID HE'S HEADIN' OUT FOR WORK, TOO.
BA-DING
YOU AND YUKITO-SAN SURE TEXT A LOT.
JUST WHEN I'M REALLY GETTIN' HUNGRY...
...THAT LITTLE DEVIL ALWAYS SENDS ME PICTURES OF THE TASTIEST-LOOKIN' FOOD!
COME TO THINK OF IT, YOUR BRO...
IS HE REALLY OKAY WORKIN' TONS OF DIFFERENT PART-TIME JOBS ON THE SIDE WHILE GOIN' TO SCHOOL?
ALL SORTS OF DIFFERENT JOBS, TOO!
DAD WAS WORRIED ABOUT THAT, TOO...

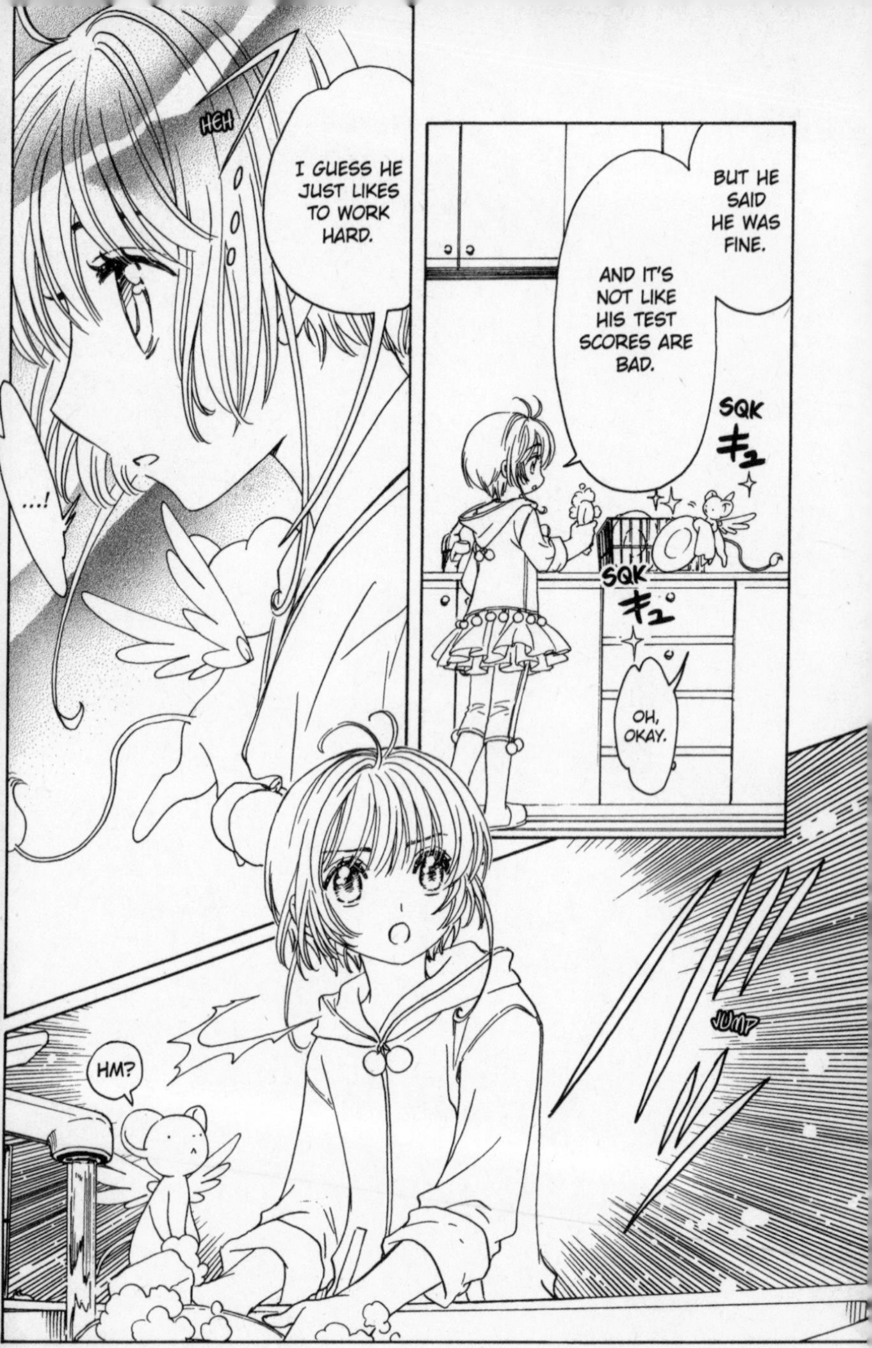
BUT HE SAID HE WAS FINE.
AND IT'S NOT LIKE HIS TEST SCORES ARE BAD.
SQK
キュ
SQK
キュ
OH, OKAY.
HEH
I GUESS HE JUST LIKES TO WORK HARD.
...!
JUMP
HM?

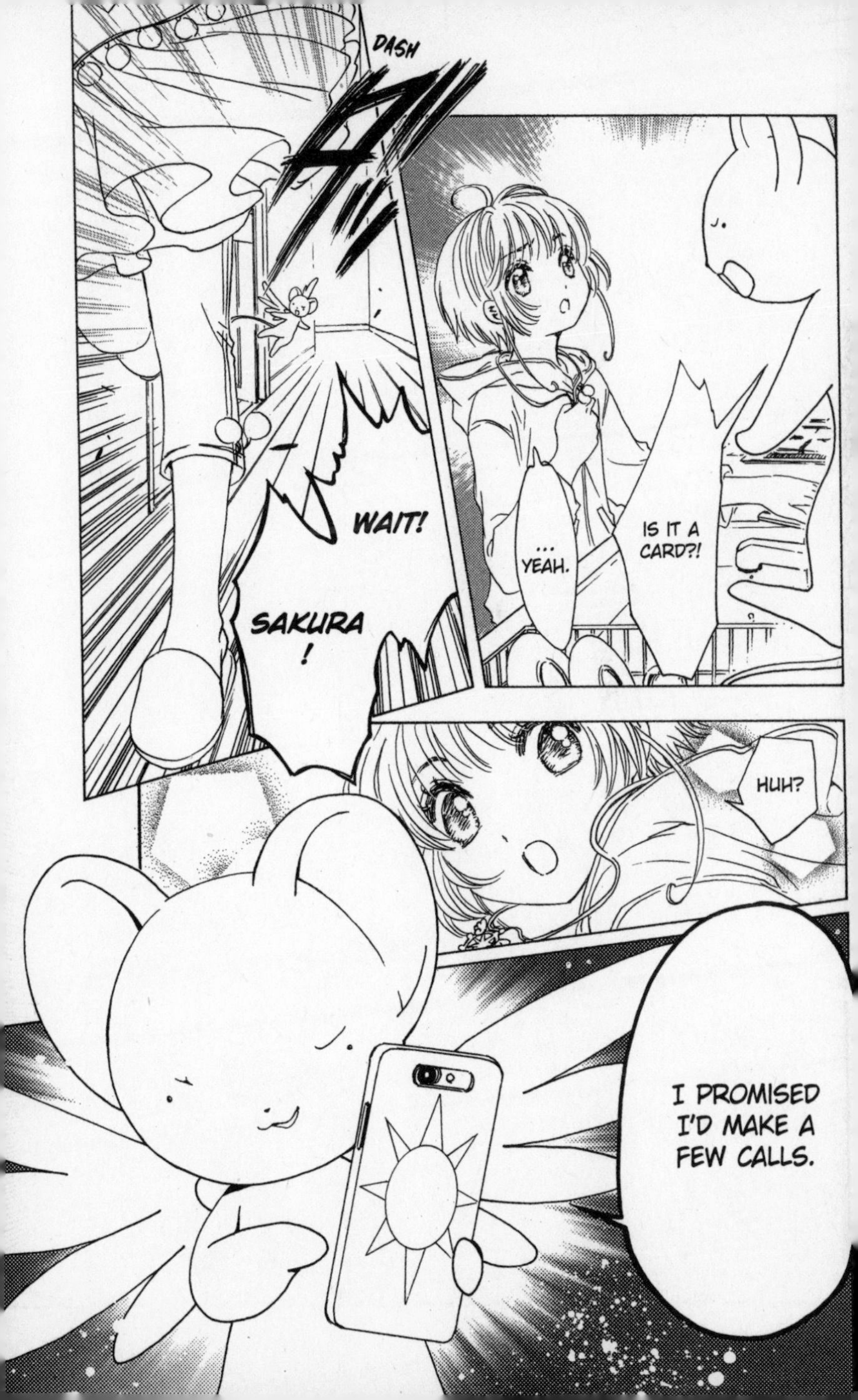
IS IT A CARD?!
... YEAH.
DASH
WAIT!
SAKURA!
HUH?
I PROMISED I'D MAKE A FEW CALLS.

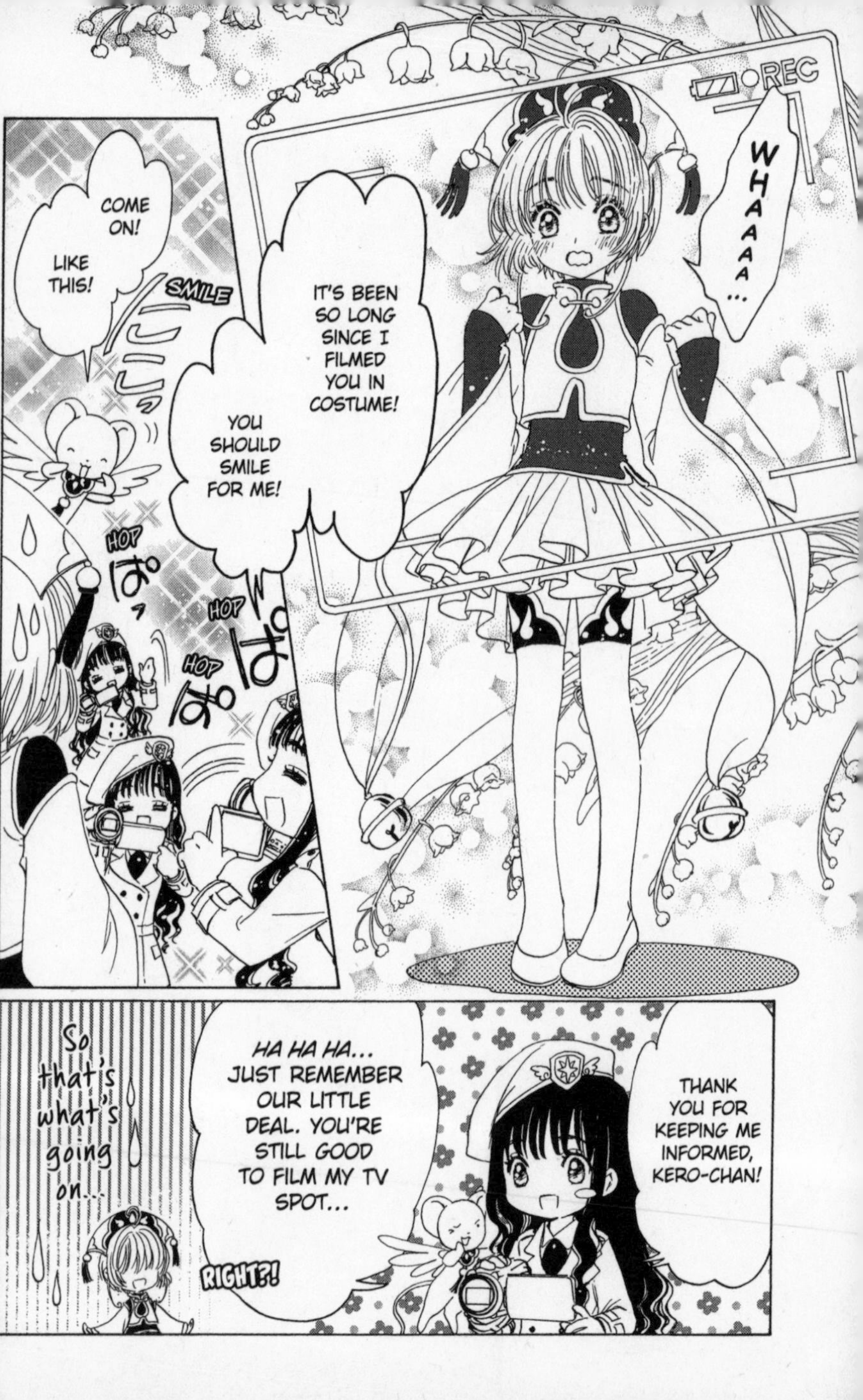
WHAAAA...
IT'S BEEN SO LONG SINCE I FILMED YOU IN COSTUME!
YOU SHOULD SMILE FOR ME!
COME ON!
LIKE THIS!
SMILE
HOP
HOP
HOP
THANK YOU FOR KEEPING ME INFORMED, KERO-CHAN!
HA HA HA... JUST REMEMBER OUR LITTLE DEAL. YOU'RE STILL GOOD TO FILM MY TV SPOT...
RIGHT?!
So that's what's going on...

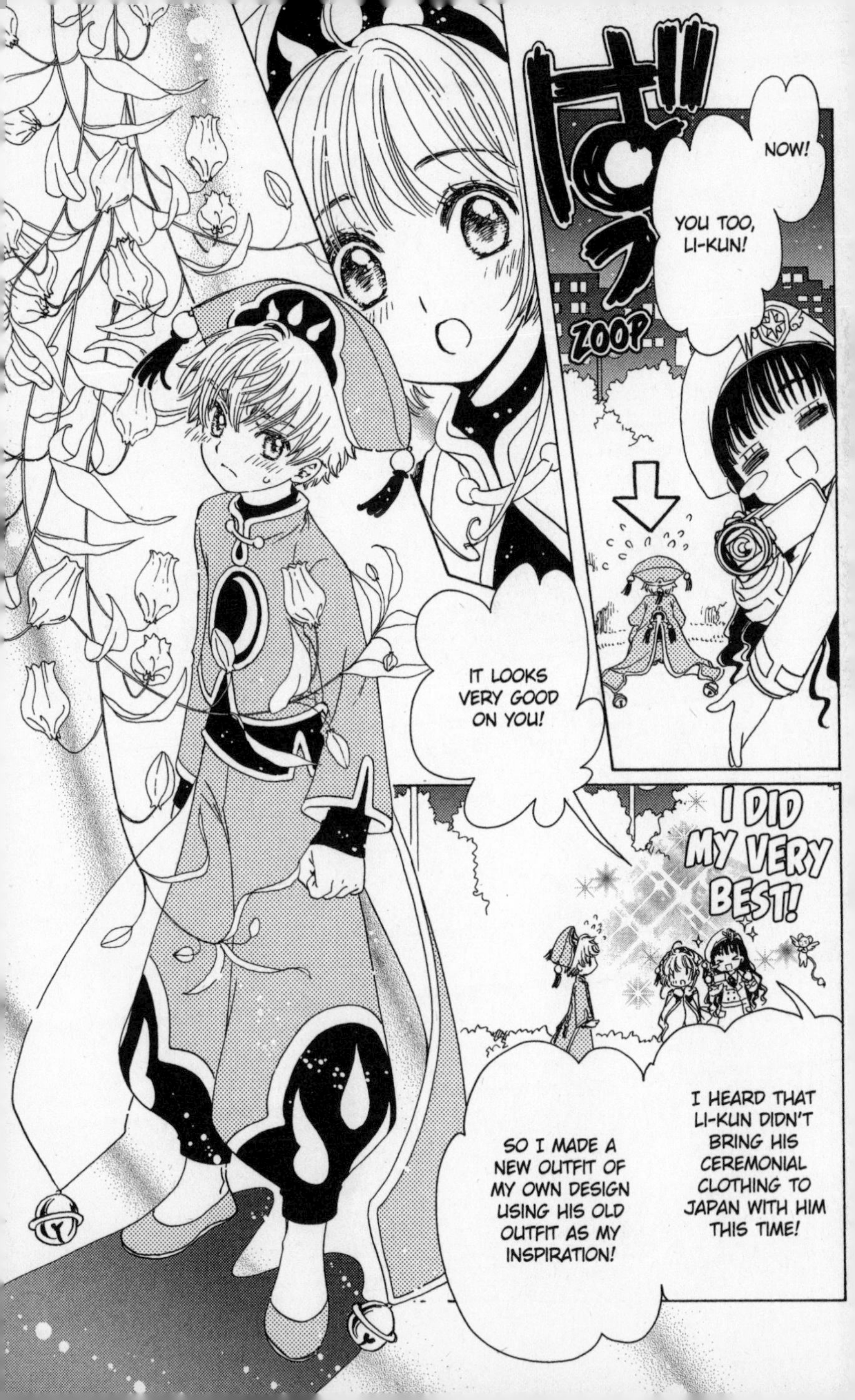

NOW!
YOU TOO, LI-KUN!
ぱっ
ZOOP
IT LOOKS VERY GOOD ON YOU!
I DID MY VERY BEST!
I HEARD THAT LI-KUN DIDN'T BRING HIS CEREMONIAL CLOTHING TO JAPAN WITH HIM THIS TIME!
SO I MADE A NEW OUTFIT OF MY OWN DESIGN USING HIS OLD OUTFIT AS MY INSPIRATION!

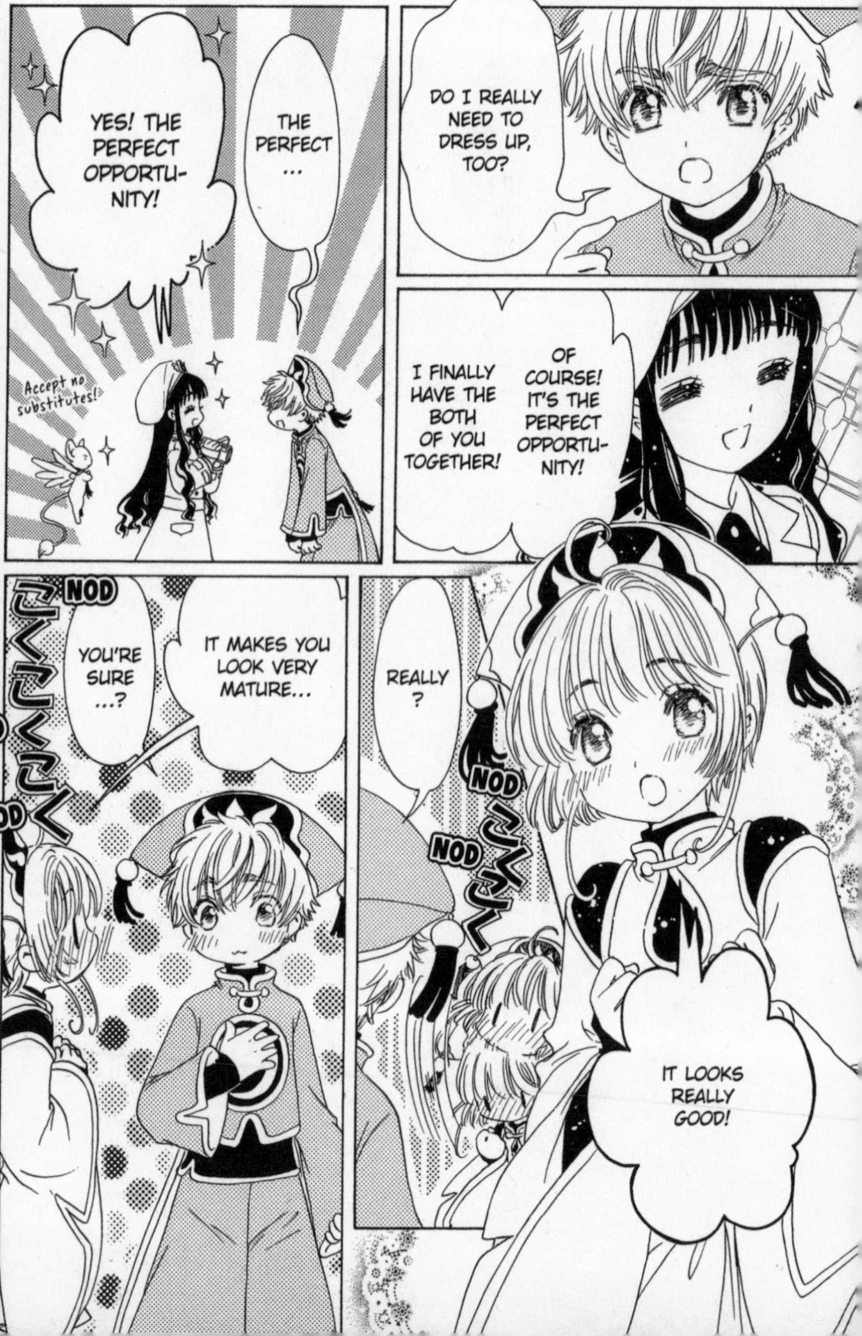
DO I REALLY NEED TO DRESS UP, TOO?
OF COURSE! IT'S THE PERFECT OPPORTUNITY!
I FINALLY HAVE THE BOTH OF YOU TOGETHER!
THE PERFECT...
YES! THE PERFECT OPPORTUNITY!
Accept no substitutes!
REALLY?
NOD
NOD
IT LOOKS REALLY GOOD!
IT MAKES YOU LOOK VERY MATURE...
YOU'RE SURE...?
NOD

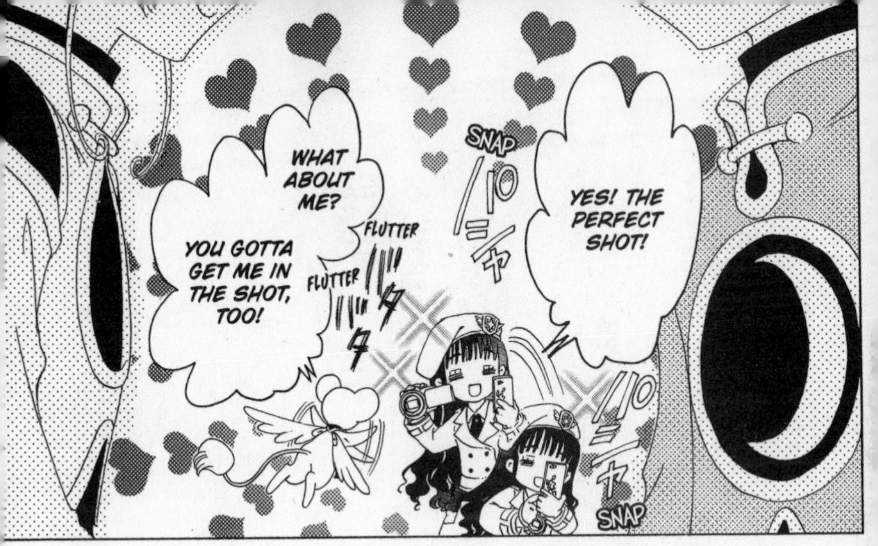
SNAP
YES! THE PERFECT SHOT!
SNAP
WHAT ABOUT ME?
YOU GOTTA GET ME IN THE SHOT, TOO!
FLUTTER
FLUTTER
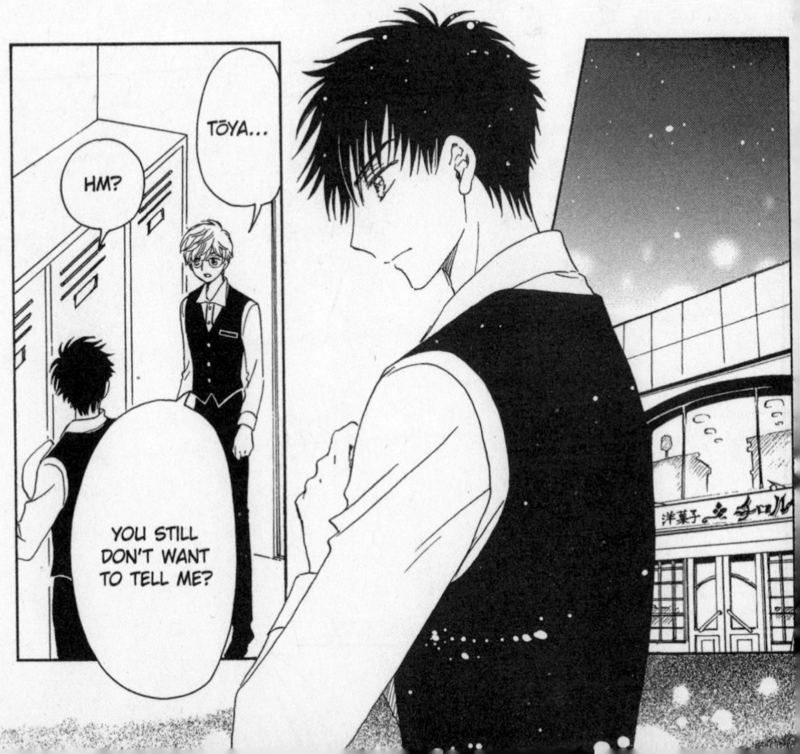
TŌYA...
HM?
YOU STILL DON'T WANT TO TELL ME?

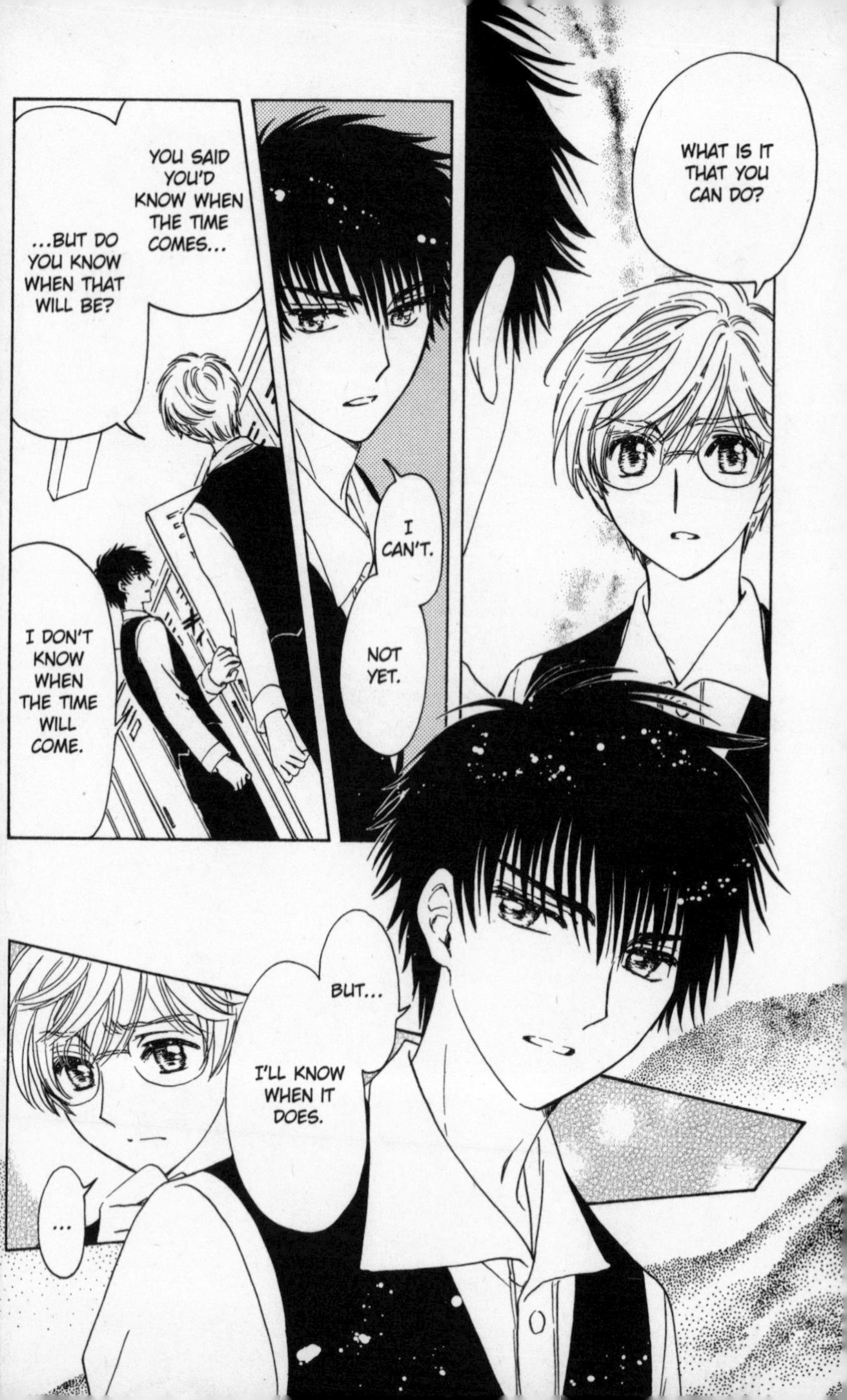
WHAT IS IT THAT YOU CAN DO?
I CAN'T.
NOT YET.
YOU SAID YOU'D KNOW WHEN THE TIME COMES...
...BUT DO YOU KNOW WHEN THAT WILL BE?
I DON'T KNOW WHEN THE TIME WILL COME.
BUT...
I'LL KNOW WHEN IT DOES.
...

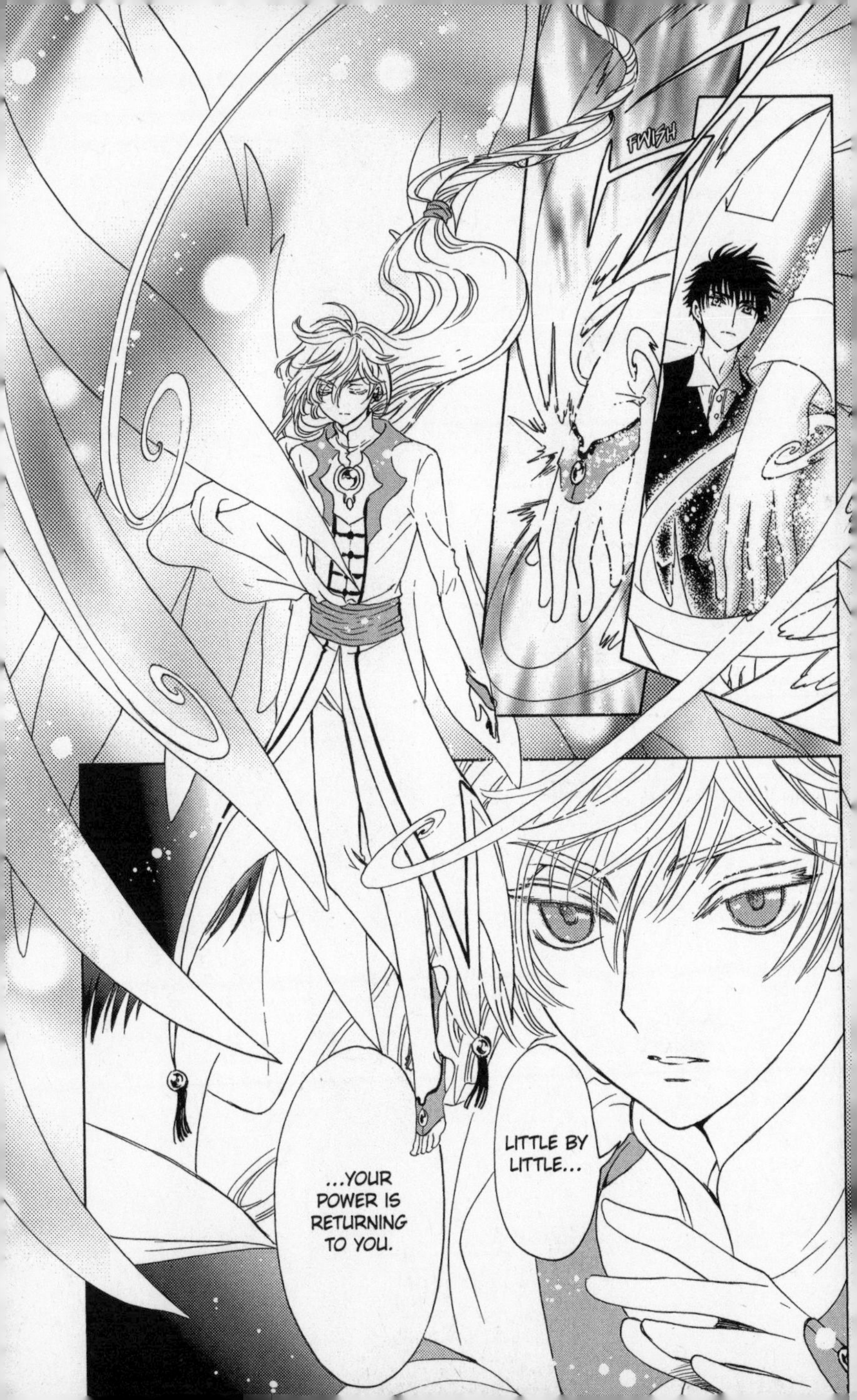
FWISH
LITTLE BY LITTLE...
...YOUR POWER IS RETURNING TO YOU.

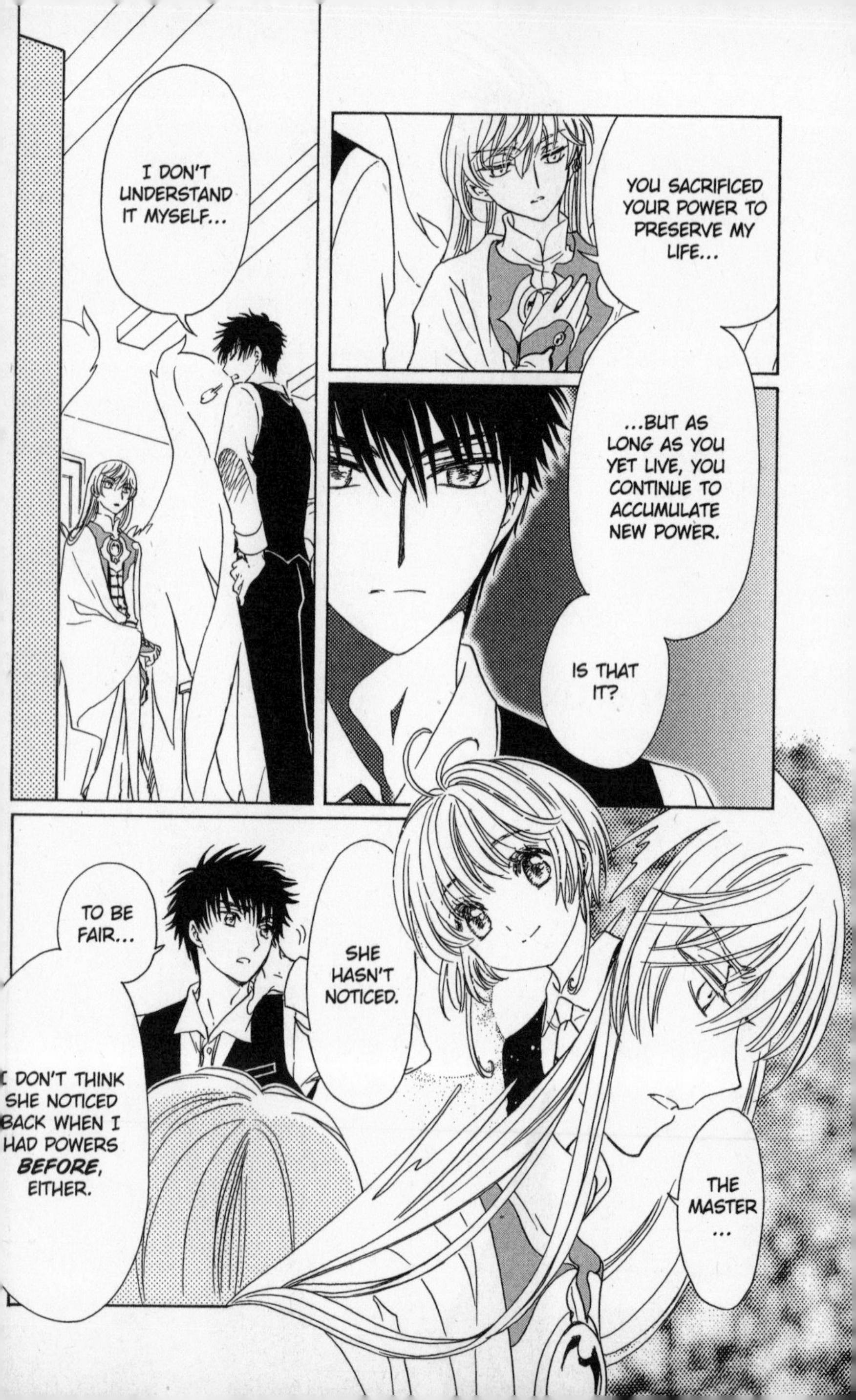
YOU SACRIFICED YOUR POWER TO PRESERVE MY LIFE...
...BUT AS LONG AS YOU YET LIVE, YOU CONTINUE TO ACCUMULATE NEW POWER.
IS THAT IT?
I DON'T UNDERSTAND IT MYSELF...
THE MASTER ...
SHE HASN'T NOTICED.
TO BE FAIR...
I DON'T THINK SHE NOTICED BACK WHEN I HAD POWERS *BEFORE*, EITHER.

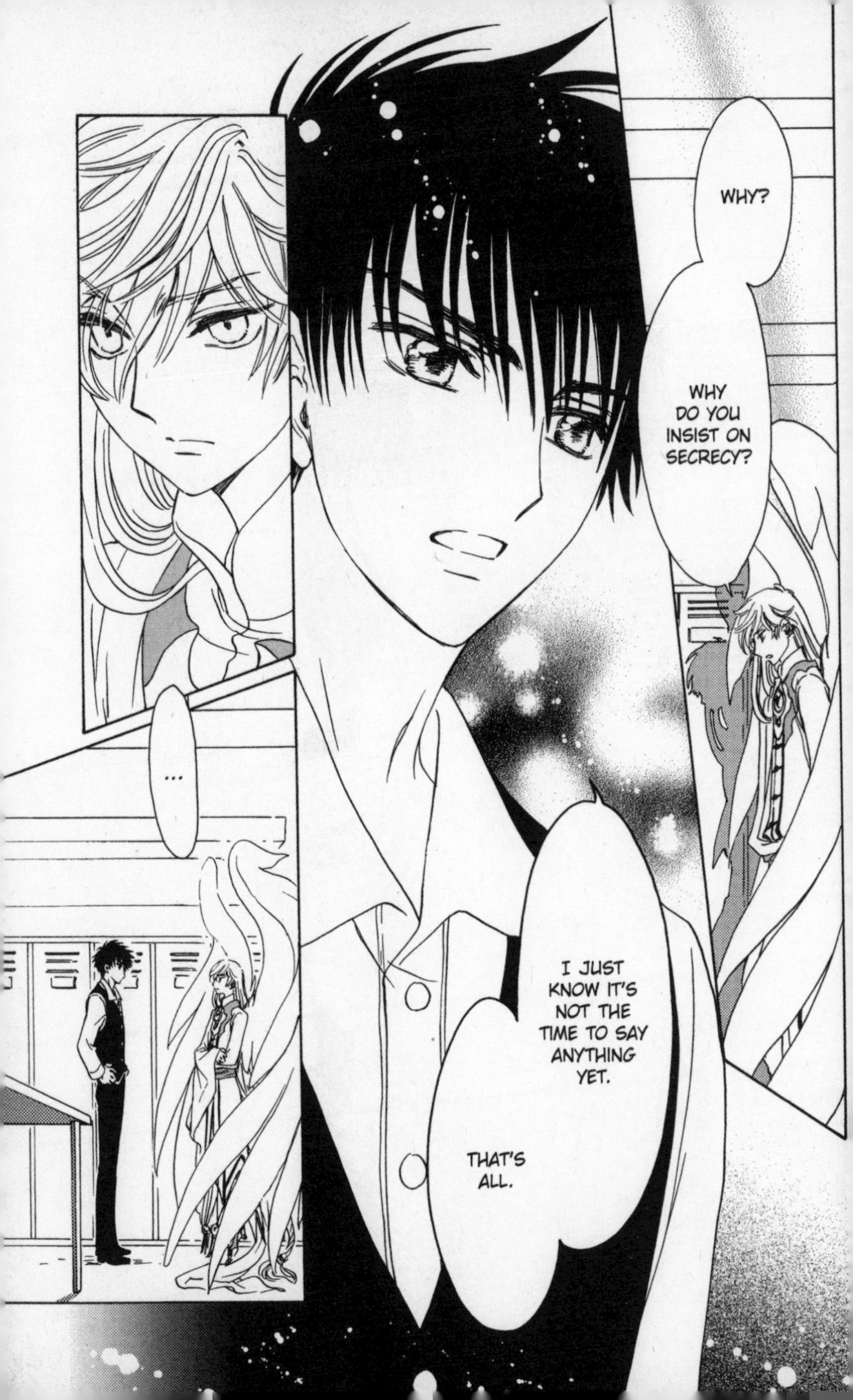
WHY?
WHY DO YOU INSIST ON SECRECY?
...
I JUST KNOW IT'S NOT THE TIME TO SAY ANYTHING YET.
THAT'S ALL.

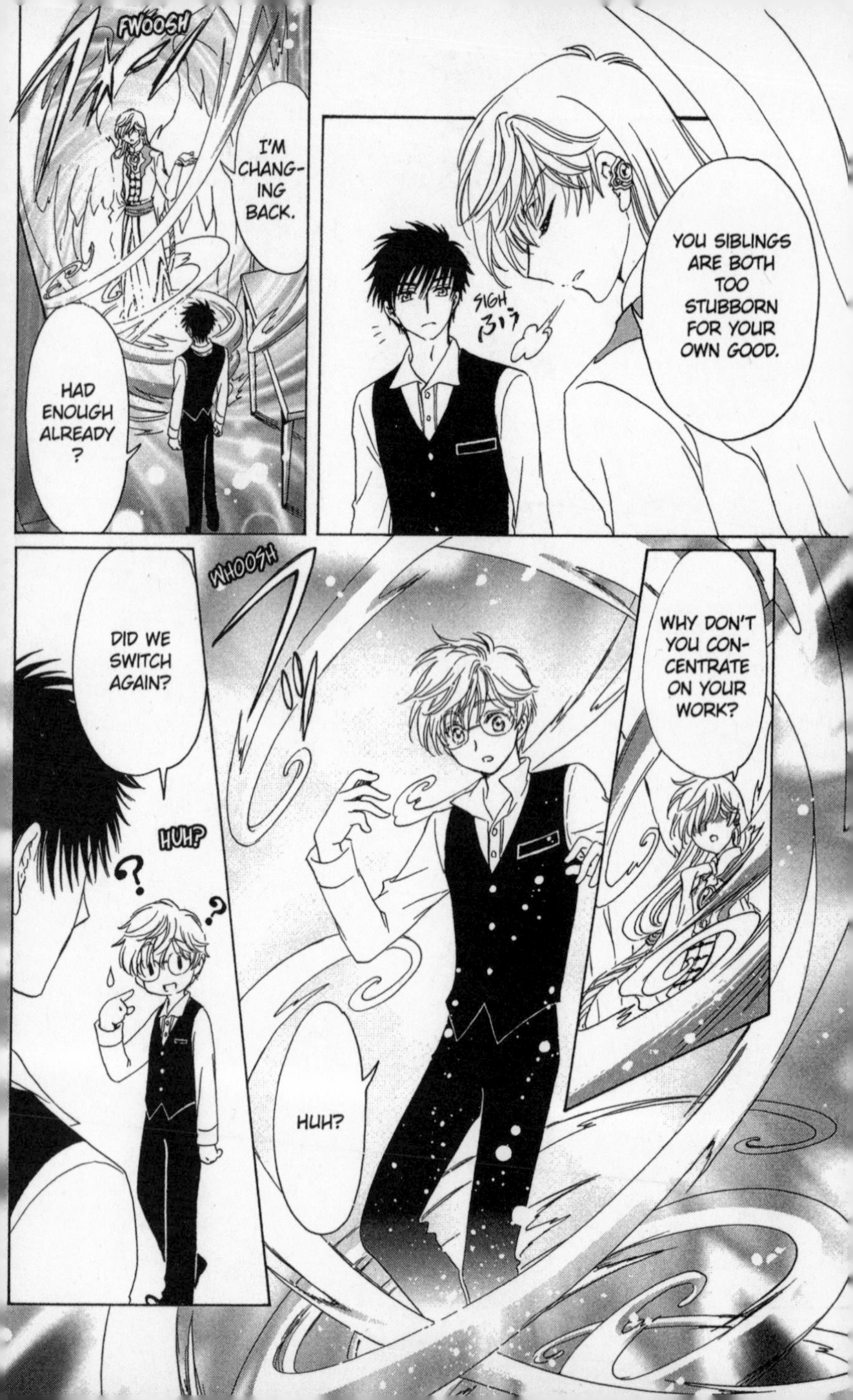
SIGH
YOU SIBLINGS ARE BOTH TOO STUBBORN FOR YOUR OWN GOOD.
FWOOSH
I'M CHANGING BACK.
HAD ENOUGH ALREADY?
WHY DON'T YOU CONCENTRATE ON YOUR WORK?
WHOOSH
HUH?
DID WE SWITCH AGAIN?
HUH?

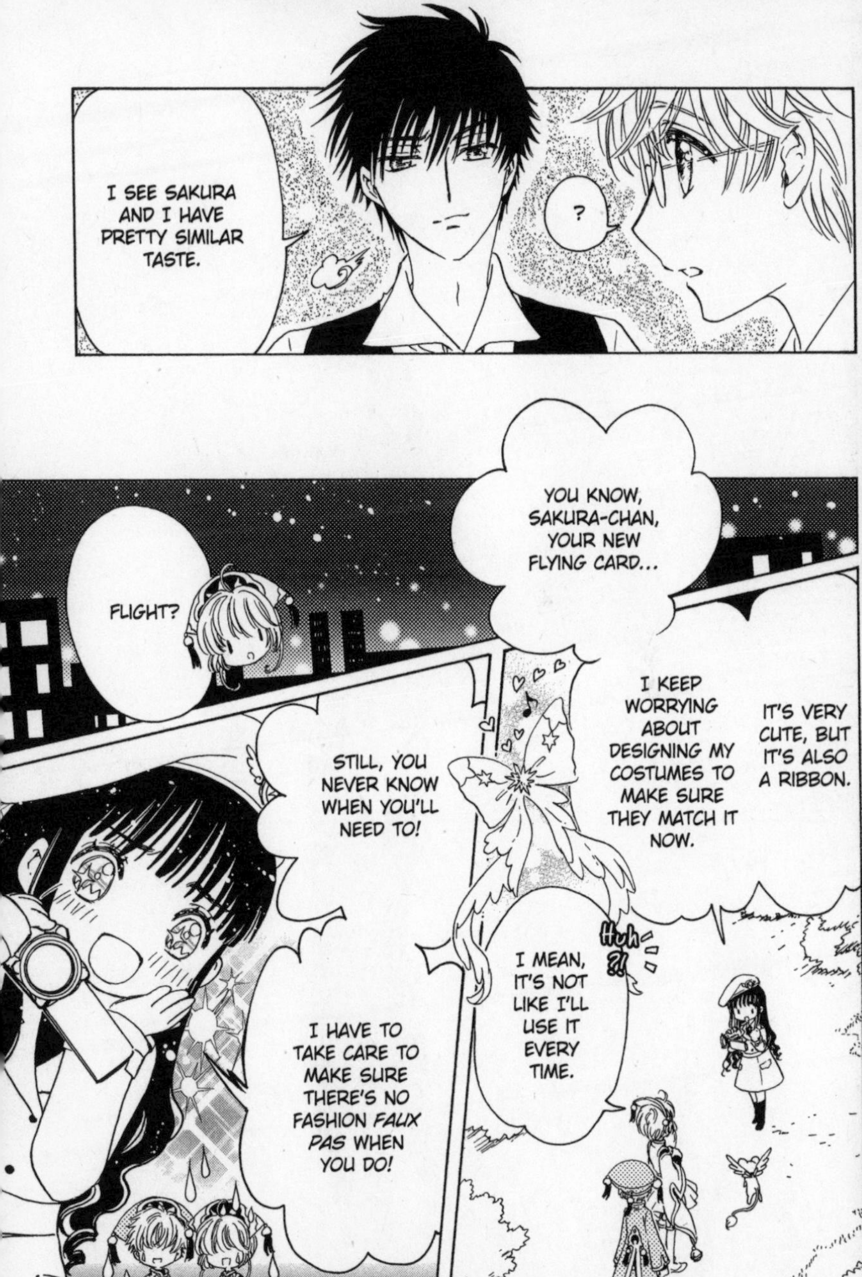
I SEE SAKURA AND I HAVE PRETTY SIMILAR TASTE.
?
YOU KNOW, SAKURA-CHAN, YOUR NEW FLYING CARD...
FLIGHT?
IT'S VERY CUTE, BUT IT'S ALSO A RIBBON.
I KEEP WORRYING ABOUT DESIGNING MY COSTUMES TO MAKE SURE THEY MATCH IT NOW.
Huh?!
I MEAN, IT'S NOT LIKE I'LL USE IT EVERY TIME.
STILL, YOU NEVER KNOW WHEN YOU'LL NEED TO!
I HAVE TO TAKE CARE TO MAKE SURE THERE'S NO FASHION *FAUX PAS* WHEN YOU DO!

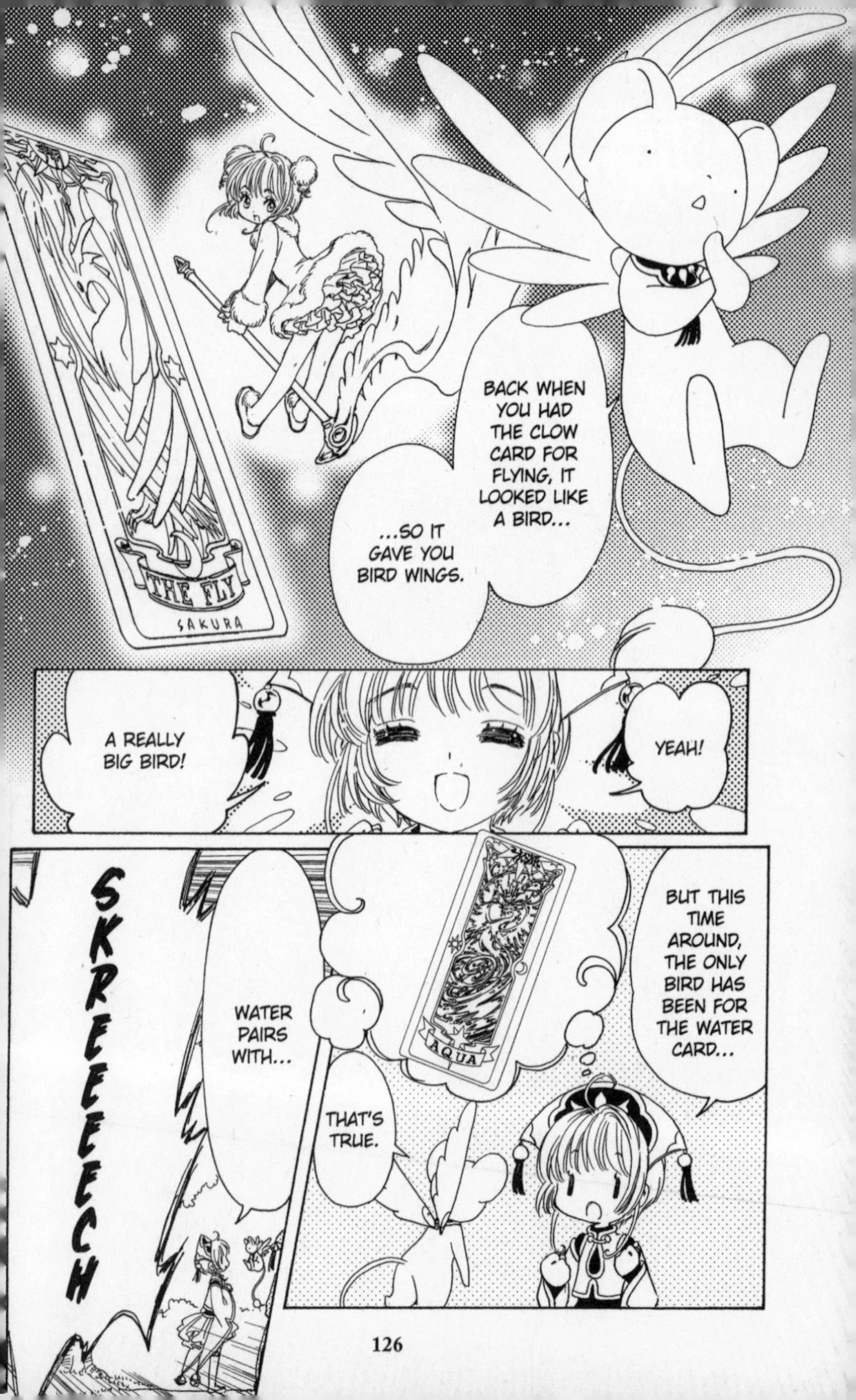
BACK WHEN YOU HAD THE CLOW CARD FOR FLYING, IT LOOKED LIKE A BIRD...
...SO IT GAVE YOU BIRD WINGS.
THE FLY
SAKURA
YEAH!
A REALLY BIG BIRD!
BUT THIS TIME AROUND, THE ONLY BIRD HAS BEEN FOR THE WATER CARD...
AQUA
THAT'S TRUE.
WATER PAIRS WITH...
SKREEEECH

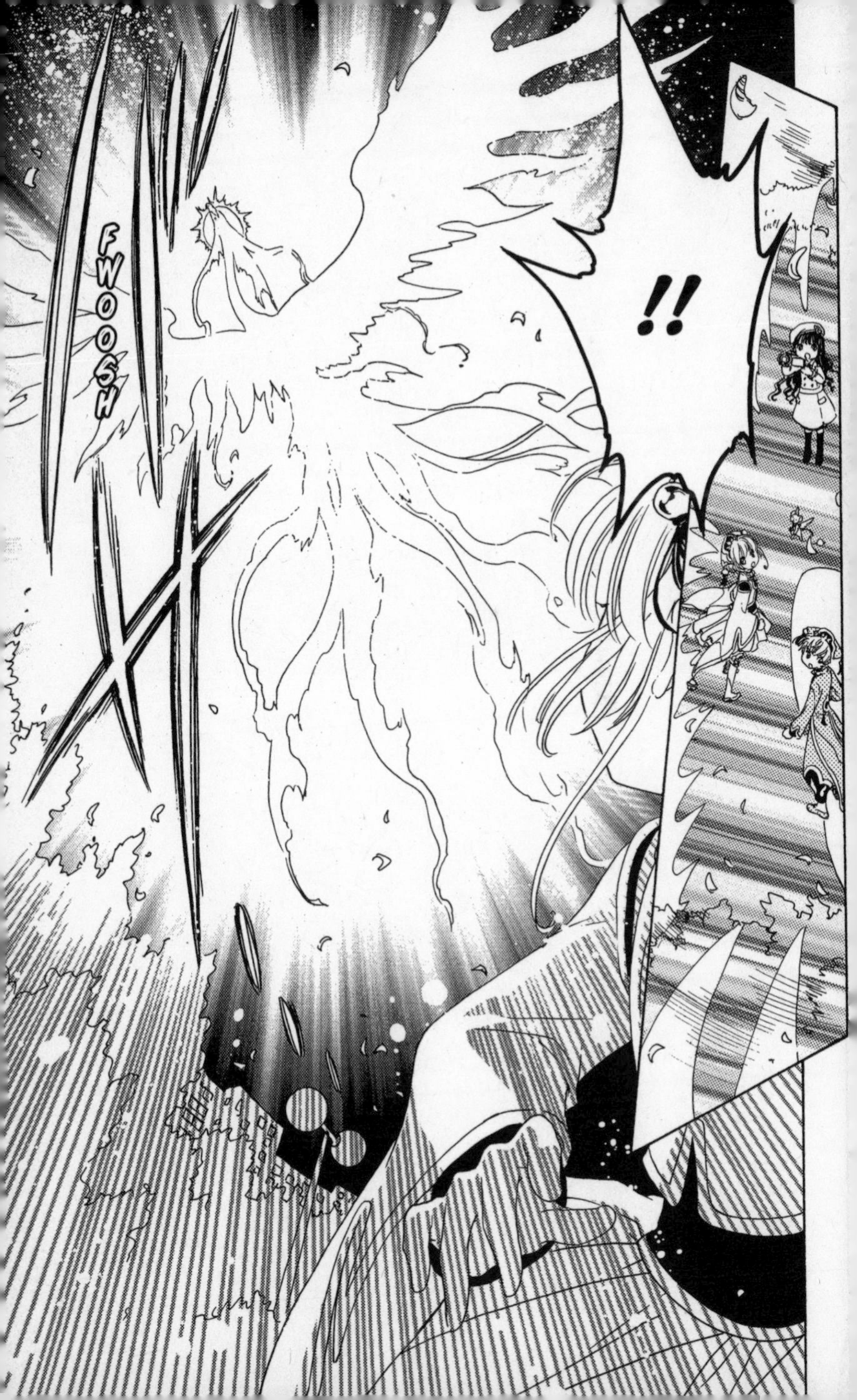
!!
FWOOSH

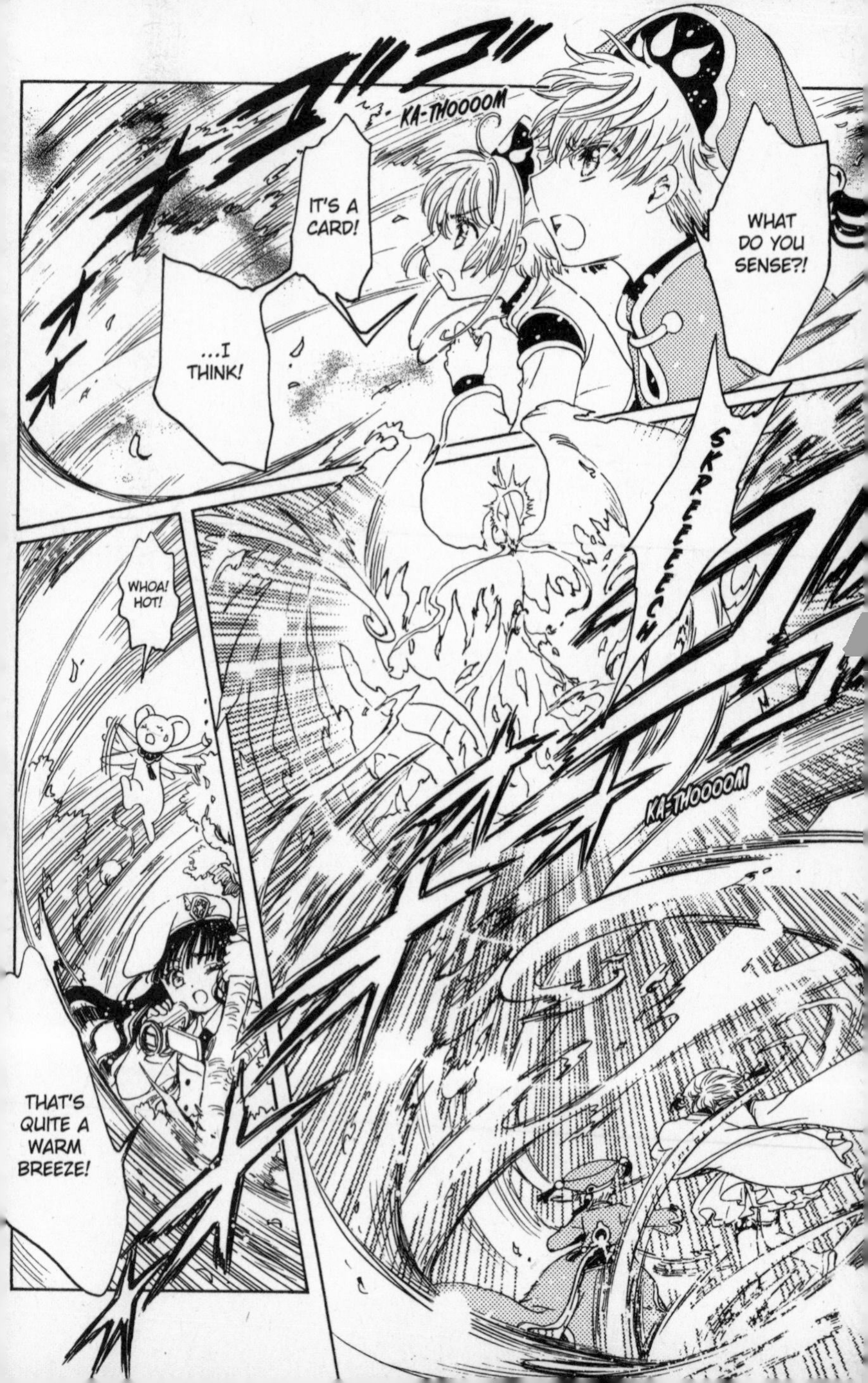
WHAT DO YOU SENSE?!
KA-THOOOOM
IT'S A CARD!
...I THINK!
SKREEEEECH
KA-THOOOOM
WHOA! HOT!
THAT'S QUITE A WARM BREEZE!

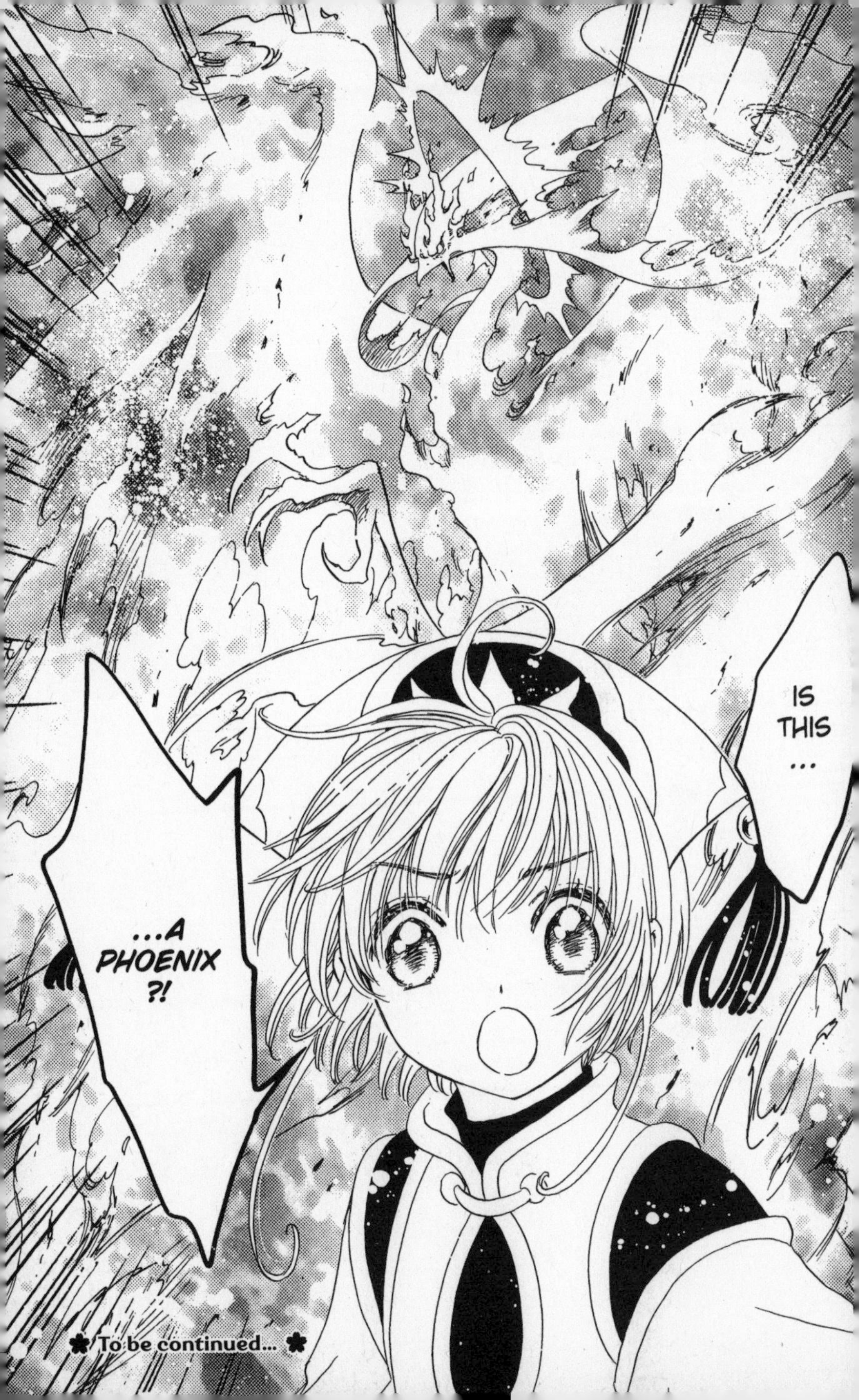
IS THIS ...
...A PHOENIX ?!
To be continued...

Cardcaptor Sakura

CLEAR CARD

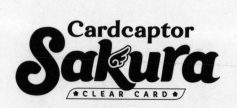

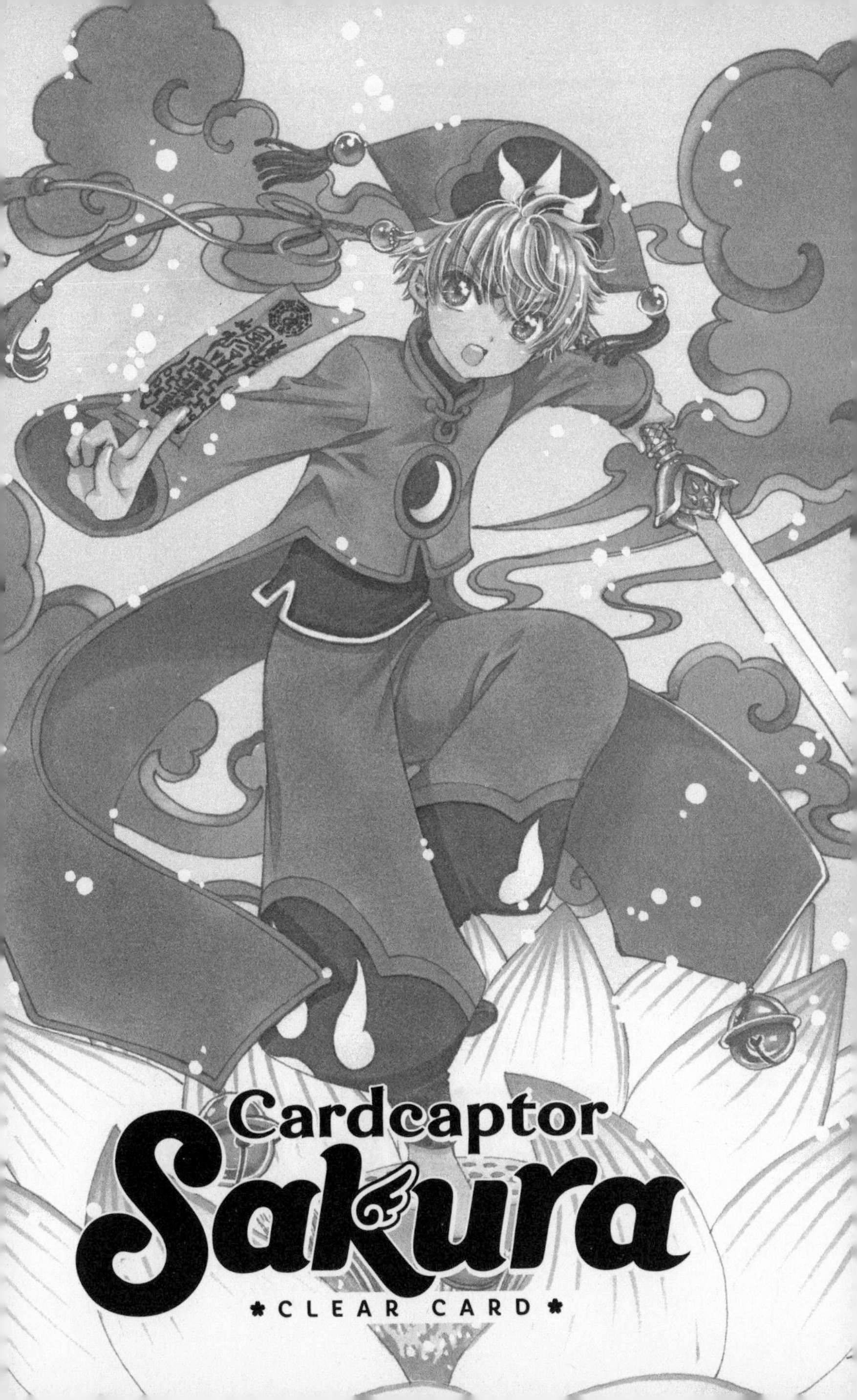
Cardcaptor
Sakura
CLEAR CARD

Cardcaptor Sakura

CLEAR CARD

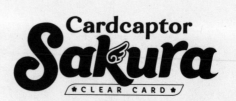

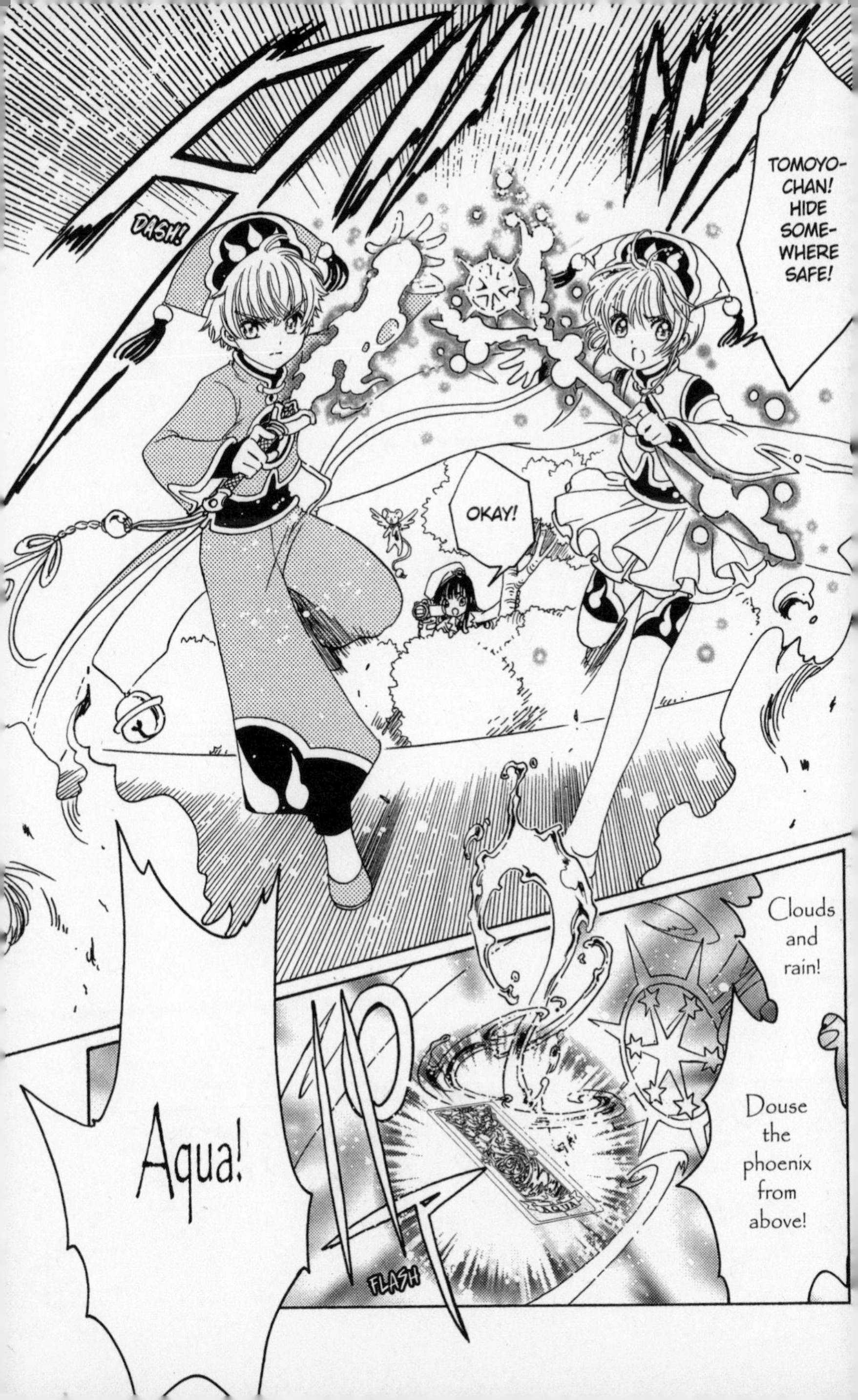
TOMOYO-CHAN! HIDE SOME-WHERE SAFE!
DASH!
OKAY!
Clouds and rain!
Douse the phoenix from above!
FLASH
Aqua!

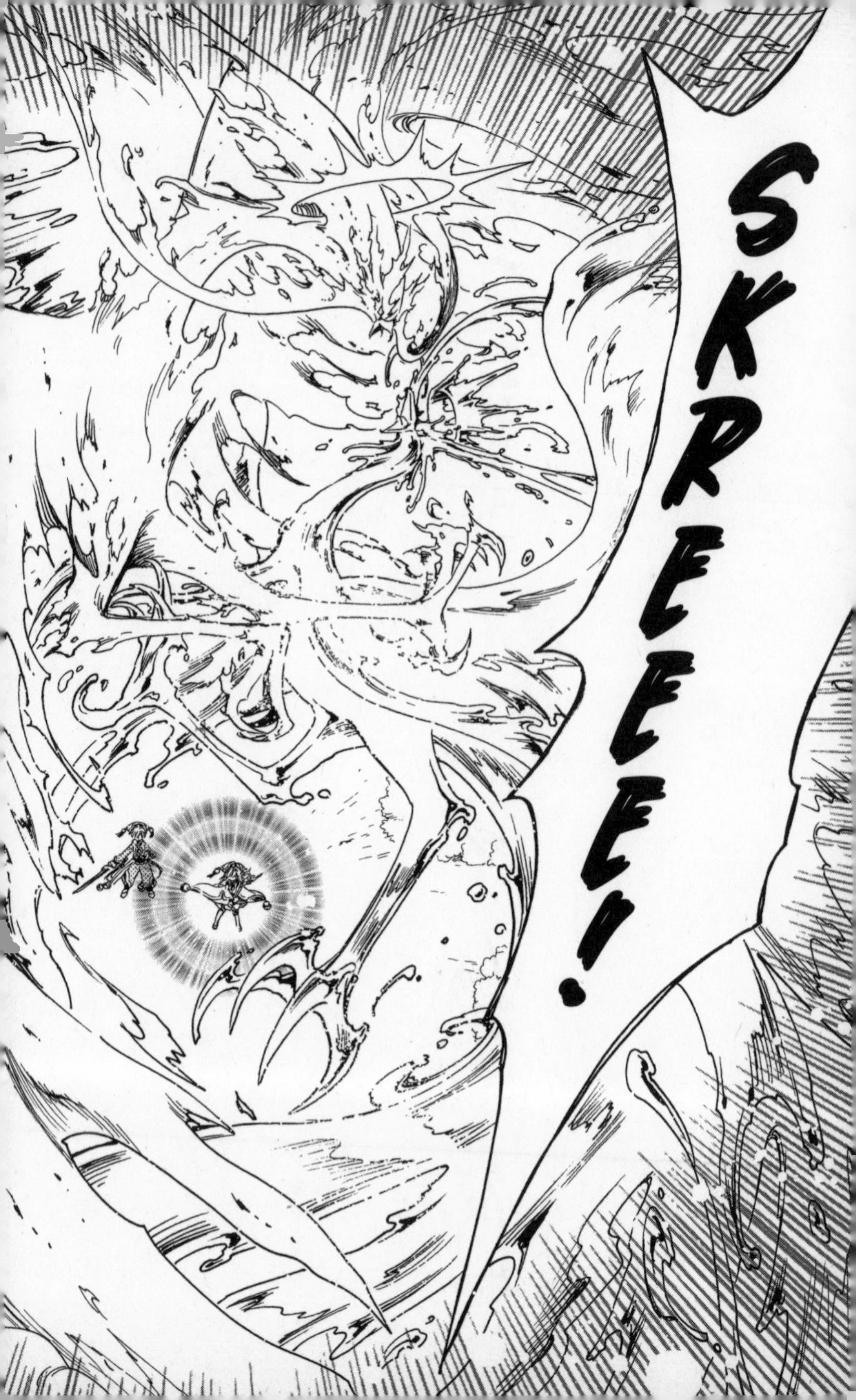
SKREEEEE!

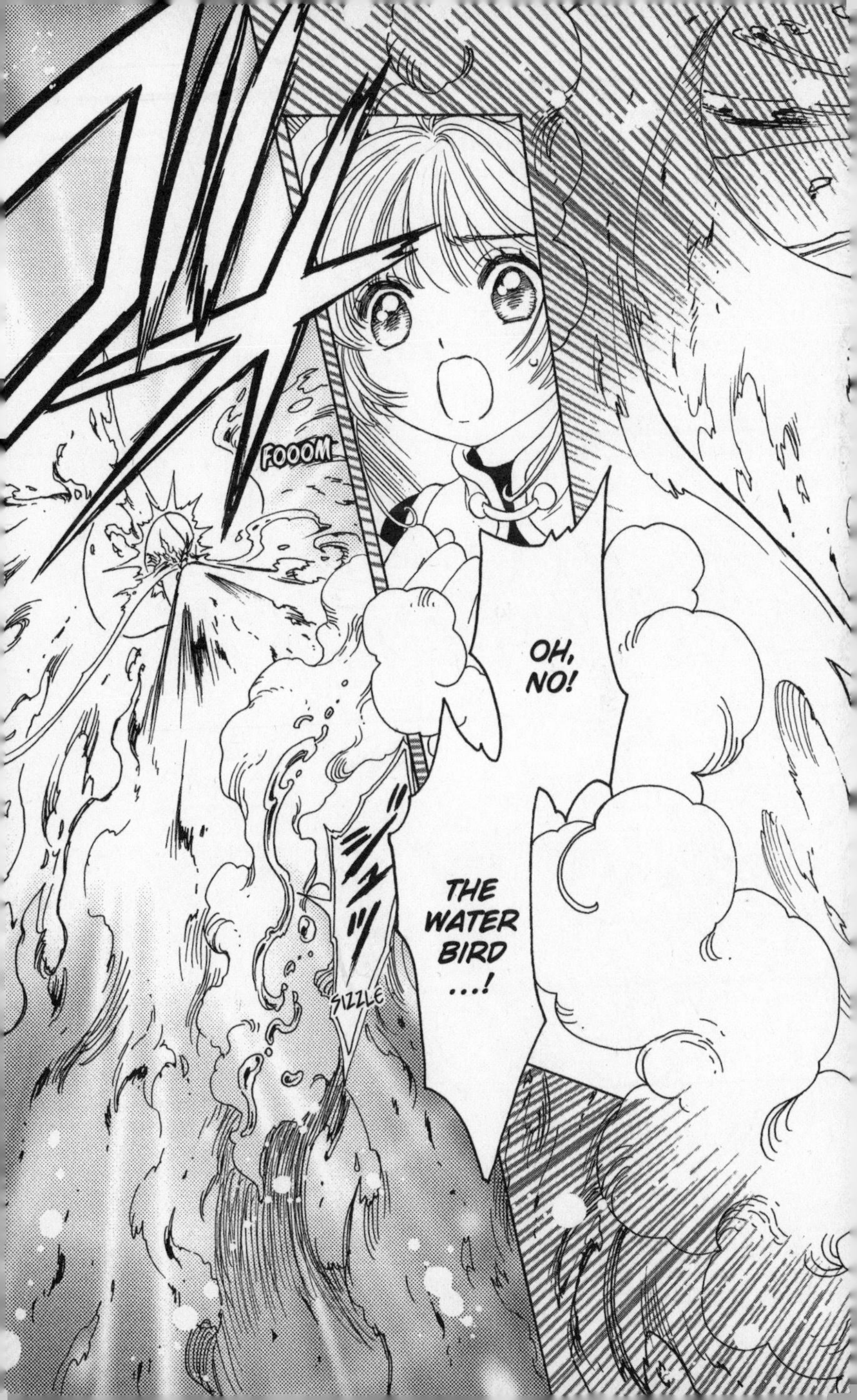
OH, NO!
THE WATER BIRD ...!
FOOOM
SIZZLE

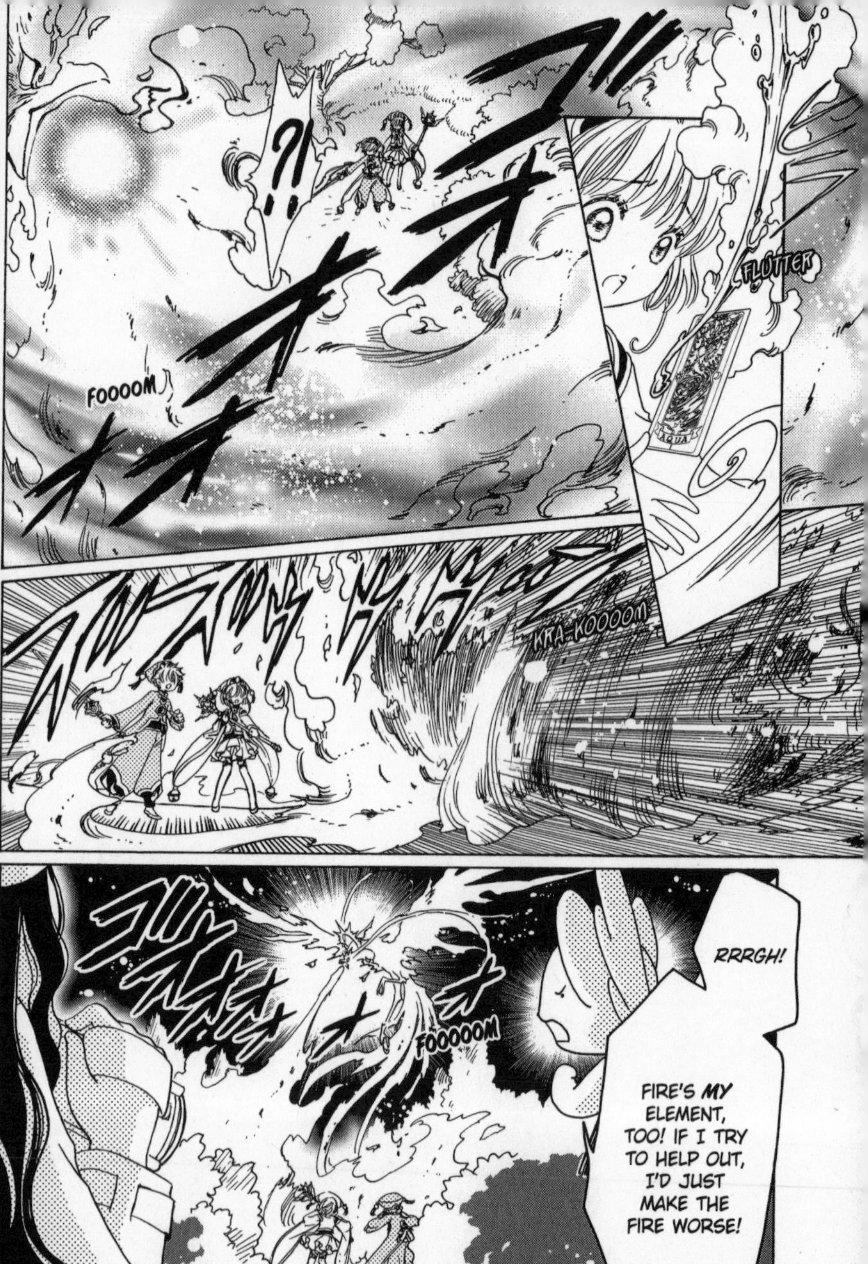
FLUTTER
AQUA
?!
FOOOOM
KRA-KOOOOM
RRRGH!
FIRE'S *MY* ELEMENT, TOO! IF I TRY TO HELP OUT, I'D JUST MAKE THE FIRE WORSE!
FOOOOOM

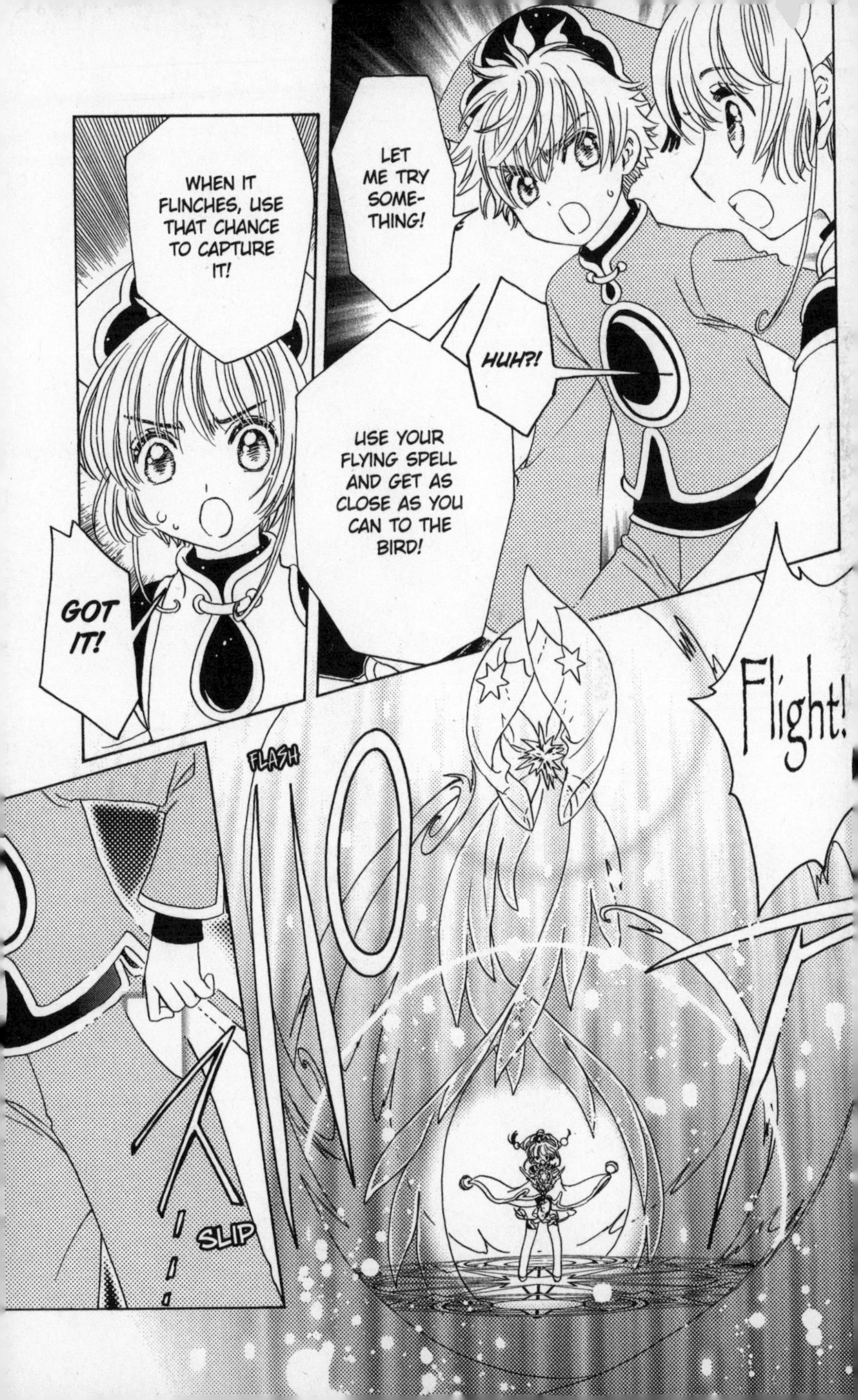

LET ME TRY SOME-THING!
HUH?!
USE YOUR FLYING SPELL AND GET AS CLOSE AS YOU CAN TO THE BIRD!
WHEN IT FLINCHES, USE THAT CHANCE TO CAPTURE IT!
GOT IT!
Flight!
FLASH
SLIP

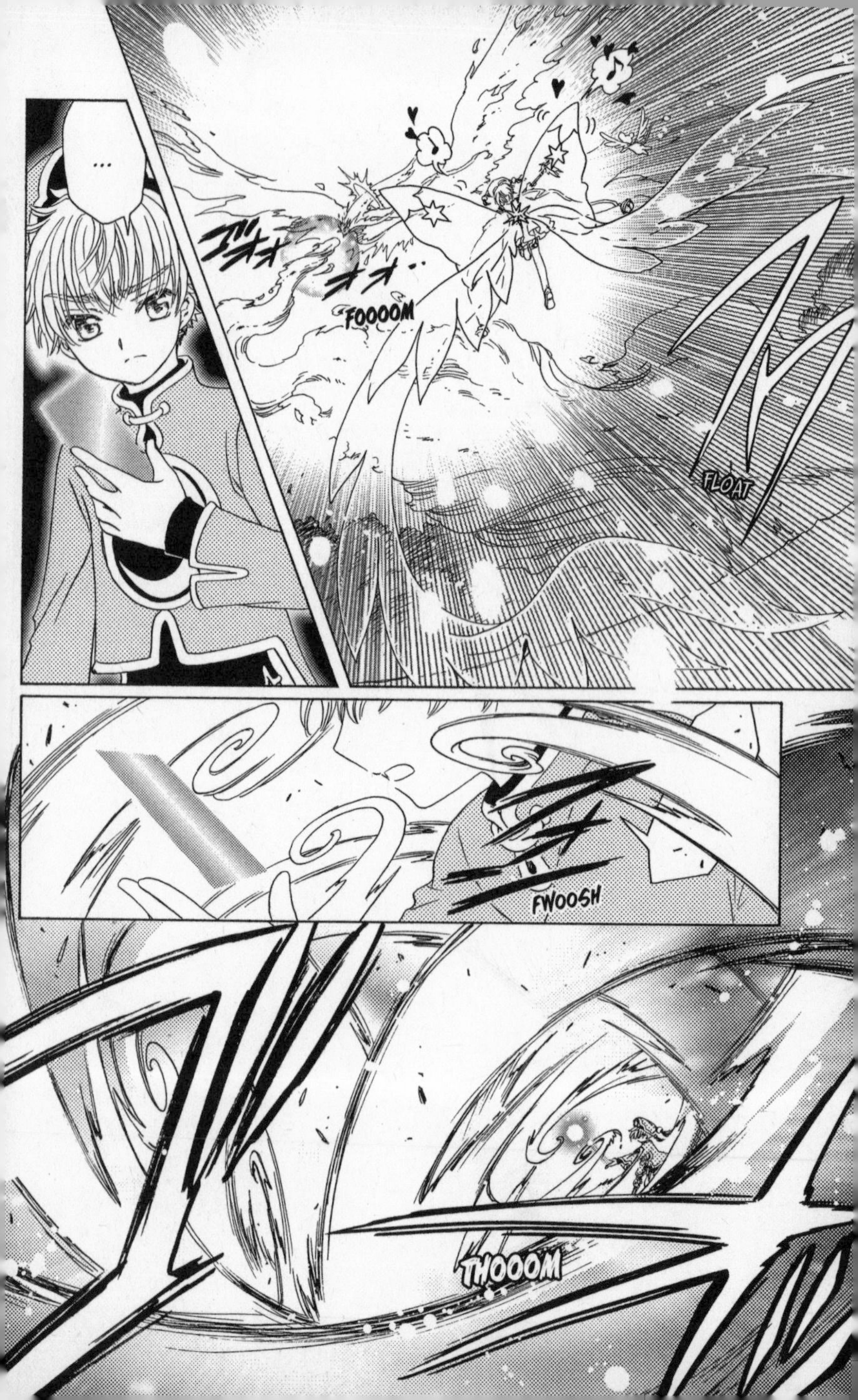
FLOAT
FOOOOM
...
FWOOSH
THOOOM

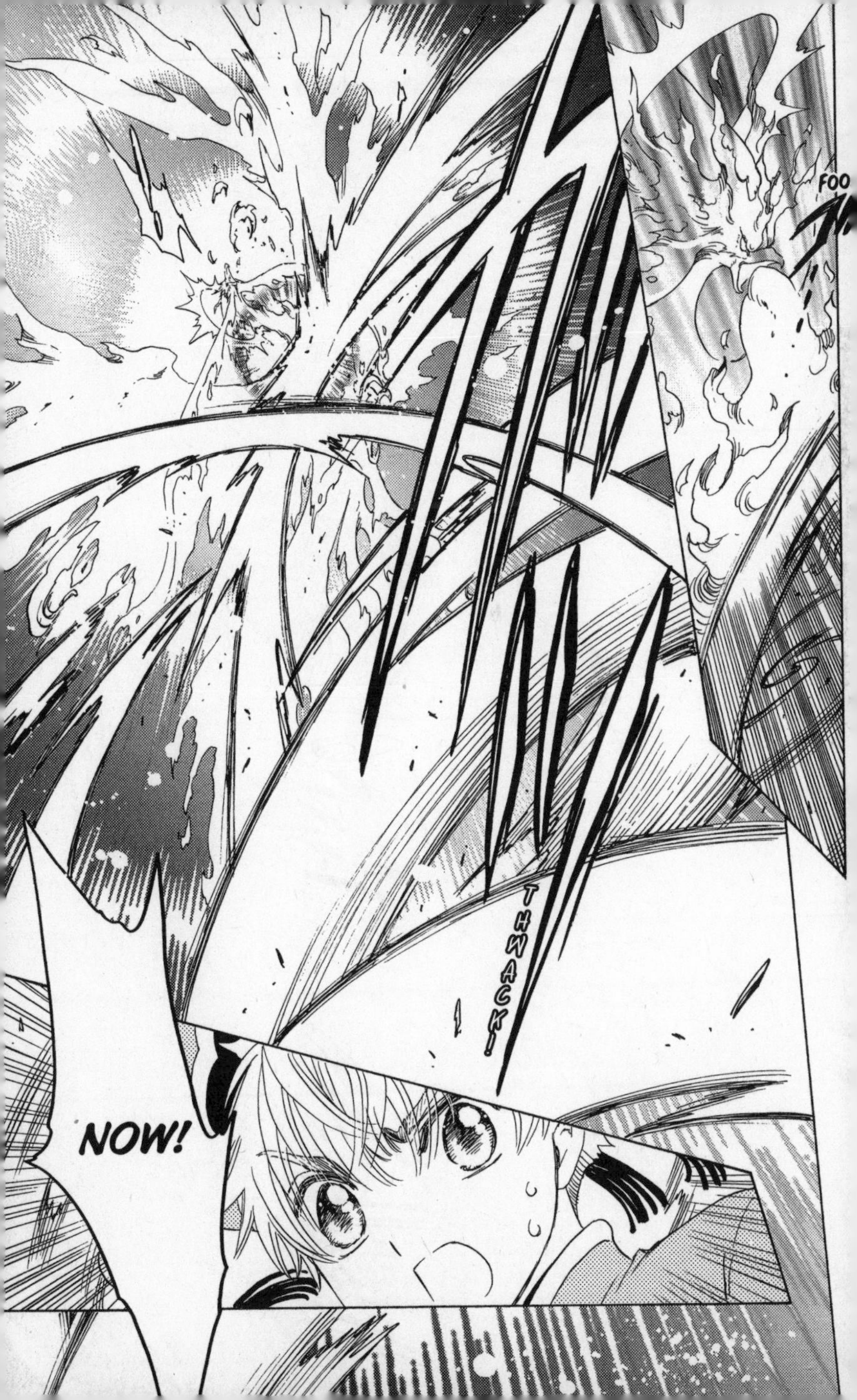
FOO
THWACK!
NOW!

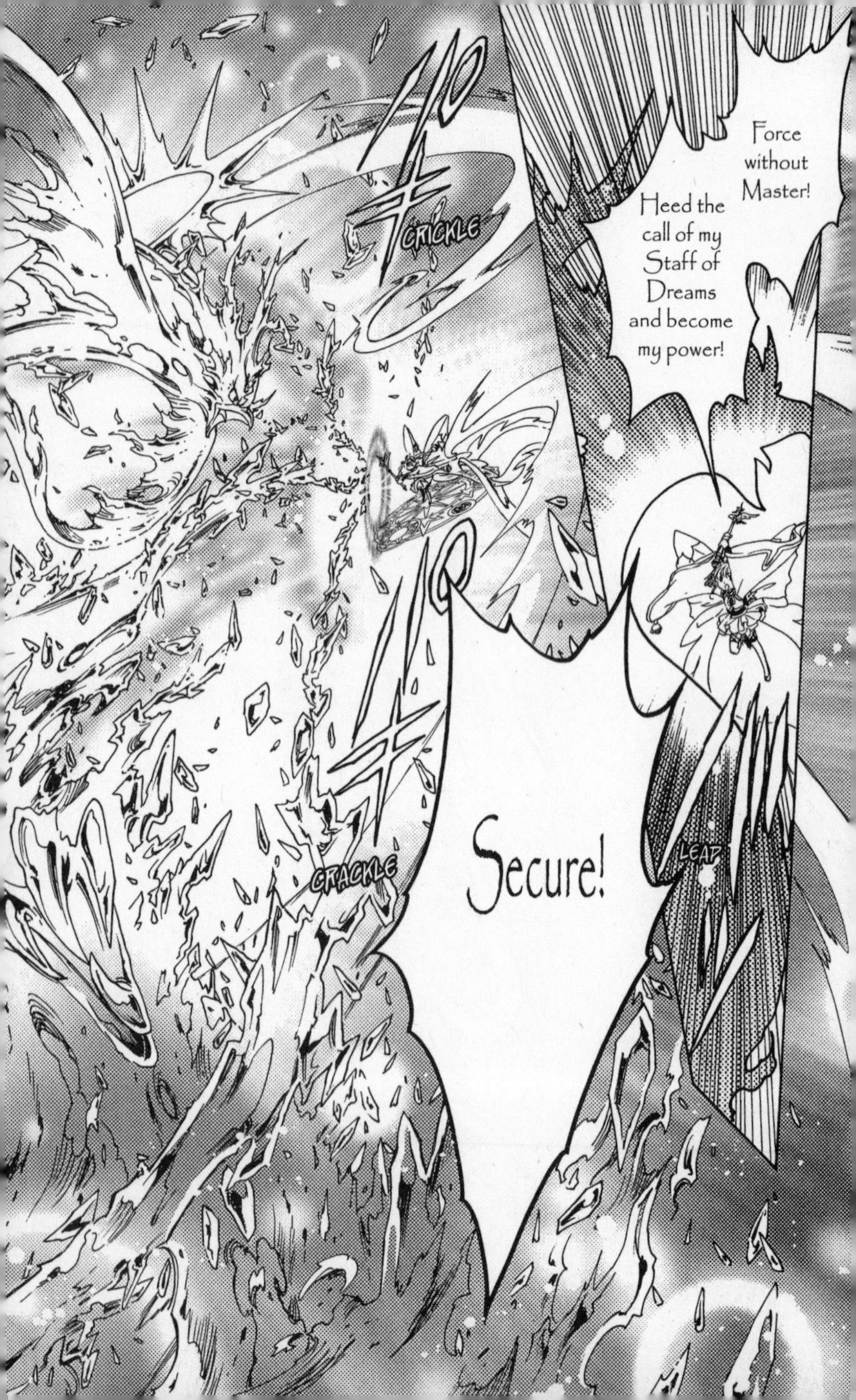
Force without Master!
Heed the call of my Staff of Dreams and become my power!
LEAP
Secure!
CRICKLE
CRACKLE

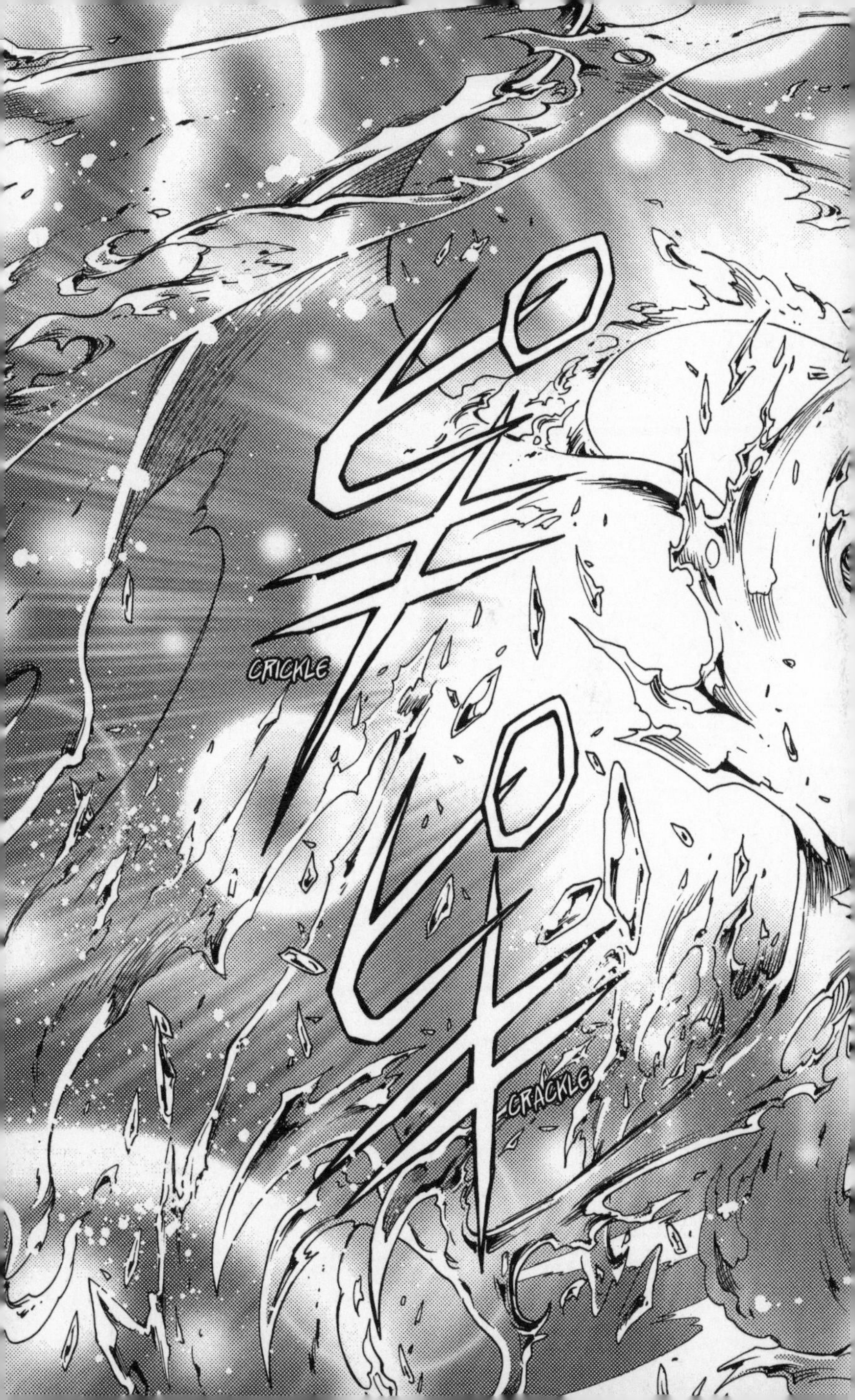
CRICKLE
CRACKLE

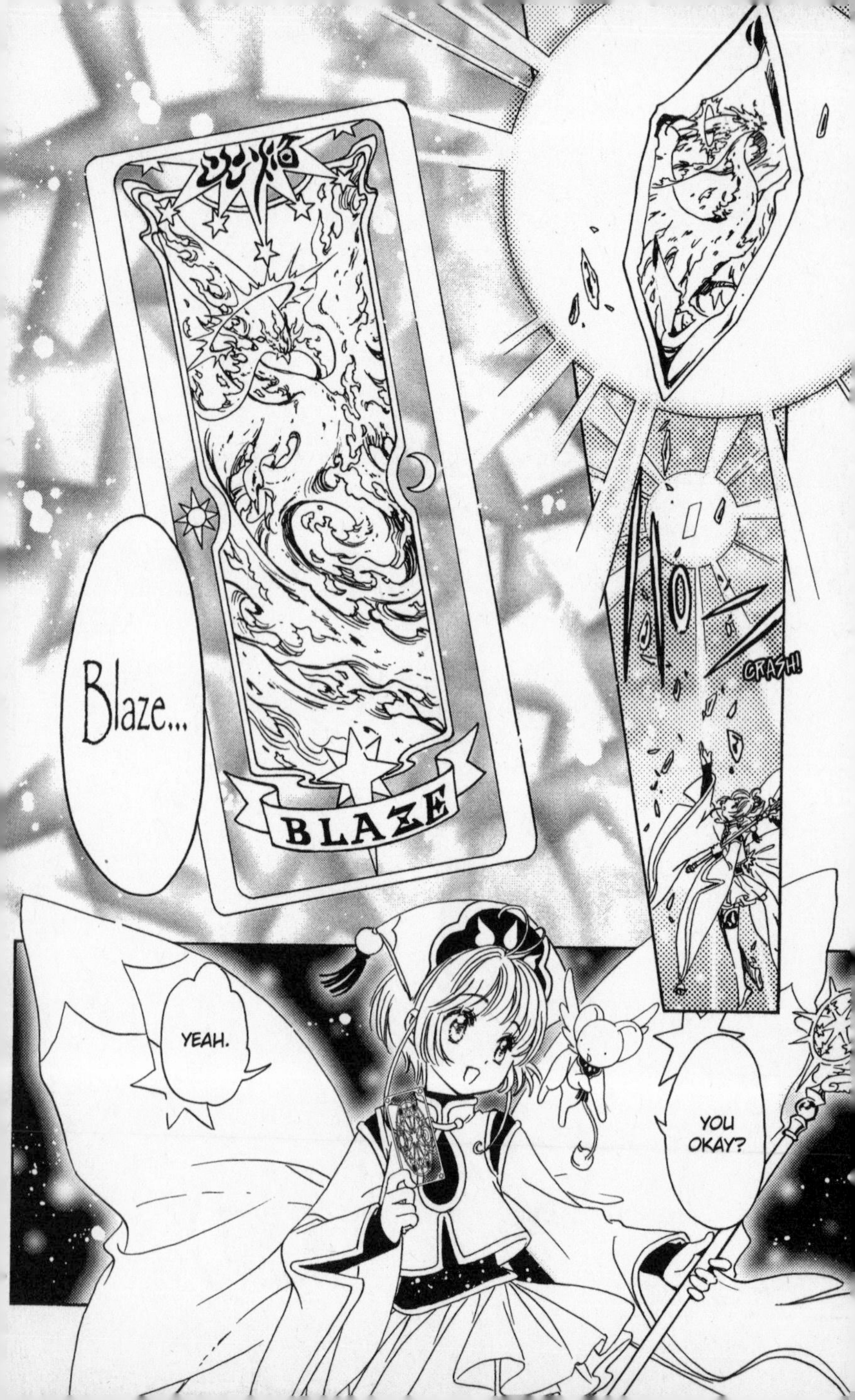
CRASH!
BLAZE
Blaze...
YOU OKAY?
YEAH.

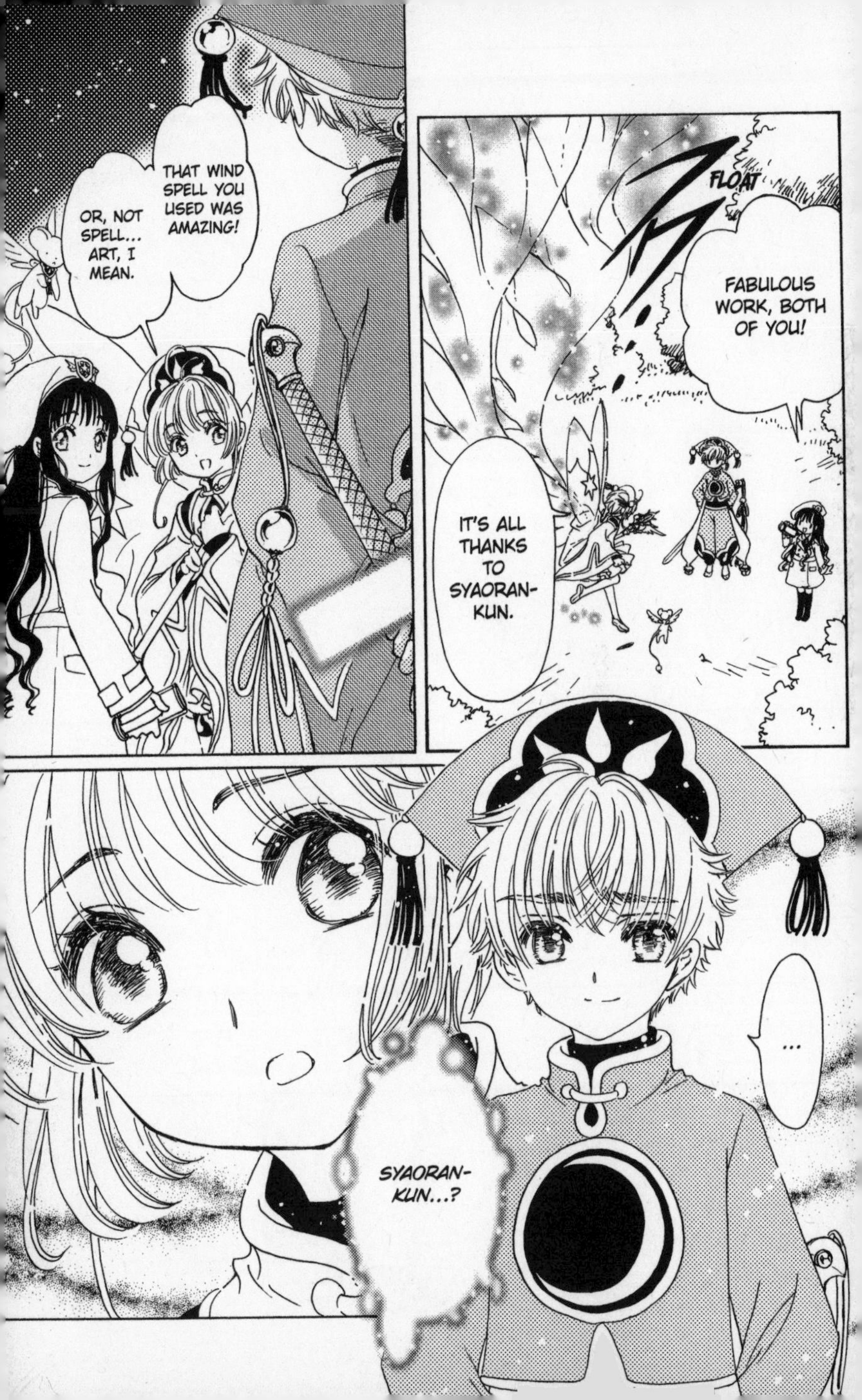
FLOAT
FABULOUS WORK, BOTH OF YOU!
IT'S ALL THANKS TO SYAORAN-KUN.
THAT WIND SPELL YOU USED WAS AMAZING!
OR, NOT SPELL... ART, I MEAN.
...
SYAORAN-KUN...?

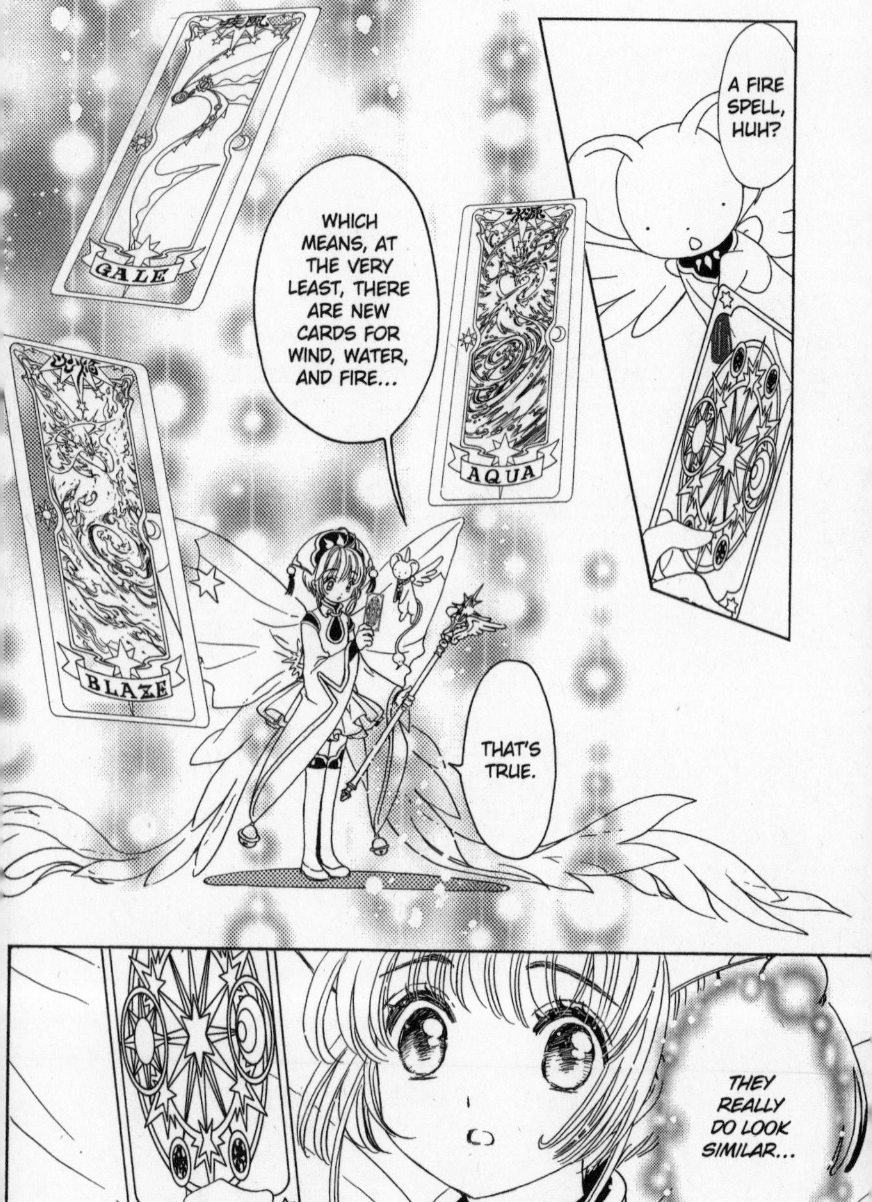
A FIRE SPELL, HUH?
GALE
AQUA
BLAZE
WHICH MEANS, AT THE VERY LEAST, THERE ARE NEW CARDS FOR WIND, WATER, AND FIRE...
THAT'S TRUE.
THEY REALLY DO LOOK SIMILAR...

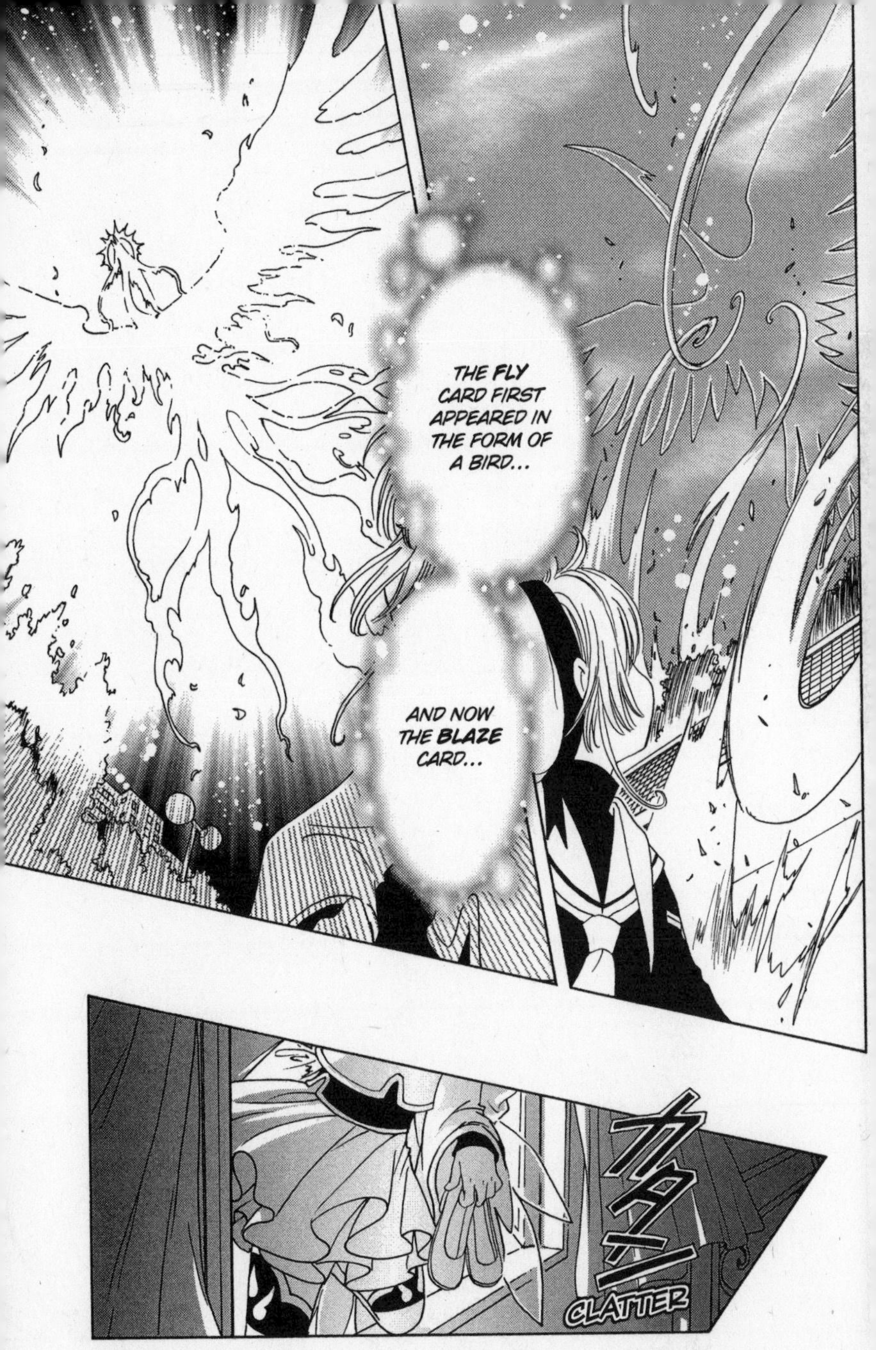
THE FLY CARD FIRST APPEARED IN THE FORM OF A BIRD...
AND NOW THE BLAZE CARD...
CLATTER

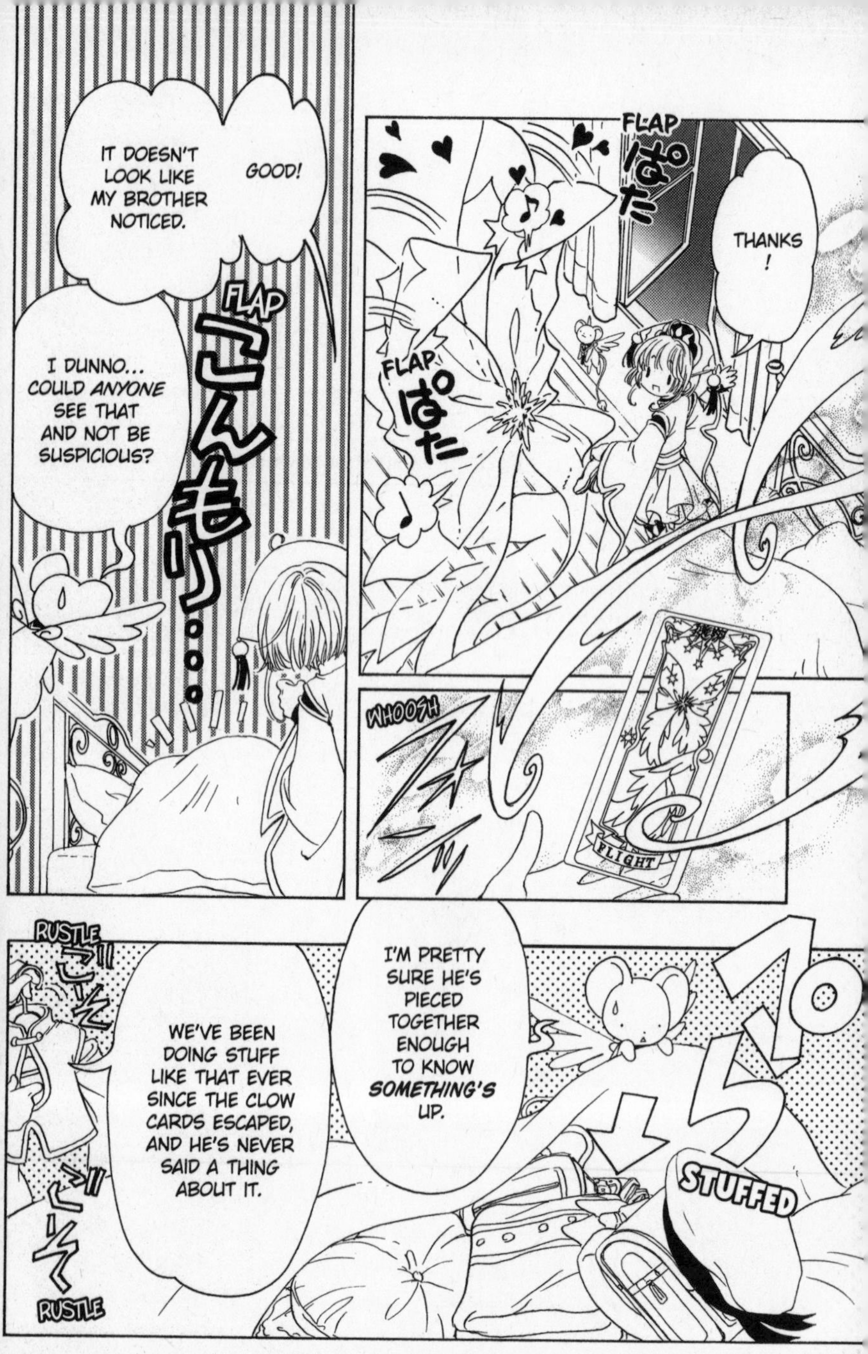
FLAP
ぱた
THANKS!
FLAP
ぱた
WHOOSH
FLIGHT
IT DOESN'T LOOK LIKE MY BROTHER NOTICED.
GOOD!
FLAP
こんもり。。。
I DUNNO... COULD *ANYONE* SEE THAT AND NOT BE SUSPICIOUS?
STUFFED
I'M PRETTY SURE HE'S PIECED TOGETHER ENOUGH TO KNOW ***SOMETHING'S*** UP.
WE'VE BEEN DOING STUFF LIKE THAT EVER SINCE THE CLOW CARDS ESCAPED, AND HE'S NEVER SAID A THING ABOUT IT.
RUSTLE
ごそごそ
RUSTLE

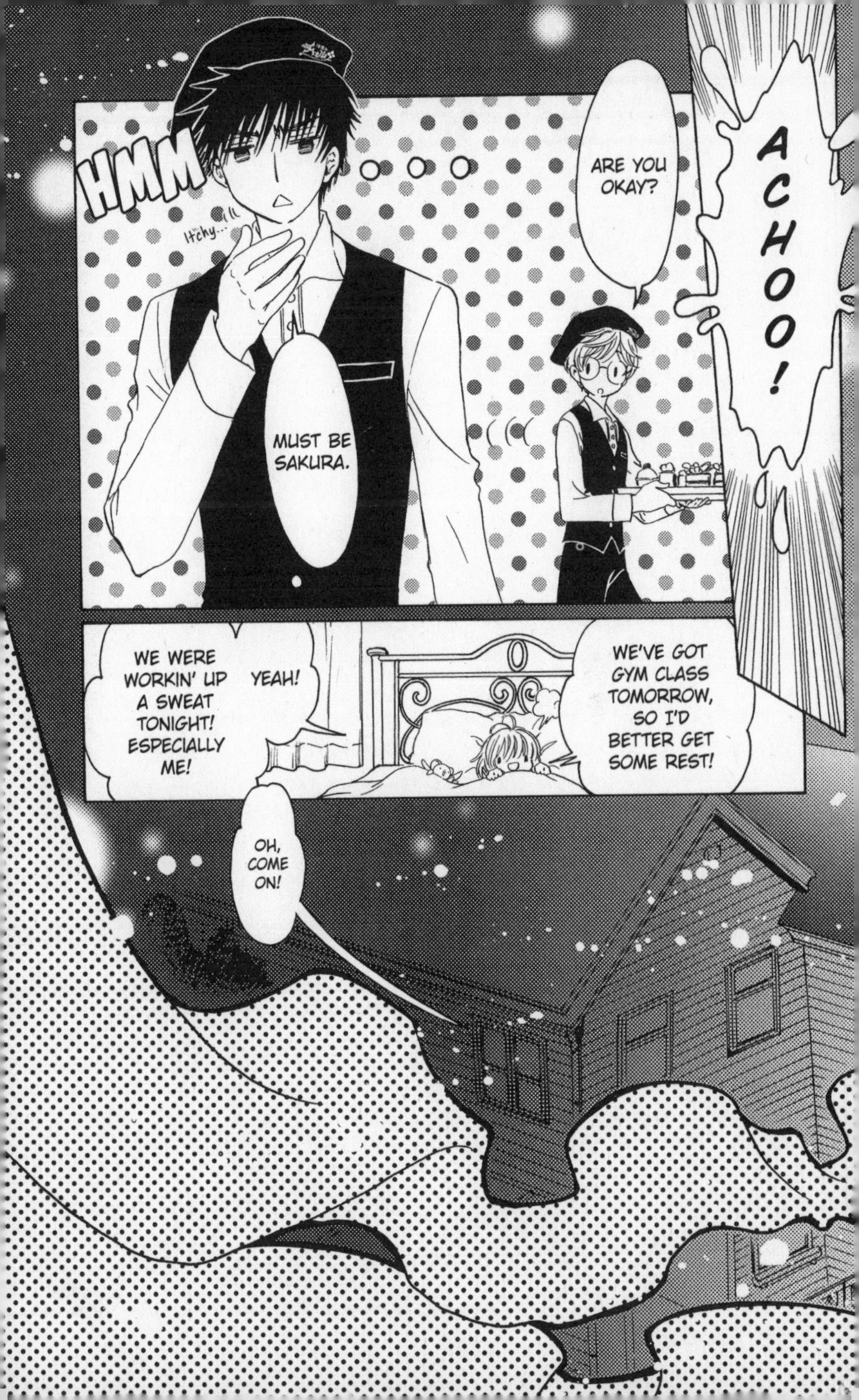
ACHOO!
ARE YOU OKAY?
HMM
Itchy...
MUST BE SAKURA.
WE'VE GOT GYM CLASS TOMORROW, SO I'D BETTER GET SOME REST!
YEAH!
WE WERE WORKIN' UP A SWEAT TONIGHT! ESPECIALLY ME!
OH, COME ON!

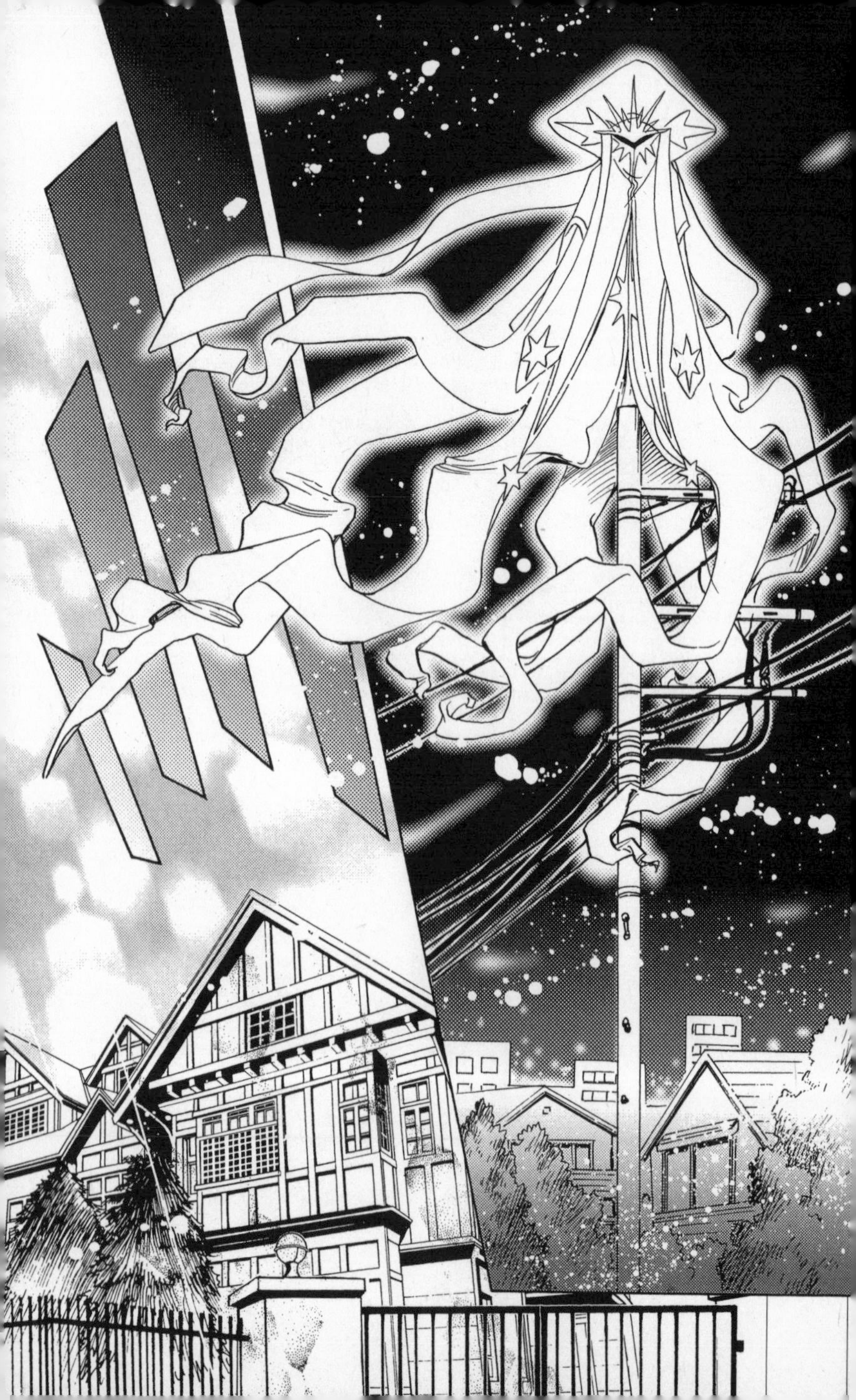

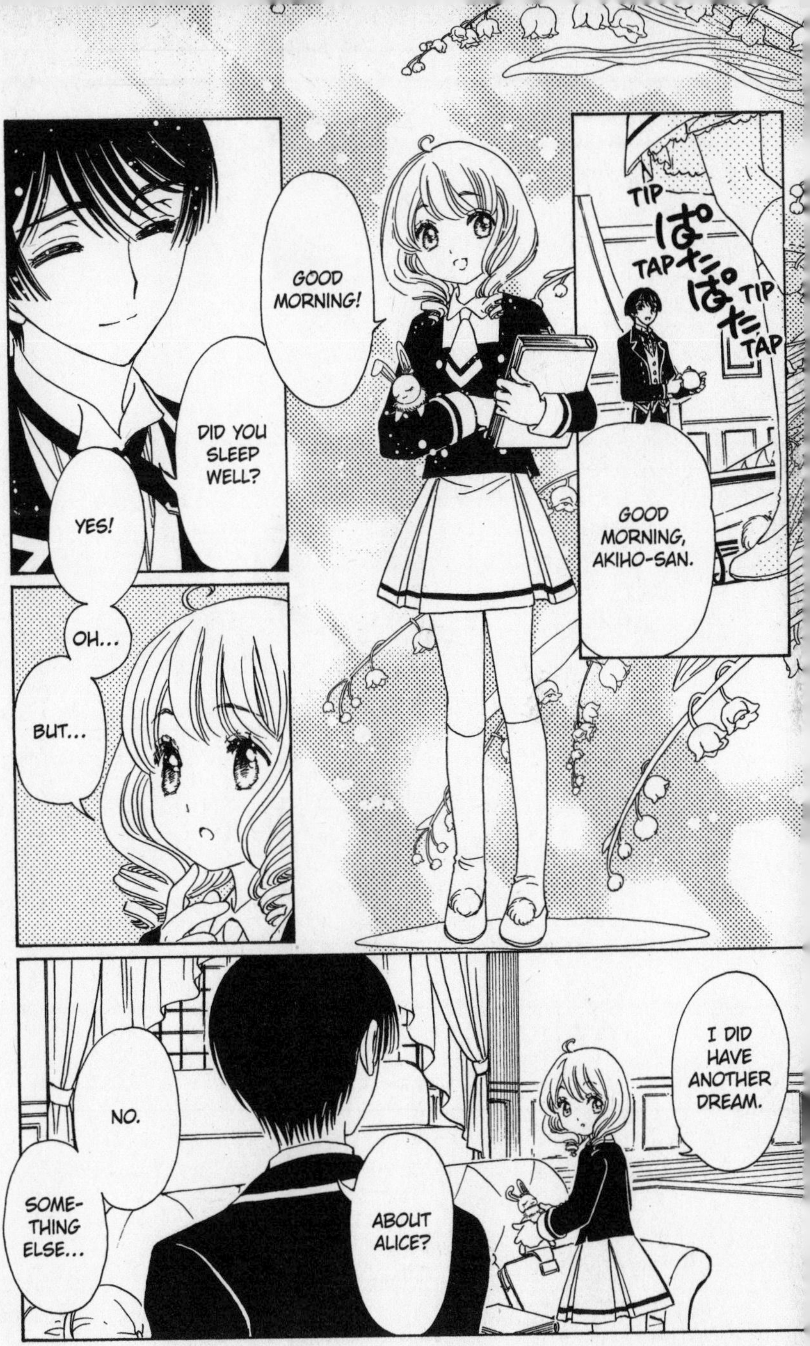
TIP TAP
ぱたぱた
TIP TAP
GOOD MORNING, AKIHO-SAN.
GOOD MORNING!
DID YOU SLEEP WELL?
YES!
OH...
BUT...
I DID HAVE ANOTHER DREAM.
ABOUT ALICE?
NO.
SOME-THING ELSE...

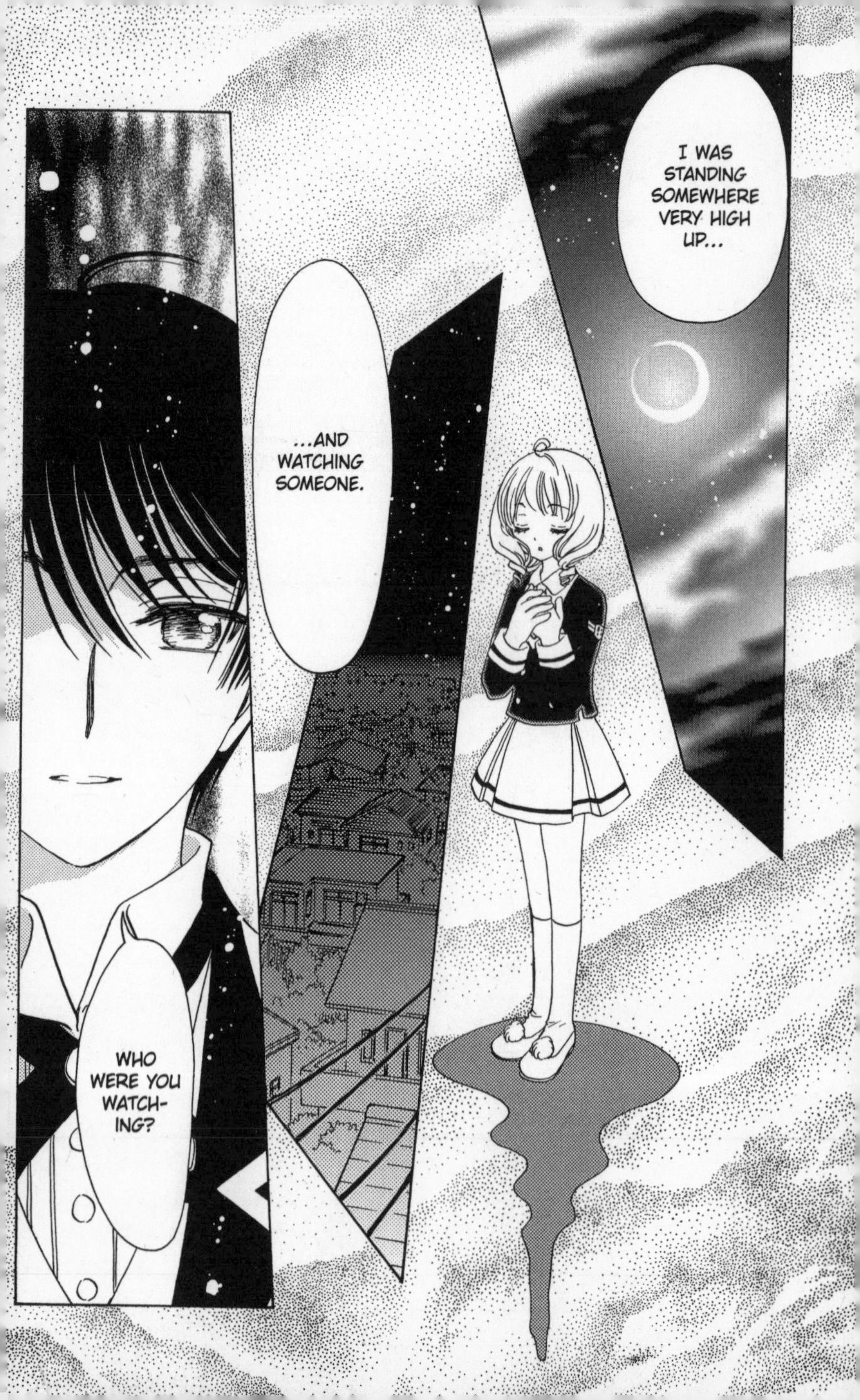
I WAS STANDING SOMEWHERE VERY HIGH UP...
...AND WATCHING SOMEONE.
WHO WERE YOU WATCH-ING?

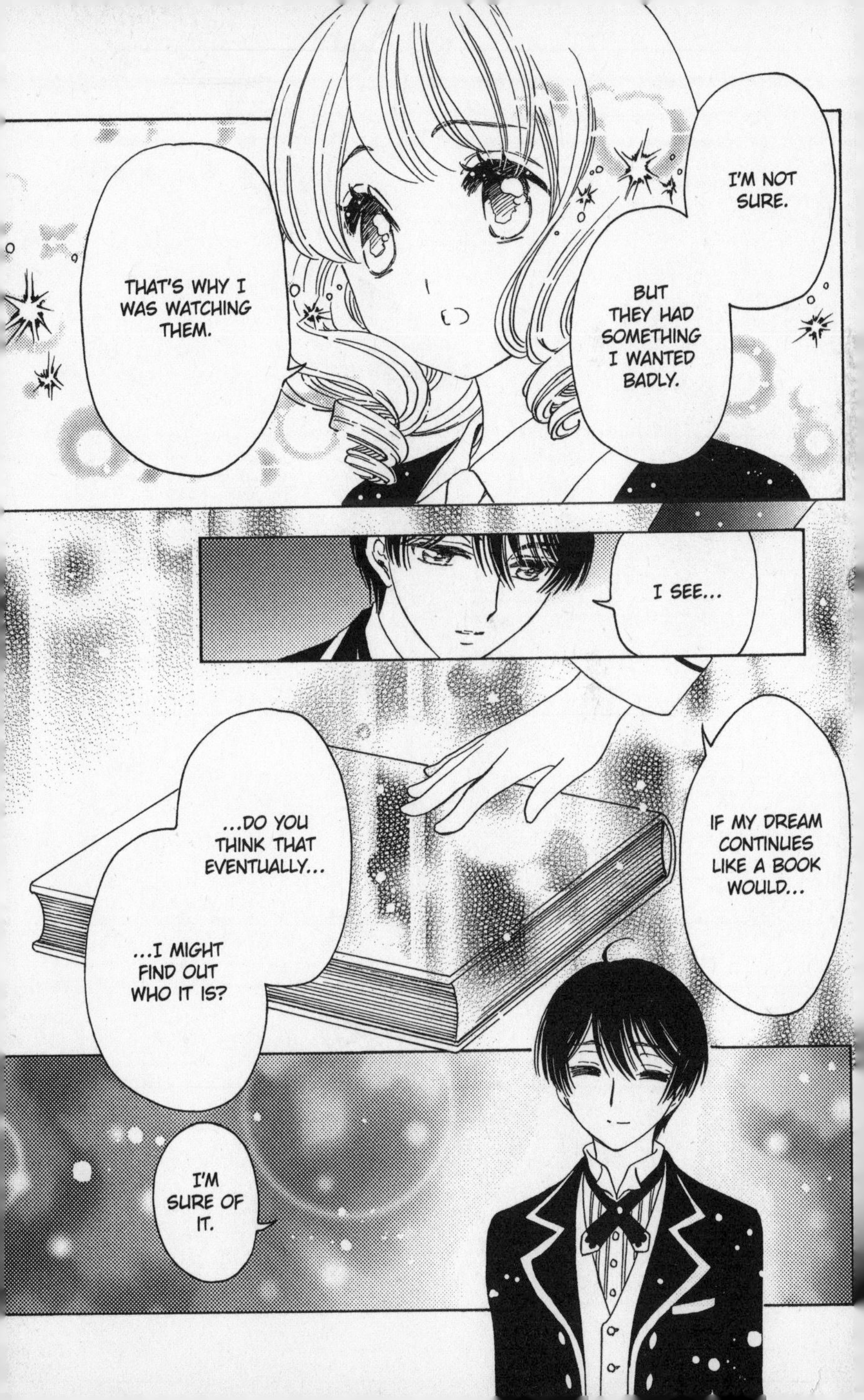
I'M NOT SURE.
BUT THEY HAD SOMETHING I WANTED BADLY.
THAT'S WHY I WAS WATCHING THEM.
I SEE...
IF MY DREAM CONTINUES LIKE A BOOK WOULD...
...DO YOU THINK THAT EVENTUALLY...
...I MIGHT FIND OUT WHO IT IS?
I'M SURE OF IT.

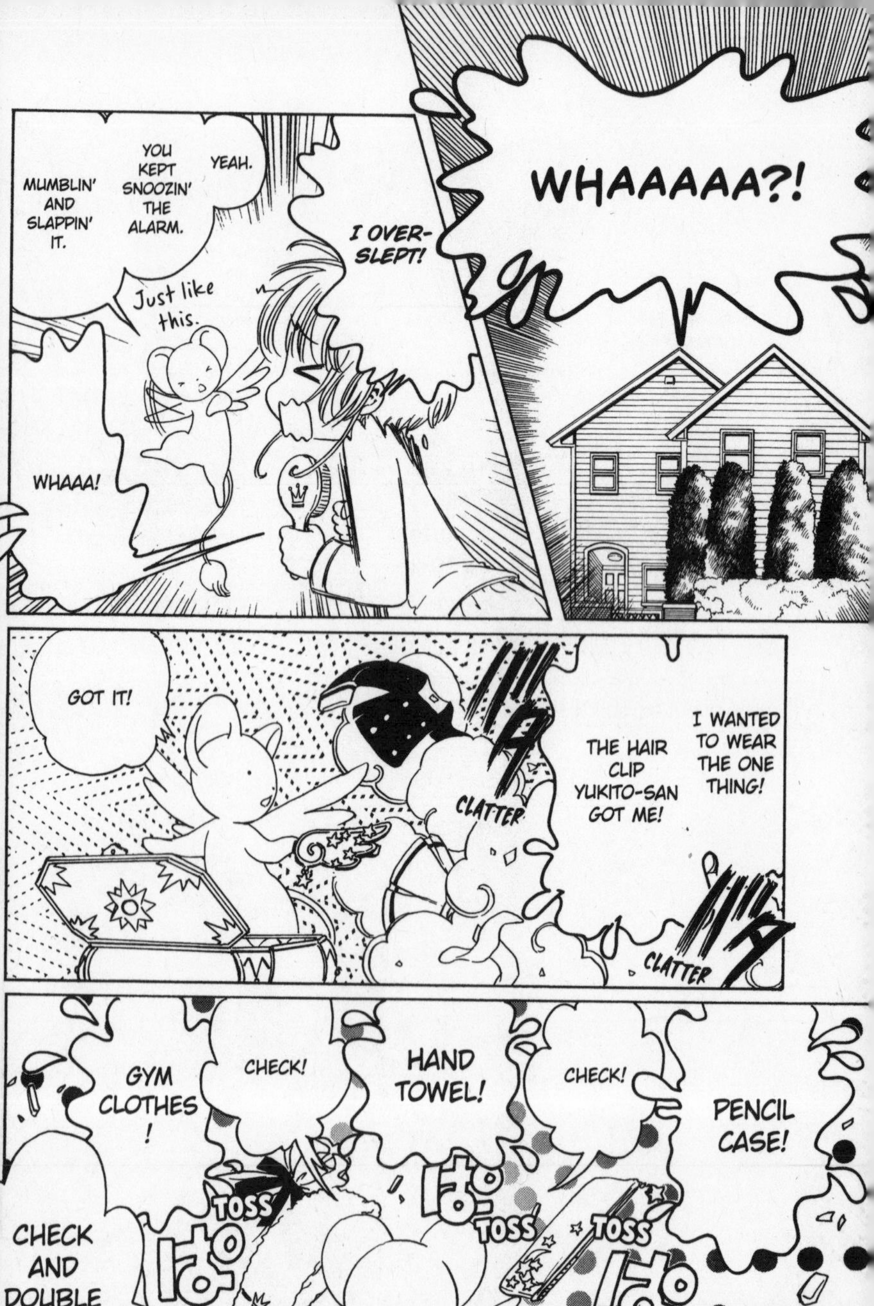
WHAAAAA?!
I OVER-SLEPT!
YEAH.
YOU KEPT SNOOZIN' THE ALARM.
MUMBLIN' AND SLAPPIN' IT.
Just like this.
WHAAA!
I WANTED TO WEAR THE ONE THING!
THE HAIR CLIP YUKITO-SAN GOT ME!
CLATTER
CLATTER
GOT IT!
PENCIL CASE!
CHECK!
TOSS
HAND TOWEL!
TOSS
CHECK!
GYM CLOTHES!
TOSS
CHECK AND DOUBLE CHECK!

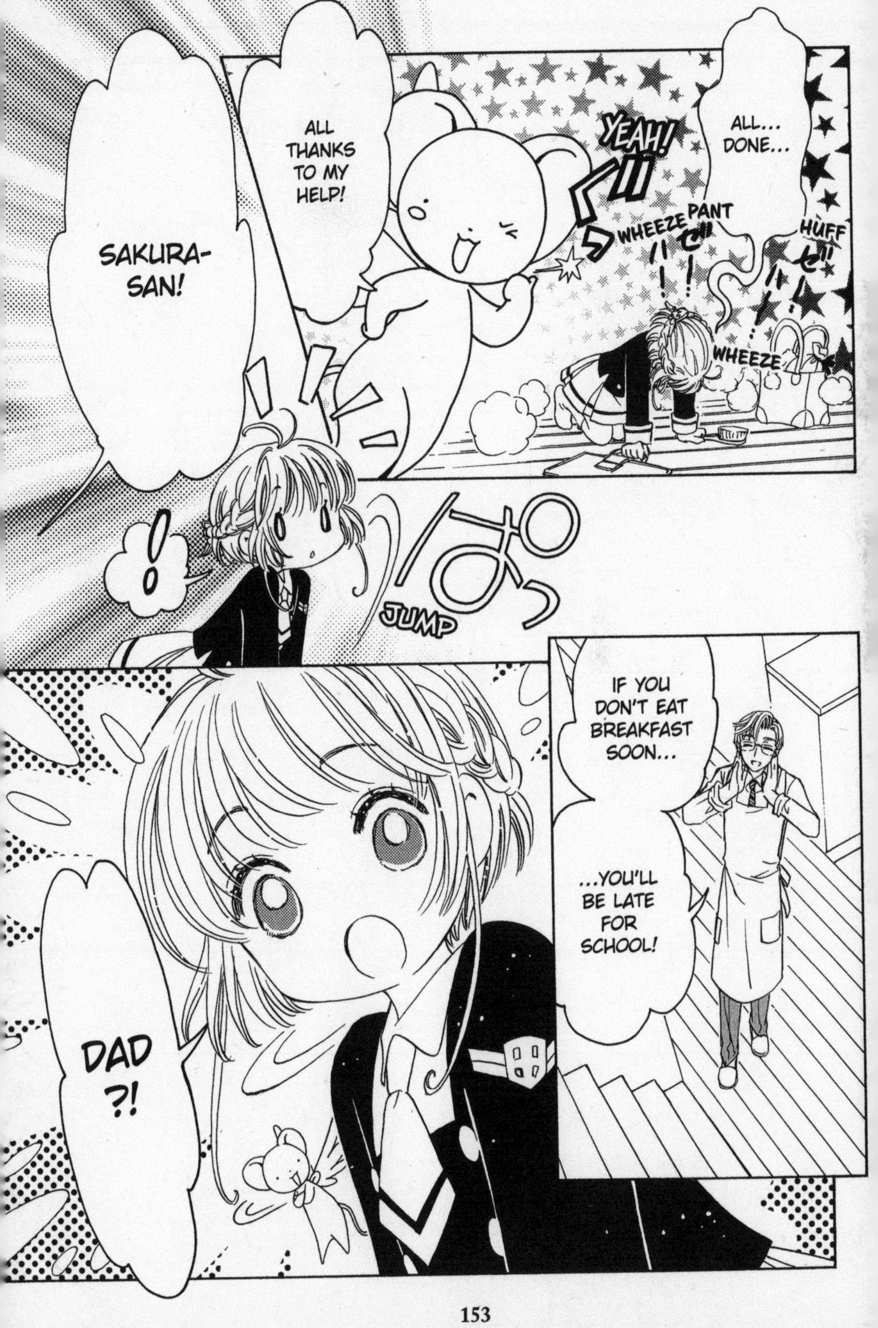
ALL... DONE...
YEAH!!
WHEEZE
PANT
HUFF
WHEEZE
ALL THANKS TO MY HELP!
SAKURA-SAN!
!
JUMP
IF YOU DON'T EAT BREAKFAST SOON...
...YOU'LL BE LATE FOR SCHOOL!
DAD?!

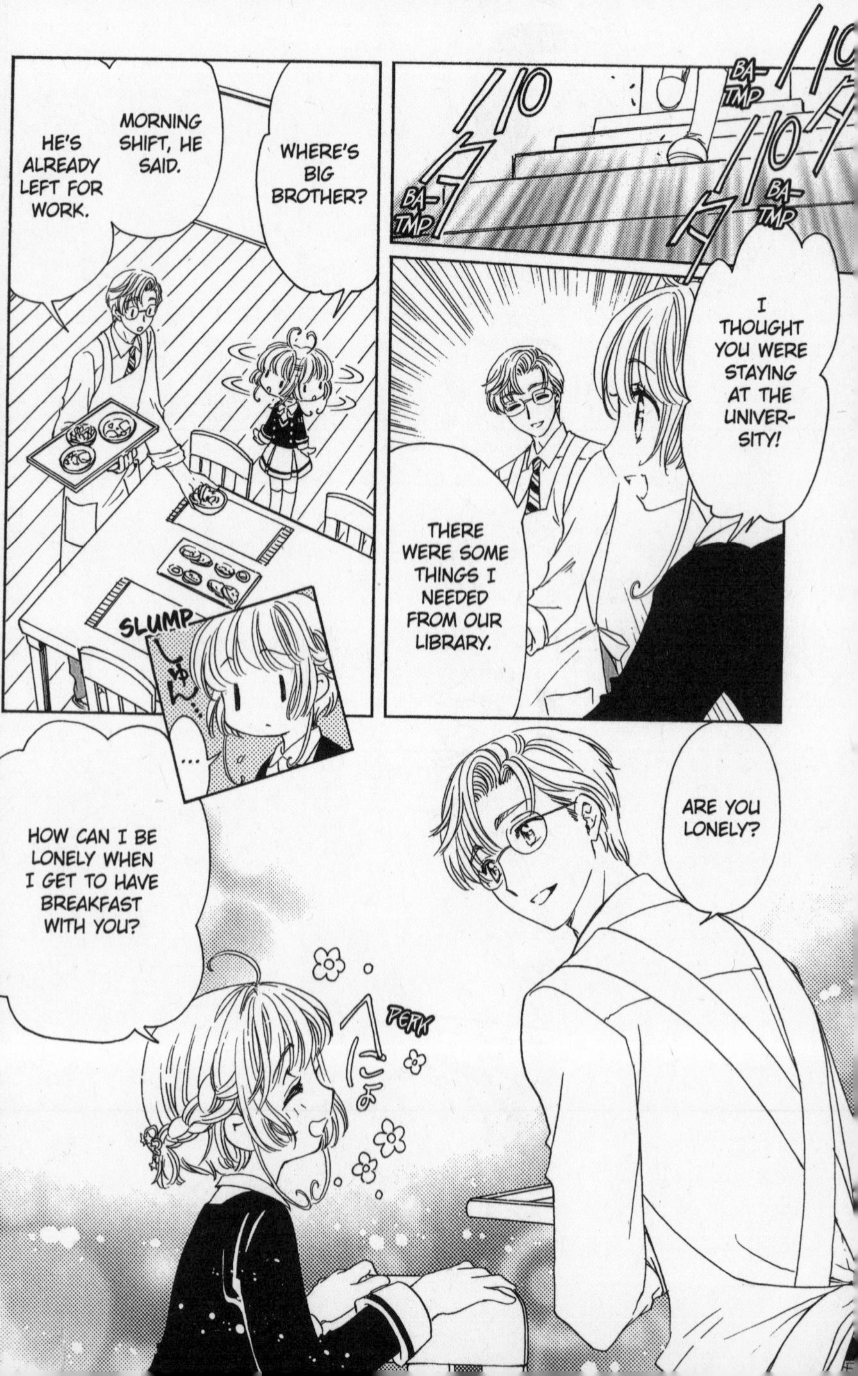
BA-TMP
BA-TMP
BA-TMP
I THOUGHT YOU WERE STAYING AT THE UNIVERSITY!
THERE WERE SOME THINGS I NEEDED FROM OUR LIBRARY.
WHERE'S BIG BROTHER?
MORNING SHIFT, HE SAID.
HE'S ALREADY LEFT FOR WORK.
SLUMP
...
ARE YOU LONELY?
PERK
HOW CAN I BE LONELY WHEN I GET TO HAVE BREAKFAST WITH YOU?

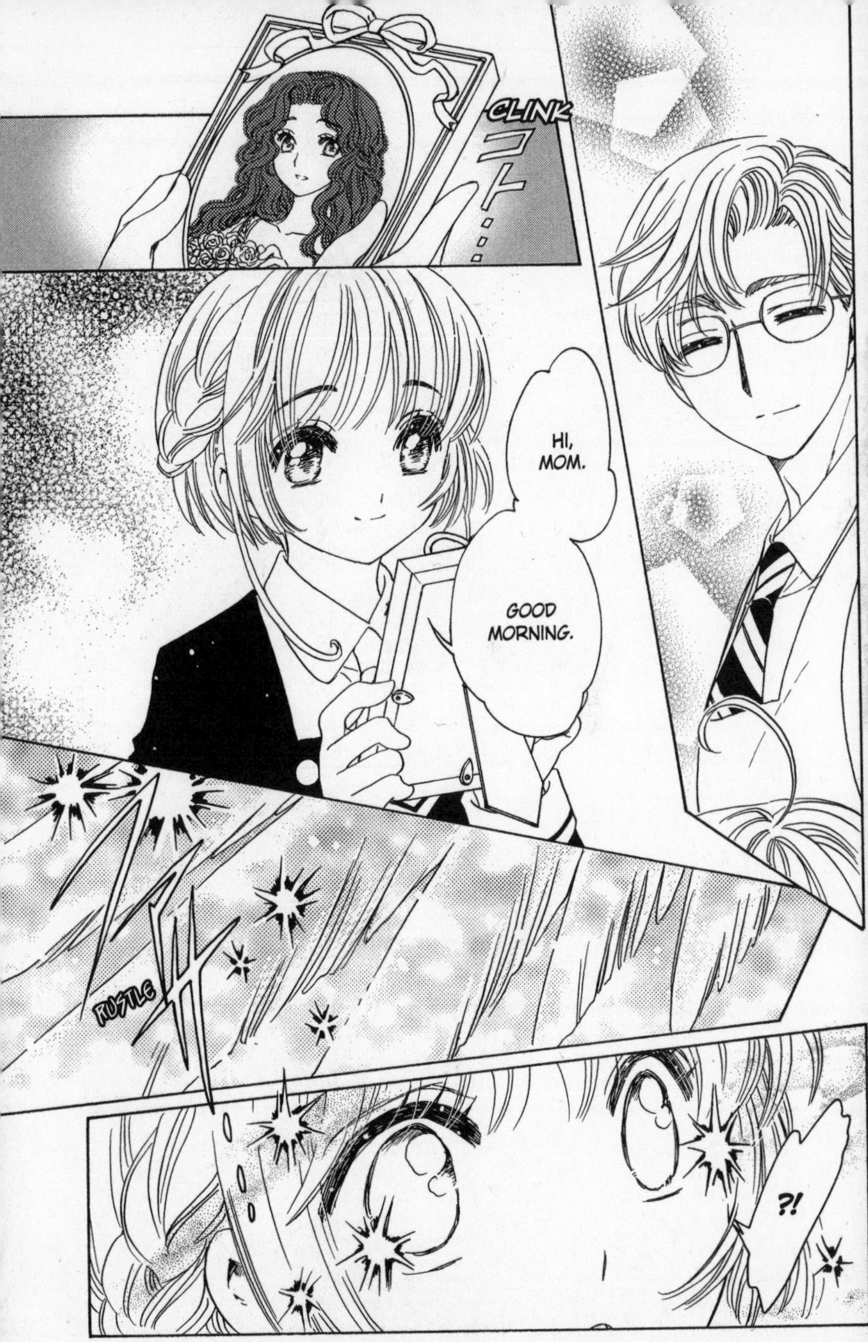
CLINK
コト・・・
HI, MOM.
GOOD MORNING.
RUSTLE
?!

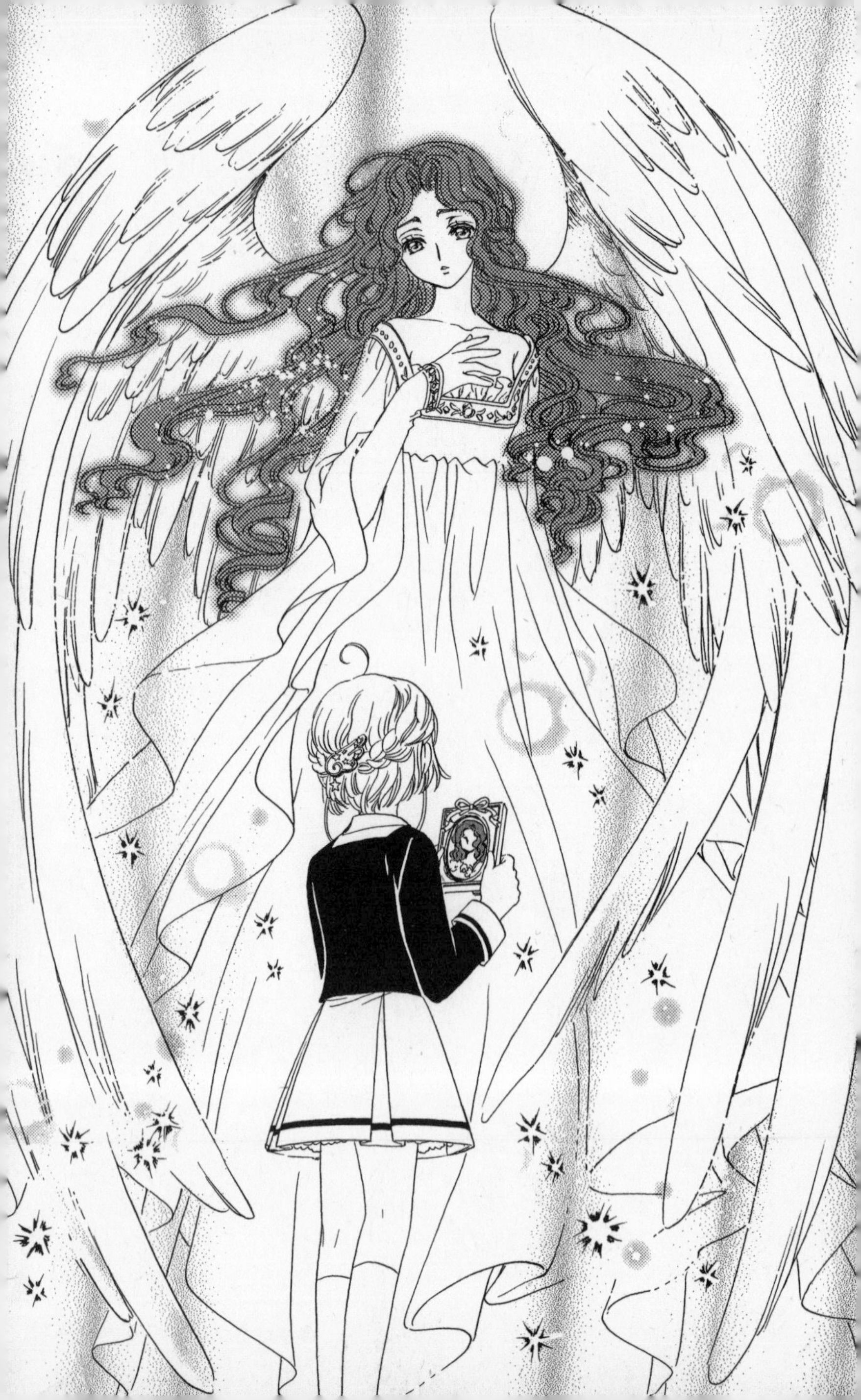

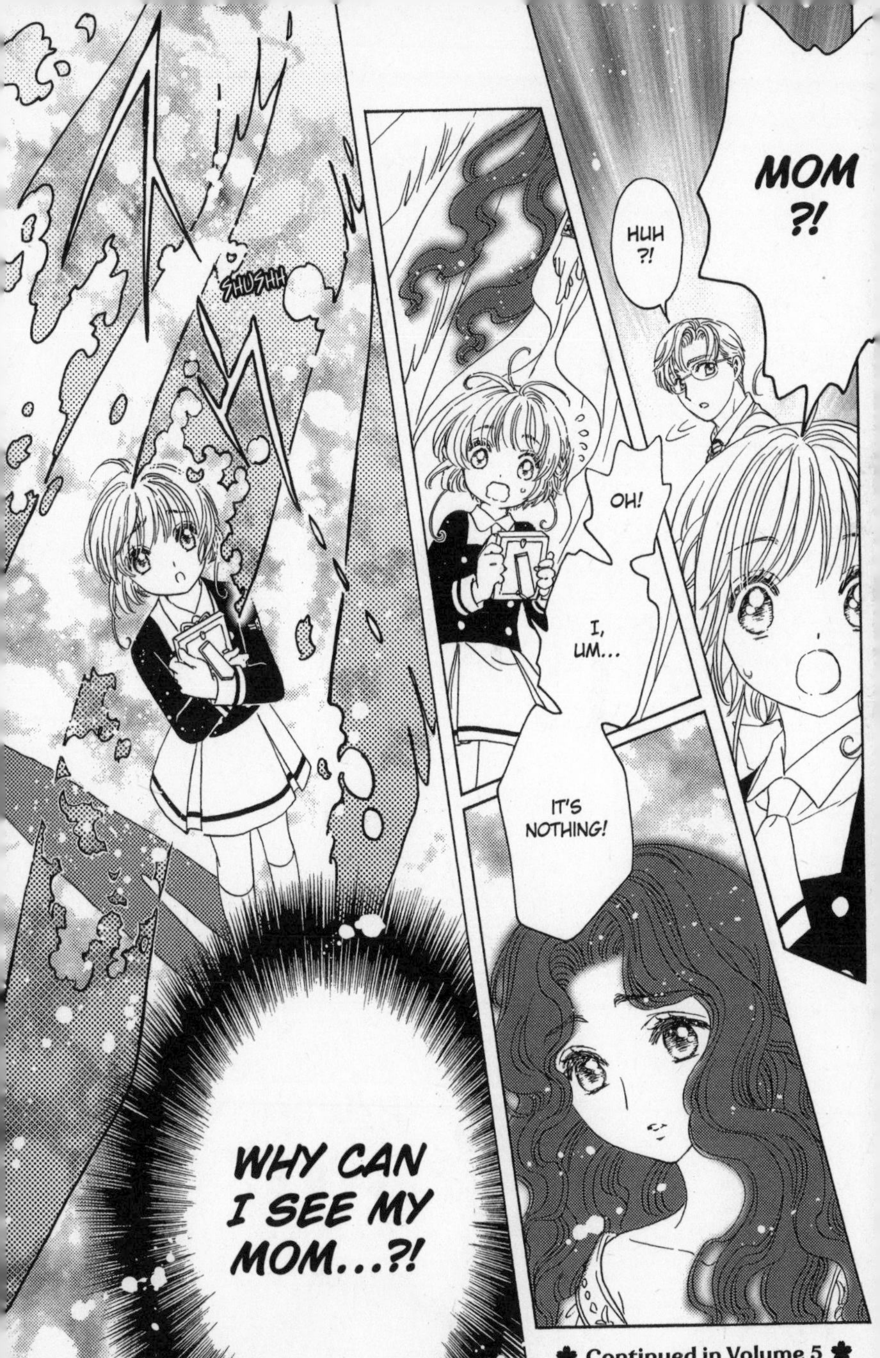
MOM ?!
HUH ?!
OH!
I, UM...
IT'S NOTHING!
SHUSHH
WHY CAN I SEE MY MOM...?!

✿ Continued in Volume 5 ✿

Cardcaptor Sakura

CLEAR CARD

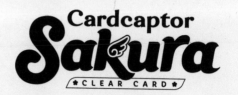